Right to Reparations

Right to Reparations

The Claims Conference and Holocaust Survivors, 1951–1964

Rachel Blumenthal

LEXINGTON BOOKS
Lanham • Boulder • New York • London

Published by Lexington Books
An imprint of The Rowman & Littlefield Publishing Group, Inc.
4501 Forbes Boulevard, Suite 200, Lanham, Maryland 20706
www.rowman.com

6 Tinworth Street, London SE11 5AL, United Kingdom

Copyright © 2021 The Rowman & Littlefield Publishing Group, Inc.

All rights reserved. No part of this book may be reproduced in any form or by any electronic or mechanical means, including information storage and retrieval systems, without written permission from the publisher, except by a reviewer who may quote passages in a review.

British Library Cataloguing in Publication Information Available

Library of Congress Cataloging-in-Publication Data

Names: Blumenthal, Rachel, 1963- author.
Title: Right to reparations : the Claims Conference and Holocaust survivors, 1951-1964 / Rachel Blumenthal.
Other titles: Claims Conference and Holocaust survivors, 1951-1964
Description: Lanham : Lexington Books, [2021] | Includes bibliographical references and index.
Identifiers: LCCN 2021018560 (print) | LCCN 2021018561 (ebook) | ISBN 9781793637871 (cloth) | ISBN 9781793637888 (epub) | ISBN 9781793637895 (pbk)
Subjects: LCSH: Conference on Jewish Material Claims Against Germany. | Holocaust, Jewish (1939-1945)—Reparations. | World War, 1939-1945—Claims. | World War, 1939-1945—Reparations.
Classification: LCC D819.G3 B58 2021 (print) | LCC D819.G3 (ebook) | DDC 940.53/18144—dc23
LC record available at https://lccn.loc.gov/2021018560
LC ebook record available at https://lccn.loc.gov/2021018561

To Aner

Contents

List of Illustrations ix

Abbreviations xi

A Note on Translations xiii

Acknowledgments xv

Introduction 1

1 Failure of Early Demands for Reparations and a New Form of Transnational Activism 19

2 Who Speaks for the Jews on Reparations?: The Genesis of the Claims Conference 41

3 From Temporary Committees to a Permanent Institution: Change of Mandate to Ensure Immortality 65

4 Reparations for Victims?: Formulation of a Policy to Strengthen the Alliance 81

5 Power Begets Power: Inclusion and Exclusion 99

6 Internal Operations: Organizational Logic and Experts 119

7 Chief Spokesman for Reparations: A Non-State Actor in the World of International Relations 141

Conclusion	161
Bibliography	179
Index	197
About the Author	207

List of Illustrations

Figure 1.1	Timeline of Evolution of Jewish Transnational Organizations	26
Figure 1.2	Nahum Goldmann	28
Figure 2.1	Chronology of Events Leading up to the Luxembourg Agreement	42
Figure 2.2	Demonstration in Israel against Direct Negotiations with West Germany on Reparations	56
Figure 3.1	Moshe Sharett Signing the Luxembourg Agreement with Nahum Goldmann on his left and Giora Josephthal on his right	69
Figure 4.1	Moses Leavitt	90
Figure 5.1	Plaque outside Nahum Goldmann's Jerusalem Apartment	102
Figure 5.2	Geographical Breakdown of Member Organizations of the Claims Conference in 1952	105
Figure 6.1	Allocation per Survivor by Country in 1952–1972	128

Abbreviations

Aguda	*Agudas* Israel World Organization
Alliance	*Alliance Israélite Universelle*
AJC	American Jewish Committee
AJCA	American Jewish Committee Archives
CAHJP	Central Archives for the History of the Jewish People
CBF	Central British Fund for German Jews now renamed World Jewish Relief
CJH	Center for Jewish History, New York
Claims Conference	the Conference on Jewish Material Claims against Germany
Comité des Délégations Juives	*Comité des Délégations Juives auprès de la Conférence de la Paix*
Conference of Presidents	Conference of Presidents of Major American Jewish Organizations
Council for Jews from Germany	Council for the Protection of the Rights and Interests of Jews from Germany
Hadassah	Hadassah, Women's Zionist Organization of America
IGO	intergovernmental organization
INGO	international nongovernmental organization
JCR	Jewish Cultural Reconstruction, Inc.
JDC	Joint Distribution Committee

JRSO	Jewish Restitution Successor Organization
NCJW	National Council of Jewish Women
UNRRA	United Nations Relief and Rehabilitation Administration
URO	United Restitution Organization
WIZO	Women's International Zionist Organization
WUPJ	World Union for Progressive Judaism
WZO	World Zionist Organization
Yishuv	The Jewish community in Palestine under the British Mandate
Zentralrat	Central Council of Jews in Germany (*Zentralrat der Juden in Deutschland*)
ZOA	Zionist Organization of America

A Note on Translations

All translations from the Hebrew and German are my own, unless otherwise stated.

Acknowledgments

On October 17, 1938, Vilma Lichtenstern, accompanied by her mother and two-year-old daughter, departed Vienna by train. Her husband Felix, my grandfather, had already left, but Vilma (known by everyone as Murki), was reluctant to abandon her home and her pharmacy on Margarete Strasse. The violence unleashed by the annexation of Austria to Germany and Adolf Eichmann's very efficient Central Office for Jewish Emigration forced her to concede. The destination of the two women and the toddler, Eva, was London. The Home Office permitted their entry after an aunt, Helena Szarvas, lay down on the pavement and refused to move until the presumably astonished official agreed to issue visas for the refugees. In retrospect, despite the plunder of all their property by Greater Germany, the imprisonment of my grandfather as an enemy alien, and the loss of his legal profession, the Lichtensterns were lucky. Jakob Maschler, my great-great-grandfather, his son Ignatz, and cousins of my grandmother who stayed behind did not survive the war. This is the reason for my interest in the Holocaust, including compensation for victims and survivors.

Over the past six years, many individuals and institutions supported my work. I am indebted to Jonathan Dekel-Chen for his advice, criticism, and guidance. Thank you to Carole Fink, Eli Lederhendler, Berel Lang, Csaba Nikolenyi, David Blumenthal, and the anonymous reader at Lexington Books who read earlier drafts and gave valuable suggestions and comments. Thank you to Aner Berger for his invaluable assistance with the diagrams and to Tamar Berger for her help with the figures. This work benefitted from fruitful discussions with Sergio Della Pergola, Yaron Tsur, Tamar Meisels, Nissan Limor, z"l, Ronald Zweig, Benjamin Ferencz, Karen Heilig, and Ofra Ross. I am also grateful to Yifat Weiss for her thought-provoking course on postwar Germany and Amos Goldberg for his course on Jewish leadership in the Holocaust. I alone bear responsibility for any errors in the text.

The Morris & Alma Schapiro Research Fellowship awarded by the Center for Jewish History funded my research in New York in the 2015–2016 academic year. I would like to thank Chris Barthel for introducing me to American academic life and for his advice on overcoming the culture shock of life in New York. The Fred & Ellen Lewis JDC Archives Fellowship facilitated research in the institution's archives in Jerusalem and New York. A travel grant from the Authority for Research Students at the Hebrew University of Jerusalem covered the costs of flights from Tel Aviv to New York. I am also grateful for a grant from the Leslie Frankel Family Trust and fellowships from the Institute of Contemporary Jewry at the Hebrew University.

Numerous archivists and librarians in Israel and the United States helped me in my search for documentary evidence. Yochai Ben-Gedalia and Beatrice Kremer of the Central Archives for the History of the Jewish People facilitated access to the Claims Conference archives. I am grateful to the Claims Conference, Wesley A. Fisher for authorizing my review of their files, and Karen Heilig, who provided updated data on the number of recipients of pensions and grants. Thank you to the librarians and archivists of the Center of Jewish History library, especially Zach, Ilya, and Leo for their advice and patience. Linda Levy, Misha Mitsel, Abra Cohen, Shahar Beer, and Anat Kutner helped me to find my way around the digitized and non-digitized JDC archives. Thank you to Sharon Kangisser-Cohen of the Hebrew University Oral History Division, the Central Zionist Archives, and Yaacov Lozowick, former Israel State Archivist. Thank you also to Gila, Laure-Lina, and Lea of the Wiener Library at Tel Aviv University. I wrote large parts of my dissertation in the Wiener Library, surrounded by artifacts from and literature on the Third Reich. The windows of the library look out on Beit Hatfutsot, the Museum of the Jewish People, another project initiated by the founder of the Claims Conference, Nahum Goldmann.

I am especially grateful to my partner Aner and our children, Yael, Abigail, Daniel, Tamar, and Jonathan for their love and longsuffering patience, to my parents Eva and Lionel who instilled in me a passion for Jewish history and to my siblings, Naomi, Harry, and David (whom I hope to see soon in the flesh) for their companionship and support.

Introduction

Meta Doran was born in Germany to an affluent Jewish family in 1926. Her father, who imported and exported scrap metal, was of Polish origin. The family lived in an expensively furnished home in Hamburg with oriental carpets, beautiful crystal, and sterling silver, "the best money could possibly buy," Meta said in a 1996 interview.[1] All this changed in 1938. In March of that year, the German government confiscated the family business. Six months later, Meta, her father and mother, Jews living in Germany without German citizenship, were put on a train and sent across the border to Poland, each with one small suitcase. From there, things got worse. Meta's father died of starvation in the Lodz ghetto. Then, in late 1943, Meta and her mother were deported from the ghetto to Auschwitz. Upon arrival, a German motioned her mother to the gas chambers. Two weeks later, Meta was sent to Bergen-Belsen and, from there, to the labor camp of Salzwedel. On April 14, 1945, American soldiers liberated Meta. She was nineteen years old, ill, and destitute.[2]

Meta and her family were among the millions of victims of Germany's war against the Jews. The National Socialist regime targeted women, men, and children living in many countries across Europe and North Africa. Little, if anything united them, except their oppression by Germany and its allies during the twelve-year reign of the Third Reich. They engaged in many different occupations and held a wide range of political and religious beliefs, or no religious beliefs at all. At the end of the war, they did not have a generally accepted spokesman to advance their claim for compensation.

The search for redress for the losses of Holocaust victims is the subject of this book. Reparations for individuals were not part of postwar planning. No country advocated for the payment of compensation to Jews, the group that suffered the most from German persecution. Politicians, jurists, and political scientists assumed that states would be the sole recipients of reparations.

As for the Germans, they emerged from the war and subsequent occupation with the belief that they, not Holocaust survivors, were Nazism's true victims. According to Robert G. Moeller, Germany made the transition from the racially defined community of the people of the Third Reich to the community of victims of the war for which they accepted no responsibility.[3] In December 1951, five percent of West Germans who were surveyed admitted to feeling "guilty" toward Jews. An additional twenty-nine percent recognized that there should be a duty to pay some restitution to the Jewish people. Twenty-one percent thought that the Jews were partly responsible for their persecution by the Third Reich, and the rest wanted only those people who had committed "something" to pay compensation.[4]

The subject of this book is the Conference on Jewish Material Claims against Germany (the Claims Conference): how it paved the way to negotiations on reparations for Holocaust survivors and acted as a dealmaker with West Germany. Prior to the 1952 round of negotiations with West Germany, Israel claimed that it alone spoke for the Jews. However, minutes of Israeli government meetings and first-hand accounts show that it was diaspora leaders who initiated the first round of negotiations with West Germany. Israel had been reluctant to conduct direct talks with the aggressors and objected to the participation of third parties in negotiations with competing claims for compensation. Help came from an unexpected quarter. West Germany supported the involvement of an entity led by American Jewish leaders and viewed the Claims Conference as a stepping-stone on the way back to the family of nations. Subsequently, Israel abandoned the campaign for reparations. The Claims Conference became the chief protagonist lobbying on behalf of Holocaust survivors and allocating reparations.

EARLIEST JUSTIFICATION FOR REPARATIONS: PLUNDER OF JEWISH PROPERTY

The earliest demands for compensation for Jewish victims of National Socialism centered on stolen property. Communal leaders and jurists drafted claims during the Second World War, before the full extent of the genocide was known. The nature of the claims did not change even after the discovery of the atrocities perpetrated against the Jews. A consensus existed between diaspora leaders that no sum of money could compensate for the loss of lives. In the words of Dr. Isaac Lewin, at the inaugural meeting of the Claims Conference: "we will not sell the memory of our parents, brothers, sisters and children . . . for any money."[5] Moreover, in the middle of the twentieth century, there was no precedent for the payment of reparations as a remedy for a mass atrocity.

Robbery was a central feature of the Nazi regime. Stuart Eizenstat has described the plunder of Jewish property as "the greatest theft in the world."[6] The official term for the confiscation (theft) of Jewish property was Aryanization (*Arisierung*). The meaning of this word has evolved over time and now encompasses the gradual expulsion of Jews from economic life.[7] Aryanization was a prolonged process involving a large number of actors and deeds and the theft of movable and immovable property, businesses, and household contents. In the first five years of the National Socialist regime, "voluntary sales" and taxes were the chief methods of expropriation. Jewish owners of businesses wishing to liquidate assets prior to emigration had to find a purchaser. Frequently, former partners and private corporations exploited the situation and acquired a business at a fraction of its true value. After selling property at a loss, the owners were subject to the Reich Flight Tax on the proceeds. In addition, the German government required emigrants transferring funds abroad to pay a special expiation levy to the German Gold Discount Bank (Dego). In August 1934, the levy amounted to sixty-five percent of the funds to be transferred abroad. By 1939, it had risen to ninety-six percent.[8]

The case of the Schocken department store chain illustrates a "voluntary sale." In 1901 Simon Schocken opened a department store in Zwickau in the state of Saxony to provide "what the housewife needed."[9] Three years later, his brother Salman opened another store in Oelsnitz, a small industrial center in the east of Germany (Erzgebirge). By 1932, the chain numbered sixteen stores and employed six thousand workers. It had a turnover of almost one hundred million Deutschmarks and was the fourth-largest department store chain in Germany.[10] When the National Socialist Party took power, a director of a German bank replaced Salman Schocken as chairman of the board of directors and dismissed the Jewish staff. In December 1937, following the government instigated boycott of Jewish stores, Salman Schocken decided to sell the enterprise. The purchaser was a German banking group, and the agreed sales price was five percent of the concern's real value.[11] The new owners renamed the stores "Merkur." The appointment of an Aryan chairman, the dismissal of Jewish employees, and a customers' boycott attest to a lack of free will and undermine the voluntary nature of the sale.[12]

In the mid-1930s, German federal and regional authorities began to participate in the expropriation of Jewish property. A revision of the foreign exchange law at the end of 1936 permitted the stripping of owners of their right to dispose of their assets if suspected of capital flight violation. The government viewed all Jews as capital flight suspects.[13] German tax authorities froze assets owned by Jews to cover taxes imposed upon them, namely the flight tax and expiation levy. Subsequently, the authorities appointed fiduciary trustees to liquidate Jewish-owned businesses.[14]

The use of violence in the theft of property increased after the annexation of Austria in March 1938. In his semi-autobiographical novel *Wohnungen* (1969), Wolfgang Georg Fischer described the loss of his family home. After entering the flat, the confiscator told his Nazi superior: "Heil Hitler, mission completed, apartment searched, excellent condition, freshly painted windows, new parquet floor, on the garden side—Thanks, I'll keep it."[15] Another description appears in Edmund de Waal's *The Hare with Amber Eyes*. On March 12, 1938, on the eve of the annexation of Austria, eight or ten brownshirts invaded the Ephrussi family home in Vienna, took the silver candlesticks, cigarette boxes, and money, heaved a dressing table to the window and sent it crashing over the handrail until, with the sound of splintering wood and gilt and marquetry, it hit the stone flags of the courtyard below. By way of explanation, the attackers added: "You think you own us, you fucking foreign shit. You'll be fucking next, you shit, you fucking Jews."[16] On the same day, German authorities confiscated the art collections of Alphonse Rothschild and the paintings and library of Baron Gutmann in Vienna. The historian William Shirer saw SS officers at the Rothschild palace removing silver and other loot from the basement.[17] One had a gold-framed picture under his arm. Another officer's arms were loaded with silver knives and forks.

The Austrian outburst of violence prompted the German government to intervene. The fear of looting by individuals, referred to in official documents as "wild Aryanizations," led to the enactment of the Decree on the Registration of Jewish Property on April 26, 1938. This decree required all Jews, as defined by the Nuremberg Laws, owning assets in excess of five thousand Reichsmarks to report, list, and value all their possessions. Later in the year, after the November pogrom, Germany issued a new decree on the exclusion of Jews from economic life and prohibiting the ownership of retail shops by Jews. In December 1938, the government imposed a Jewish property levy, namely a compulsory contribution of one billion Reichsmarks (equivalent to four hundred million US dollars, in nominal terms). In 1935, between a fifth and a quarter of an estimated 102,000 Jewish-owned businesses in Germany had been liquidated or transferred to Aryan hands. On the eve of the November pogrom, fewer than 4,000 retail outlets in Greater Germany remained in Jewish hands.[18] Jewish banks underwent a similar process of forced transfer of ownership.

The outbreak of the Second World War and the deportation of Jews from Germany and Austria to the East offered new opportunities for plunder. Heinrich Himmler oversaw the transfer of Jewish household goods abandoned by owners to deserving German families. In a 1941 meeting, Joseph Goebbels said that *Volksgenossen* (racial comrades) "would lunge at the

Jews' warm rolls like vultures."[19] One example that illustrates the scope of the plunder is a delivery order of the finance ministry in Baden-Württemberg dated October 6, 1942. The order provided for the transfer of the contents of the homes of (presumably deported Jews) Isak Strauss, Isak Gottlieb, and Sarah Grünstein to the Alois Jereb family in neighboring Berlichingen including two bedsteads, two nightstands, one pull-out table, three chairs, one chaise longue, two feather beds, a tablecloth, hand towels, and lamps.[20] German residents of demolished apartments and buildings bombed by the Allied forces also benefited from abandoned Jewish household goods.

In Poland, the confiscation of businesses owned by Jews commenced immediately after the German invasion. The German-run General Government confiscated 112,000 Jewish-owned businesses in the region.[21] German administrative agencies froze the bank accounts of Polish Jews in both the annexed parts and occupied territories of Poland. Pillage by German and Austrian officials was an everyday phenomenon throughout the war, conducted in homes, at killing sites, and at concentration camps. On October 22, 1939, a German officer accompanied by two policemen entered an apartment in Lodz and took away radios, mattresses, comforters, and carpets.[22] In Riga, in the summer of 1941, no fewer than 5,800 Jewish homes were plundered.[23]

Germany and its collaborators benefitted from the stolen property. One example is the Mennonite community. Following the division of Poland, Mennonites who resided in the territory under Soviet control relocated to summer homes that had belonged to Jewish vacationers in the vicinity of Lodz. Heinrich Hamm, a member of the Mennonite Central Committee, wrote that he and true Germans "thank God and the *Führer* daily with tears in their eyes for the great privileges they enjoy."[24] The occupying forces shipped valuable items back to Germany, and from 1942 onward, deposited stolen valuables in the Reichsbank. In Galicia alone, the looting included 206 kilograms of gold objects, 5,400 kilograms of silver objects, and thirty-five freight cars filled with furs and fur coats.[25]

Survivors who returned home to search for relatives and property encountered homes possessed by others and hostile neighbors. Helen Fagin from Radomski in Poland recounted how after liberation, friends who had looked after her family's possessions when they fled, refused to return the items: "they wouldn't recognize us, they wouldn't give them back to us, and they just totally dismissed us."[26] Ruth Klüger told the joke that was current in postwar Vienna about two people to whom Jews had entrusted their belongings before deportation. One said to the other: "You are lucky, your Jew didn't return. Mine did."[27]

Estimates of the value of property expropriated from Jewish owners during the twelve-year reign of the Third Reich varied. One of the earliest assessments put the damage caused to the Jews of Germany and Austria at four billion marks.[28] In 1944, the jurist Dr. Nehemiah Robinson stated that the probable value of Jewish wealth in eighteen Axis or Axis-dominated countries was between 8.23 million and 8.63 million US dollars.[29] Raul Hilberg valued the total wealth of German Jews in 1933 at between ten and twelve million marks.[30] A 1999 investigation of six countries estimated that before the Second World War, the 4.95 million Jewish residents of Germany, Austria, Holland, France, Poland, and Hungary owned property totaling approximately twelve billion US dollars. By 1945, nine billion dollars' worth of this property was lost.[31]

A NOVEL FORM OF INTERNATIONAL ACTIVISM

The Claims Conference played (and continues to play) a unique role in international law. It is a private corporation created by one person, Dr. Nahum Goldmann, to negotiate on behalf of Holocaust victims and survivors. After the successful conclusion of two agreements with West Germany (Protocols 1 and 2 to the Luxembourg Agreement), the international non-governmental organization (INGO) administered and distributed funds according to criteria it prescribed. In addition, it liaised with governmental officials and negotiated follow-up agreements, chiefly with West Germany. Almost seventy years later, the organization still lobbies for compensation and distributes funds received from states and foundations. It is one of the largest public organizations (in terms of revenues and assets) in the Jewish world.[32]

The Claims Conference presents a different model of non-state diplomacy. Traditionally, communities entered the international arena to promote social reform or to engage in relief work. More recently, they have acted as consultants to states and intergovernmental organizations, generating and sharing knowledge or providing development aid. The Claims Conference fills a void in state-to-state relations. It sought and received reparations for a transnational community, namely Jewish victims of the Third Reich. Subsequently, it determined a system for the allocation of German funds. This form of activism extends the barriers of communities' involvement in global politics.

Since its inception, the Claims Conference has been surrounded by controversy. Scholars have dismissed the Claims Conference, as well as other organizations created by Goldmann. One assessment of Goldmann's diplomatic activities concluded that "All these oligarchic structures with fancy titles, where the same group of Jewish notables fulfilled similar functions under diverse headings, had neither broad backing nor real influence."[33] The creation of an entity claiming to speak in the name of world Jewry on reparations by one person supports the charge of a lack of broad backing. The evidence does not support the second charge regarding a lack of real influence. German recognition and the funds provided to it granted the Claims Conference considerable power and a very real influence on the postwar diaspora.

POINT OF DIVERGENCE FROM EXISTING LITERATURE

The belief that international agreements were made by states may have colored the perception of scholars in their study of post-Holocaust financial reckoning. The earliest accounts centered on the two states involved. They chronicled the reparations process in the context of relations between West Germany and Israel. Historians and political scientists viewed the Claims Conference as an agent of minor importance or a go-between, liaising and smoothing the way between the principal actors.[34] This approach is derived from the traditional view of states as the sole players in global politics.[35] In his 1985 revised edition of *The Destruction of the European Jews*, Hilberg described the formation of the Claims Conference in one sentence.[36] Other studies that treated the Claims Conference as Israel's sidekick are Ralph Vogel's collection of documents, entitled *The German Path to Israel*, Lily Gardner Feldman's book *The Special Relationship between West Germany and Israel*, and research by Yechiam Weitz on the events leading up to the commencement of negotiations.[37] These accounts ended with the signing of the Luxembourg Agreements on September 10, 1952, and did not review subsequent rounds of negotiations.

The reunification of Germany in 1990 generated renewed interest in the subject of legal redress for Holocaust crimes. Scholars either overlooked the Claims Conference or repeated the statist version of two main players and one tag-along. Reviews of the postwar model of transitional justice in Germany limited their examination to the question of criminal accountability for Nazi barbarity.[38] Histories of the 1990s campaign for restitution and compensation to slave laborers omitted the agreements made with Israel and the Claims Conference.[39] Other authors broadened the scope of their review to include the precedent created by the Luxembourg Agreement but did not challenge the narrative of negotiations between two states. Michael Marrus, Elazar Barkan, and Tom Segev have noted the historical importance of the 1952 Luxembourg Agreement on reparations but focused on other subjects: justice and morality after the end of the Cold War, negotiating historical injustices, and the impact of the Holocaust on Israel.[40] Michael Bazyler, in his 2006 book *Holocaust Restitution: Perspectives on the Litigation and its Aftermath*, described the Claims Conference as a "pass-through entity," by which West Germany could make payment to a limited class of survivors living in the West.[41] This assessment ignores the fact that the Claims Conference was and is an autonomous organization, and in the first decade of its existence, distributed reparations according to criteria it—not West Germany—determined. Regula Ludi's analysis of the evolution of reparations in different national contexts described the central role played by Goldmann, not the Claims Conference, in the 1952 negotiations. She did not question the participation of a new diaspora alliance in the talks or the justification for its claim to speak in the name of world Jewry.[42]

German and German-speaking scholars examined the issue of reparations for individual victims of the Third Reich. Their analysis of federal legislation and central and local government records highlighted the reluctance of German politicians and administrators to provide compensation and the fear of establishing precedents that would enable other groups to demand redress. Constantin Goschler is a leading authority on the subject and has published numerous works including his 2005 book, *Schuld und Schulden: Die Politik der Wiedergutmachung für NS-Verfolgte seit 1945*.[43] In 2009, Goschler, together with Norbert Frei and José Brunner, edited *die Praxis der Wiedergutmachung* on the attempts of Nazi victims to obtain compensation.[44] This literature does not explain the genesis of the Claims Conference or the manner in which the organization distributed German funds.

Literature on the Claims Conference is limited to portrayals of its activities commissioned by the organization or diatribes against it. The leading account is Ronald Zweig's *German Reparations and the Jewish World, A History of the Claims Conference*, first published in 1987. It reviewed the impact of German reparations on the rehabilitation of Jewish life.[45] The Claims Conference also sponsored a history of the organization by the journalist Marilyn Henry. Her book, *Confronting the Perpetrators: A History of the Claims Conference*, published in 2007, is an uncritical evaluation of the organization. It contains a chapter on "Sacred Spending" based entirely on discussions with executives and a limited range of documents from the organization.[46] A recently published anthology contains an article by senior officials of the Claims Conference listing the agreements they negotiated.[47] Less favourable and highly polemical accounts of the organization appear in Norman Finkelstein's *The Holocaust Industry: Reflections on the Exploitation of Jewish Suffering* and Raul Teitelbaum's *The Biological Solution* (in Hebrew and German).[48] Finkelstein recycled Jewish stereotypes, reinforcing rather than challenging antisemitic tropes on the connection between Jews and money. Both advocates and critics did not explain the leading role taken by the Claims Conference in the reparations process or compare it to other forms of transnational activism inside or outside the Jewish world.

This analysis of the Claims Conference is intended to contribute to research on post-Holocaust and reparative justice. There is a growing body of literature on survivors and transitional justice.[49] Advocacy by the Claims

Conference highlights the strengths and weaknesses of a non-state actor seeking redress for a transnational community. Moreover, the allocation of German funds by the organization explains how the money was used and why survivors played a limited role in the distribution process. Restitution of looted assets is another topic that has received considerable attention and is on the agendas of governments and individuals. In 1998, the US Department of State and the US Holocaust Memorial Museum hosted a conference in Washington on Holocaust era assets.[50] An understanding of the conflict between individuals and leaders of a community that accompanied the Claims Conference will, hopefully, enrich research on restitution and ownership of "heirless" property.

The Claims Conference is one of a myriad of institutions that governments, communities, and individuals established after the war. Interest in international and transnational organizations and their impact on global politics is a relatively recent development reflected in a growing body of literature. Authors from different disciplines including political science, history, and law have examined forms of non-state governance and diplomacy. Examples of this work include Bob Reinalda's *Routledge History of International Organizations: From 1815 to the Present Day*, Mark Mazower's *Governing the World*, and "Nongovernmental Organizations and International Law," an article by Steve Charnovitz.[51] This research has provided a theoretical basis for analyzing the Claims Conference, a Jewish institution, in a wider context. The Claims Conference shares many qualities of international agencies established in the same period. These include American domination, exclusion of large sectors of the community they purportedly represent, emphasis on the professional nature of their conduct, and a lack of transparency. Patricia Clavin, a scholar of international relations in the twentieth century, stated that the question of how the institutions operated has "dogged attempts to assess the role of international organizations in the modern world."[52] She added that an understanding of this issue is important for both historians and international relations scholars. A description of the genesis and evolution of the Claims Conference is intended to enhance the study of non-state actors.

The reparations alliance is absent from recent studies of Jewish internationalism. In the pre-1948 world, there was a long history of intercessions by individuals and associations with rulers and governments to prevent persecution of coreligionists and provide humanitarian aid.[53] Attempts to build a single broad common coalition in the century preceding the negotiations on German reparations failed.[54] The Claims Conference presents a new model of leadership: transnational, supra-denominational, and non-ideological. Its stability and longevity are striking. The choice of constituent members and the culture that directed their joint operations explain how the alliance overcame differences in ideologies and practices. This study contributes to an understanding of Jewish diplomacy and intra-communal politics.

Finally, this book fills a gap in research on Israel-diaspora relations. The existing literature on the subject rarely mentions the Claims Conference.[55] The first years after the establishment of the state were a period of acrimonious exchanges between statesmen and communal leaders. Prime Minister David Ben-Gurion charged the heads of the Zionist movement with moral bankruptcy for remaining in the diaspora and not joining the efforts to build the new state.[56] At the same time, leaders of non-Zionist associations in America objected strongly to Israeli references to the term "the Jewish nation" and calls for "the ingathering of exiles."[57] Cooperation in the field of German reparations demonstrated the adjustment of diaspora activism to the new reality of operations alongside a state. In addition, the state's focus on security needs convinced those Israeli politicians who had criticized life in the diaspora of the benefits of diplomacy by a non-state actor.

SOURCES

Documents of the Claims Conference from 1951 to 1964 constitute the main source of this study. The difficulty of accessing these documents is one reason for the very limited research on the organization and its omission from accounts of post-Holocaust financial reckoning. The Claims Conference shipped its archives for the first long decade of its operations to Israel, although its offices are in New York. The geographical distance and need to obtain permission in advance to access the material explain the lack of research on the organization. It took me three and a half months and many emails to receive approval from the Claims Conference to access their archives, located at the time in a crowded asbestos hut on the Givat Ram campus. Documents on the internal proceedings of the organization for the period after 1964 are located in New York and have not yet been classified. Shortly before the publication of this book, the Claims Conference began to digitize its records from the 1950s. Hopefully, the availability of the documents will encourage academic interest in the organization.

Goldmann's autobiographies and interviews are another source. In this context, it should be noted that he was an interested and non-objective party and therefore not a totally reliable source of information. Shlomo Shafir, an Israeli historian, argued that Goldmann's autobiography "should be used with caution."[58] Most of the documents in Goldmann's personal archive relate to the World Zionist Organization and very few are directly connected to the Claims Conference. Documents of member organizations of the Claims Conference provide a valuable source of information. Finally, archival material from the Israeli Foreign Ministry contributes to an understanding of the evolving relationship between the state and the diaspora alliance.

The voices of Holocaust survivors on the advocacy agency that demanded compensation for their losses are an essential part of the Claims Conference history. Many institutions collected and digitized testimonies of people who lived through the horrors of the Second World War. I searched but found extremely limited direct references to personal reparations and no mention of the Claims Conference. There are several reasons for this omission. Institutions and survivors limited their questions and answers to life before the war and the persecution and loss of family members and friends. Interviewers did not always ask survivors about their lives after the war.[59] When asked, the intended beneficiaries explained how small payments received many decades after the end of the war did not begin to cover their losses or compensate for their suffering and injuries. In the words of Eva Weiner who survived the war in Poland in a ghetto and in hiding, "We never get paid for what we went through."[60] Dina Dzialowski, who was born in Cologne and was hidden in a Belgian convent, asked whether reparations could heal a soul or pay for a destroyed childhood.[61] Another survivor, Horst Weiss, who was born in Dresden in 1913 and escaped without his family before the war, said in a 1996 interview that occasionally he received a few marks and added that "for your mother and sister who were sent to Auschwitz they paid a certain amount for each day. . . . My whole life would have been completely different if nothing else had happened."[62] In addition, the impact of reparations on the lives of survivors depended on their financial situation. Interviewees generally refrained from sharing private information on their wealth or poverty with a large audience of strangers. Finally, restrictions imposed due to the COVID-19 pandemic limited access to testimonies. Writing the survivors into the history of reparations and the Claims Conference requires further research. This will have to wait until the post-pandemic return to normality.

OUTLINE

The refusal of the Allied nations to recognize Jewish claims for compensation at the end of the Second World War set the scene for a new form of activism. Jewish individuals and associations decided to concentrate their efforts on restitution instead of reparations. The first chapter describes the coalitions between Zionist and non-Zionist groups operating in occupied Germany. They constituted a prototype for a spokesman on behalf of a transnational community. Restitution work and the distribution of proceeds between member organizations served as an essential training ground for officers and executives of the much longer-lasting reparations agency.

The emergence of an alliance claiming to speak in the name of "world Jewry" on reparations, the Claims Conference, is the subject of the second chapter. A major distinction between democratic states and communities relates to the assumption of control and the change of status from a subject to a leader. In a democracy, the rules and procedures for the election of leaders are determined in advance and made public to all. Communities of coreligionists, compatriots, professionals, or political activists frequently lack guidelines on the appointment of individuals to act on their behalf. Consequently, leadership emerges behind closed doors. The Claims Conference exemplifies this practice.

The third chapter examines the role of the diaspora delegation in the first round of negotiations on reparations. The agreements reached by the Claims Conference with West Germany transformed the delegation comprised of two committees with a lifespan of six months and a limited mandate into a permanent and powerful organization. The adaptation of mandates and methods to ensure immortality is a common phenomenon. In the 1940s and 1950s, individuals and communities set up a broad range of institutions directly connected to the cataclysmic consequences of the Second World War. Within a decade, many had completed their mission. Seventy years later, they continue to function. The chapter discusses the tactics applied by members and officers of the Claims Conference and the interplay between external and internal pressures that enabled its survival.

The fourth chapter describes the formulation of a policy for the allocation of German funds. This policy was tailored to the needs of the Claims Conference and its members. Paradoxically, survivors controlled only a minority stake. The structure of the alliance and its operations illuminate the divergence between its alleged purpose of representing "world Jewry" in the claim for reparations for survivors and its actual conduct.

Distribution of reparations by a non-state actor raises questions of inclusion and exclusion. The Claims Conference boasted that it included among its members a broad range of Jewish groups, geographically and ideologically. The accuracy of this portrayal is examined in the fifth chapter as well as the sectors excluded from the umbrella organization.

The penultimate chapter analyzes the internal operations of the reparations agency. The Claims Conference adopted the language of progressive management based on rational norms and objective criteria. It published a list of rules and guidelines on entitlement to German funds. The intention was to project an image of disbursement of reparations by experts in accordance with neutral standards. Minutes of meetings and correspondence of the organization and its members reveal the actual workings of the allocations. They illustrate the similarity between the entity and much earlier forms of self-governance.

The last chapter focuses on the lobbying activities of the Claims Conference after the execution of the Luxembourg Agreement. No state volunteered to represent a transitional community in their demands for compensation. The ongoing negotiations between Germany and the Claims Conference illustrate the involvement of non-state actors in global politics and a new form of diplomacy.

NOTES

1. Meta Doran, Interview 10878. Tape 1: 4:14–5:06. USC Shoah Foundation Visual History Archive. USC Shoah Foundation. January 13, 1996. Accessed December 30, 2020.
2. Meta Doran, Interview 10878. Tape 2: 17:56–20:52.
3. Robert G. Moeller, "The Politics of the Past in the 1950s: Rhetorics of Victimisation in East and West Germany," in Bill Niven, ed., *Germans as Victims: Remembering the Past in Contemporary Germany*. (New York: Palgrave Macmillan, 2006), 33. There is a considerable literature on German self-perception as victims. See, for example, Robert C. Holub, "Germans as Victims in 1995," *Colloquia Germanica* 48, no. 1/2 (2015): 23–33. https://www.jstor.org/stable/44478221.
4. Tony Judt, *Postwar: A History of Europe Since 1945* (New York: Penguin, 2005), 271–272.
5. See Minutes of the Conference on Jewish Material Claims against Germany held at the Waldorf-Astoria Hotel – New York City on October 25–26, 1951 (Minutes of the Conference on Jewish Material Claims held on October 25–26, 1951), Central Archives for the History of the Jewish People (CAHJP), Claims Conference File no. 16600, p. 64.
6. Eizenstat, Stuart. Interview 55687. USC Shoah Foundation Visual History Archive. USC Shoah Foundation. 2016. Accessed 23 November 2020.
7. Franz Bajohr, "Aryanization and Restitution in Germany," in Martin Dean, Constantin Goschler, and Philipp Ther, eds., *Robbery and Restitution: The Conflict over Jewish Property in Europe* (New York and Oxford: Berghahn Books, 2007), 33.
8. Bajohr, "Aryanization and Restitution in Germany," 35.
9. Siegfried Moses, "Salman Schocken: His Economic and Zionist Activities," *Leo Baeck Institute Yearbook* 5 (1960): 77.
10. André Krajewski, *Die Geschichte der jüdischen Warenhäuser in Deutschland* (*The History of Jewish Department Stores in Germany*), Self-published, 2011, p. 9, https://andre-krajewski.de/content/pdf/warenhaus.pdf.
11. Krajewski, *Die Geschichte der jüdischen Warenhäuser*, p. 15.
12. Another example of a voluntary sale appears in Géraldine Schwarz, *Those Who Forget: One Family's Story – A Memoir, A History, A Warning*, trans. Laura Marris (London: Pushkin Press, 2020), 47–50.
13. Bajohr, "Aryanization and Restitution in Germany," 36.
14. Ingo Köhler, "Business as Usual? Aryanization in Practice, 1933–1938," in Hartmut Berghoff, Jürgen Kocka, and Dieter Ziegler, eds., *Business in the Age of*

Extremes: Essays in Modern German and Austrian Economic History (Cambridge, New York: Cambridge University Press, 2013), 176.

15. Wolfgang Georg Fischer, *Wohnungen (Apartments)* (Munich: C. Hanser, 1969), 207.

16. Edmund de Waal, *The Hare with Amber Eyes: A Family's Century of Art and Loss* (New York: Farrar, Straus and Giroux, 2010), 240–241.

17. William Shirer, *Berlin Diary: The Journal of a Foreign Correspondent, 1934–1941* (New York: Alfred A. Knopf, 1941), 189.

18. Helen B. Junz, "Report on the Pre-War Wealth Position of the Jewish Population in Nazi-Occupied Countries, Germany and Austria," Appendix S to *Report on Dormant Accounts of Victims of Nazi Persecution in Swiss Banks* (Berne: Staempfli, 1999), A-165.

19. Carolin Dorothée Lange, "After they Left: Looted Jewish Apartments and the Private Perception of the Holocaust," *Holocaust and Genocide Studies* 34, no. 3 (2020): 436. https://doi.org/10.1093/hgs/dcaa042.

20. H. G. Adler, *Der verwaltete Mensch: Studien zur Deportation der Juden aus Deutschland (The Administered Human: Studies on Deportation of Jews from Germany)* (Tübingen: J.C.B. Mohr, 1974), 599.

21. Dieter Pohl, "The Robbery of Jewish Property in Eastern Europe under German Occupation, 1939–1942," in *Robbery and Restitution*, 71–72.

22. Saul Friedlander, *Nazi Germany and the Jews, 1933–1945* (New York: HarperCollins, 2009), 155.

23. Pohl, "The Robbery of Jewish Property in Eastern Europe," 71.

24. Ben Goossen, "The Real History of the Mennonites and the Holocaust," *Tablet Magazine, tabletmag.com,* November 17, 2020, accessed November 17, 2020, https://www.tabletmag.com/sections/history/articles/heinrich-hamm-mennonite-holocaust.

25. Yitzhak Arad, "Plunder of Jewish Property in the Nazi-Occupied Areas of the Soviet Union," *Yad Vashem Studies* 29 (2001): 146.

26. Oral history interview with Helen Fagin dated February 13, 1995, United States Holocaust Memorial Museum (USHMM) Accession Number: 1995.A.1269.4, RG Number: RG-50.470.0004.

27. Ruth Klüger, *Still Alive: A Holocaust Girlhood Remembered* (New York: Feminist Press, 2012), 59.

28. Nana Sagi, *German Reparations: A History of the Negotiations*, trans. Dafna Alon (Jerusalem: Magnes Press, 1980), 15.

29. Nehemiah Robinson, *Jewish Post-War Claims* (New York: Institute of Jewish Affairs of AJC and WJC, 1944), 83.

30. Raul Hilberg, *The Destruction of the European Jews*, rev. and definitive ed. (New York and London: Holmes & Meier, 1985), 135.

31. Junz, "Report on the Pre-War Wealth Position of the Jewish Population," A-130.

32. See the organization's 2018 financial reports at "Conference on Jewish Material Claims Against Germany, Inc. Financial Statements," *Claims Conference*, December 31, 2018 and 2017, accessed on October 20, 2019, http://www.claimscon.org/wp-content/uploads/2019/08/Audited-FS-FYE-12-31-18.pdf.

33. Jehuda Reinharz and Evyatar Friesel, "Nahum Goldmann, Jewish and Zionist Statesman - An Overview," in Mark A. Raider, ed., *Nahum Goldmann: Statesman without a State* (Albany: SUNY Press, 2009), 36.

34. See, for example, Sagi, *German Reparations*; Nicholas Balabkins, *West German Reparations to Israel* (New Brunswick, NJ: Rutgers University Press, 1971).

35. Darren Hawkins, David Lake, Daniel Nielson, and Michael Tiernet, eds., *Delegation and Agency in International Organization* (New York: Cambridge University Press, 2006), 4–5.

36. Hilberg, *The Destruction of the European Jews*, vol. 3, 1178.

37. Rolf Vogel, ed., *The German Path to Israel: A Documentation* (London: Oswald Wolff, 1969); Lily Gardner Feldman, *The Special Relationship between West Germany and Israel* (Boston: George Allen & Unwin, 1984); Yechiam Weitz, "HaDerech LeWassenaar: Keitsad Ushra Hahachlata al Masa umatan Yashir ben Yisrael leGermania," (The Way to Wassenaar: How the Decision on Negotiations between Israel and Germany was Approved) *Yad Vashem* 28 (2000): 247; Balabkins, *West German Reparations to Israel*; Yeshayahu A. Jelinek, "Political Acumen, Altruism, Foreign Pressure or Moral Debt – Konrad Adenauer and the 'Shilumim,'" *Tel Aviv Jahrbuch für deutsche Geschichte* 19 (1990): 77–102: Moshe Zimmermann and Oded Heilbronner, *"Yahasim Normaliim:" Yahasei Israel-Germania* (*"Normal Relations:" Israeli-German Relations*) (Jerusalem: Magnes Press, 1993).

38. See, for example, Berel Lang, *Post-Holocaust: Interpretation, Misinterpretation, and the Claims of History* (Bloomington: Indiana University Press, 2005); Alan E. Steinweis and Robert D. Rachlin, eds., *Ideology, Opportunism, and the Perversion of Justice* (New York and Oxford: Berghahn, 2013); John Michalczyk, ed., *Nazi Law: From Nuremberg to Nuremberg* (London: Bloomsbury Academic, 2018); Devin O. Pendas, *Democracy, Nazi Trials, and Transitional Justice in Germany, 1945–1950* (New York: Cambridge University Press, 2020); Philippe Sands, *East West Street: On the Origins of Genocide and Crimes Against Humanity* (London: Weidenfeld + Nicolson, 2016).

39. Stuart Eizenstat, *Imperfect Justice: Looted Assets, Slave Labor, and the Unfinished Business of World War II* (New York: Public Affairs, 2003); Leora Bilsky, *The Holocaust, Corporations, and the Law: Unfinished Business* (Ann Arbor: University of Michigan Press, 2017).

40. Michael R. Marrus, *Some Measure of Justice: The Holocaust Era Restitution Campaigns of the 1990s* (Madison, Wisconsin: University of Wisconsin Press, 2009), 70–73; Elazar Barkan, *The Guilt of Nations: Restitution and Negotiating Historical Injustices* (New York: Norton, 2000), 11; Tom Segev, *The Seventh Million: The Israelis and the Holocaust*, trans. Haim Watzman (New York: Henry Holt, 1991), 229–236.

41. Bazyler did not cite any reference for his description of the Claims Conference as a "pass-through" entity. See Michael J. Bazyler, *Holocaust, Genocide, and the Law: A Quest for Justice in a Post-Holocaust World* (New York: Oxford University Press, 2016), 158.

42. Regula Ludi, *Reparations for Nazi Victims in Postwar Europe* (Cambridge: Cambridge University Press, 2012), 111–114.

43. Constantin Goschler, *Schuld und Schulden: Die Politik der Wiedergutmachung für NS-Verfolgte seit 1945* (*Guilt and Debts: The Politics of Reparations for Victims of National Socialism since 1945*) (Göttingen: Wallstein, 2005). Other studies include Christian Pross, *Paying for the Past: The Struggle over Reparations for Surviving Victims of the Nazi Terror*, trans. Belinda Cooper (Baltimore and London: John Hopkins University Press, 1998); Hans Günter Hockerts, "Wiedergutmachung in Deutschland: Eine historische Bilanz 1945–2000," (Reparations in Germany: A Historical Balance, 1945–2000) *Vierteljahrshefte für Zeitgeschichte* 49, no. 2 (2001): 167–170; Claudia Moisel and Tobias Winstel, eds., *Grenzen der Wiedergutmachung: Die Entschädigung für NS-Verfolgte in West- und Osteuropa 1945–2000* (*Limits of Reparations: Compensation for Victims of National Socialism in Western and Eastern Europe 1945–2000*) (Göttingen: Wallstein Verlag, 2006).

44. Norbert Frei, José Brunner, and Constantin Goschler, eds., *Die Praxis der Wiedergutmachung: Geschichte, Erfahrung und Wirkung in Deutschland und Israel* (*Compensation Practice: History, Experience, and Outcome in Germany and Israel*) (Göttingen: Wallstein Verlag, 2009). See also Elazar Barkan, Constantin Goschler, and James Waller, eds., *Historical Dialogue and the Prevention of Mass Atrocities* (New York: Routledge, 2020).

45. Ronald W. Zweig, *German Reparations and the Jewish World, A History of the Claims Conference*, 2nd ed. (London: Portland, 2001). See also Karen Heilig, "From the Luxembourg Agreement to Today: Representing a People," *Berkeley Journal of International Law*, 20, no. 1 (2002): 176–196.

46. Marilyn Henry, *Confronting the Perpetrators: A History of the Claims Conference* (London: Vallentine Mitchell, 2007). A critical review of this book appears in Ronald W. Zweig, "Review of *Confronting the Perpetrators. A History of the Claims Conference* by Marilyn Henry," *American Jewish History* 94 (2008): 344–346. https://www.jstor.org/stable/23887743.

47. Carla Ferstman, Mariana Goetz, and Alan Stephens, eds., *Reparations for Victims of Genocide, War Crimes, and Crimes against Humanity: Systems in Place and Systems in the Making* (Leiden and Boston: Nijhoff, 2020), 203–214.

48. Norman Finkelstein, *The Holocaust Industry: Reflections on the Exploitation of Jewish Suffering* (London: Verso, 2000); Raul Teitelbaum, *The Biological Solution* (Israel: Hakibbutz Hameuchad, 2008).

49. On survivors see Leonard Dinnerstein, *America and the Survivors of the Holocaust* (New York: Columbia University Press, 1982); Margarete Myers Feinstein, *Holocaust Survivors in Postwar Germany, 1945–1957* (Cambridge and New York: Cambridge University Press, 2010); Mark Wyman, *Displaced Persons: Europe's Displaced Persons, 1945–1951* (Philadelphia: Balch Institute Press, 1989); Eva Kolinsky, *After the Holocaust: Jewish Survivors after 1945* (London: Pimlico, 2004); Ben Shephard, *The Long Road Home: The Aftermath of the Second World War* (London: Vintage Books, 2011); Tara Zahra, *The Lost Children: Reconstructing Europe's Families after World War II* (Cambridge, MA: Harvard University Press, 2011); David Nasaw, *The Last Million: Europe's Displaced Persons from World War to Cold War* (New York: Penguin Press, 2020); Rebecca

Clifford, *Survivors: Children's Lives after the Holocaust* (New Haven, CT: Yale University Press, 2020).

50. Larissa Allwork, *Holocaust Remembrance between the National and the Transnational: the Stockholm International Forum and the First Decade of the International Task Force* (London: Bloomsbury Academic, 2015), 23–25; Chris Hopkinson, *Terezín Declaration—Ten Years Later: 7th International Conference: The Documentation, Identification and Restitution of the Cultural Assets of WWII Victims: Proceedings of an International Academic Conference Held in Prague on 18–19 June, 2019* (Prague: Documentation Centre for Property Transfers of Cultural Assets of WWII Victims, 2019); Elisabeth Gallas, Anna Holzer-Kawalko, Caroline Jessen, and Yfaat Weiss, eds., *Contested Heritage: Jewish Cultural Property after 1945* (Göttingen: Vandenhoeck & Ruprecht, 2020).

51. Bob Reinalda, *Routledge History of International Organizations: From 1815 to the Present Day* (Oxford: Routledge, 2009); Mark Mazower, *Governing the World: The History of an Idea* (New York: The Penguin Press, 2012); Steve Charnovitz, "Nongovernmental Organizations and International Law," *The American Journal of International Law* 100, no. 2 (2006): 348–372. https://www.jstor.org/stable/3651151. See also Michael Barnett and Martha Finnemore, *Rules for the World: International Organizations in Global Politics* (Ithaca and London: Cornell University Press, 2004); Geoffrey Allen Pigman, "Making Room at the Negotiating Table: The Growth of Diplomacy between Nation-State Governments and Non-State Economic Entities," *Diplomacy and Statecraft* 16 (2005): 385–401. https://doi.org/10.1080/0959229059 0948414; Teresa La Porte, "The Impact of 'Intermestic' Non-State Actors on the Conceptual Framework of Public Diplomacy," *The Hague Journal of Diplomacy* 7 (2012): 441–458. https://doi.org/10.1163/1871191X-12341241.

52. Patricia Clavin, "Defining Transnationalism," *Contemporary European History* 14, no. 4 (2005): 424. https://doi.org/10.1017/S0960777305002705.

53. See, for example, Jonathan Frankel, *The Damascus Affair: "Ritual Murder," Politics and the Jews in 1840* (Cambridge: Cambridge University Press, 1997); Jonathan Dekel-Chen, "Philanthropy, Diplomacy, and Jewish Internationalism," in Mitchell Hart and Tony Michels, eds., *Cambridge History of Judaism*, vol. 8 (Cambridge: Cambridge University Press, 2017): 505–528; Lisa Moses Leff, *Sacred Bonds of Solidarity: The Rise of Jewish Internationalism in Nineteenth Century France* (Stanford: Stanford University Press, 2006).

54. Carole Fink, *Defending the Rights of Others: The Great Powers, the Jews, and International Minority Protection, 1878–1938* (Cambridge: Cambridge University Press, 2004).

55. See, for example, Charles S. Lieberman, "Diaspora Influence on Israel: The Ben-Gurion-Blaustein 'Exchange' and its Aftermath," *Jewish Social Studies* 36, no. 3/4 (1974): 271–280; Ilan Troen, *Jewish Centers and Peripheries: Europe between America and Israel Fifty Years after World War II* (New Brunswick, NJ: Transaction, 1998); Yossi Shain and Aharon Barth, "Diasporas and International Relations Theory," *International Organization* 57, no. 3 (2003): 449–479. https://www.jstor.org/stable/3594834; Zvi Ganin, *An Uneasy Relationship: American Jewish Leadership and Israel, 1948–1957* (New York: Syracuse University Press, 2005);

Ofer Shiff, Adi Sherzer, Talia Gorodess, "The Ben-Gurion-Blaustein Exchange: Ben-Gurion's Perspective Between an Ideological Capitulation and a Strategic Alliance," *Israel Studies* 25, no. 3 (2020): 15–32. https://www.jstor.org/stable/10.2979/israelstudies.25.issue-3.

56. *Divrei Haknesset* 10 (12 December 1951), 634–637. The charges were reported in the *New York Times* on December 13, 1951.

57. Ganin, *An Uneasy Relationship*, 27.

58. Shlomo Shafir, "Nahum Goldmann and Germany after World War II," in Raider, *Nahum Goldmann: Statesman without a State*, 224.

59. The USC Shoah Foundation includes questions on restitution in their questionnaire to survivors.

60. Weiner, Eva. Interview 21648. Tape 3. 13:01–13:34. USC Shoah Foundation Visual History Archive. USC Shoah Foundation. October 22, 1996. Accessed December 30, 2020.

61. Dzialowski, Dina. Interview 15806. Tape 3: 19:37–19:56. USC Shoah Foundation Visual History Archive. USC Shoah Foundation. May 30, 1996. Accessed December 30, 2020.

62. Weiss, Horst. Interview 7971. Tape 3: 13:25–16:13. USC Shoah Foundation Visual History Archive. USC Shoah Foundation. January 13, 1996. Accessed December 30, 2020.

Chapter 1

Failure of Early Demands for Reparations and a New Form of Transnational Activism

Reparations for a transnational community was a novel concept in the aftermath of the Second World War. International law recognized the right of a state intentionally wronged by another state to obtain reparations for the damage incurred.[1] This remedy was intended, as much as possible, to wipe out the consequences of the illegal act.[2] The concept of postwar reparations dates back to the seventeenth-century philosopher Hugo Grotius, the founder of international legal theory. To this day, it is generally accepted that states are the primary actors in negotiations on reparations. In the words of the philosopher Larry May in his 2012 book *After War Ends*, "reparations typically concern States."[3] Even when individuals had claims for reparations, these were advocated by states.

Reparations figured in the program of the Allied Powers for the post-Hitler era. From 1943 onward, Britain, the United States, and the Soviet Union planned to exact compensation to cover their losses. Jewish lawyers and communal leaders also published demands for compensation for the war waged against them. However, at the time, no state recognized the right of Jewish victims to reparations.

The rebuttal of claims for reparations indicated the failure of traditional Jewish diplomacy. After the Paris Peace Conference, organizations and individuals formed new broad alliances that cut across denominational and ideological divisions. The purpose was to trace and claim property formerly owned by Jews in occupied Germany. These coalitions provided a blueprint for cooperation in the framework of an alliance promoting claims for reparations for Holocaust victims. This chapter describes the steps preceding the formation of the Claims Conference, namely the failure of Jewish diplomatic efforts to obtain compensation in the immediate aftermath of the war and the establishment of new alliances engaged in restitution work.

Chapter 1
JEWISH DEMANDS FOR REPARATIONS

Shortly after the outbreak of the Second World War, jurists and communal leaders began to draw up claims for the compensation of Jewish victims. The proponents were mainly German émigrés and victims themselves. They demanded compensation for the expropriation of Jewish property by the Third Reich. The legal basis they put forward to support their claims was an extension of generally accepted principles on postwar remedies to cover the damage perpetrated by a state against its own citizens and residents. By the end of the war, most of the surviving members of the German Jewish community no longer lived in Germany and therefore lacked the political power required to obtain compensation. The solution proposed by the authors of Jewish reparations claims was to apply to the international community for support.

Shalom Adler-Rudel submitted the first demand for compensation for stolen Jewish property. Adler-Rudel was director of the Berlin Jewish Community's Department of Productive Welfare from 1930 to 1934 and director of the Central British Fund for German Jews (CBF, now renamed World Jewish Relief) from 1939. In 1941, he drew up a memorandum addressed to David Ben-Gurion, leader of the Jewish community in Palestine (the *Yishuv*) and to Sir Herbert Emerson, the head of the League of Nations Inter-Governmental Committee for Refugees, on the scope of damage to the property of German and Austrian Jews perpetrated by the Nazi regime.[4]

In 1944, several Jewish jurists published treatises on the legal justification for the payment of reparations to Jews after the war. Nehemiah Robinson of the New York-based Institute of Jewish Affairs described the discriminatory measures exercised by Germany against Jews and explained that indemnification for losses "is not only a requirement of justice but also the only sound policy for the United Nations and the individual states to pursue."[5] This indemnification should cover claims of individuals and communities. Robinson called for the United Nations to intervene on behalf of former citizens of Axis countries and stateless persons.

Dr. Siegfried Moses, who was active in Jewish communal affairs first in Berlin and later in Palestine, also published an essay on the Jewish aspects of postwar claims. In his view, the basis of the demand for compensation was that "a very large part of the economic assets of the Jews have been destroyed and the work of rebuilding Palestine . . . urgently requires complementary economic assets."[6] Consequently, the Jewish people should be allowed a claim for reparations if Germany were to pay reparations at all. Moses advocated individual and collective claims against Germany. He argued that Jews who had emigrated from Germany should be recognized as members of a nation that was at war with Germany since 1933. Another writer called for new creative ideas, not positive law, to do justice for the unprecedented events.[7]

A different approach intended to promote Jewish claims was to draft laws on compensation for property expropriated by Germany on racist grounds. In 1944, Emilio von Hofmannsthal drafted a "Restoration Law for Axis and Axis occupied countries" with the motto *Pirata non mutat dominium* (a pirate does not change ownership, namely goods should be restored to their original owners).[8] The proposed legislation afforded the rightful owner a choice between restitution and compensation and gave priority to the individual over the state on the grounds that it was the former who had been deprived of his property and therefore should recover it. Again, the author called for international protection against arbitrary national laws and decisions. The newly formed Council for the Protection of the Rights and Interests of Jews from Germany (the Council of Jews from Germany), an organization representing German Jewish émigrés, published a similar draft indemnification law in 1947.[9] The bill proposed a presumption that all transfers and renunciations of properties, rights, and interests by discriminated persons during the critical period were made under duress and were consequently void. Leaders and jurists hoped their proposals would be adopted by the Allied states after the defeat of Germany.

DISREGARD OF JEWISH CLAIMS BY THE INTERNATIONAL COMMUNITY

No state presented Jewish claims for compensation at the end of the Second World War. A majority of Holocaust survivors were stateless or citizens of countries that denied the singling out of Jewish citizens and residents by Germany and its allies. Jewish groups lobbied the Allied Powers for the recognition of their unparalleled damage, with very limited success. American and British politicians and diplomats concentrated their efforts on promoting national interests. They refused to discuss compensation for individual losses. The American and British refusal to address the plunder of Jewish property commenced in the 1930s and did not end after their victory over Germany. Throughout the war, the Allies ignored the expropriation of Jewish property by Germany carried out in broad daylight. So, for example, in the midst of the war, they published the Inter-Allied Declaration against Acts of Dispossession committed in Territories Under Enemy Occupation or Control. This declaration warned all concerned of the intention to do the utmost to defeat the methods of dispossession practiced by enemy governments against countries and peoples.[10] Neither the declaration nor the diplomatic correspondence that preceded its drafting specified the expropriation of property (or murder) of Jews throughout Europe.

Allied leaders first discussed reparations at the Yalta Conference. In February 1945, after the liberation of Auschwitz, Prime Minister Churchill, President Roosevelt, and General Secretary Stalin met to discuss the new world order. Their agreements included a protocol requiring Germany to pay in kind for the losses caused to the Allied nations. The designated recipients of reparations, in the first instance, were those countries that had borne the main burden of the war.[11] The protocol omitted any mention of damage suffered by individuals in general, and Jews in particular.

After the defeat of Germany, the Allied leaders convened, this time at Potsdam, a suburb of Berlin. The agreement reached by President Truman, Stalin, and Churchill centered on the treatment of Germany. It also provided for reparations to be made, mainly by the removal of equipment from the Soviet-occupied zone of Germany to the Soviet Union.[12] Again, the agreement did not contain any provisions on the restitution of property expropriated from individuals, Jews and non-Jews, or compensation for their suffering.

Studying the Allied leaders at the Potsdam Conference draws attention to the absence of the murder and plunder of Jews or the question of the future of European Jews from their deliberations. Truman's briefing books for the conference contained 163 separate topical briefs; only one mentioned Palestine and none discussed the genocide of Jews. The State Department advised Truman to discuss Palestine "in general terms only" and to agree to nothing that the British or the Soviets might propose.[13] The author Michael Neiberg wrote that "Palestine and the Jews seemed a peripheral issue to the central problems of Potsdam, most importantly the maintenance of good relations among the Big Three."[14]

The 1946 Paris Peace conference was the last opportunity to present demands to the international community for the payment of reparations for Jewish losses. Representatives of twenty-one Allied nations met with representatives of Germany's former allies—Bulgaria, Romania, Hungary, Finland, and Italy—over a period of ten weeks. The purpose was to resolve outstanding issues in the peace treaties drawn up by the newly established Council of Foreign Ministers of the Allied Powers. Jewish organizations viewed the conference as an opportunity to be heard by the international community on their claims for justice and protection in the shadow of the Holocaust.

Building on their experience at the end of the Great War, Jewish organizations drew up statements and sent delegations to lobby the participants in the 1946 conference. Prior to the conference, the Council of Jews from Germany submitted a memorandum to the Allied states on restitution for German Jewish émigrés. According to the memorandum:

> The dead cannot be brought to life again, but the principle of justice can be upheld. Private property and its protection are dependent on the legal principle

that stolen property which has been recovered must be restored to its rightful owner or his successor. Robbery committed against individuals and communities would appear in the future legitimate if the robberies perpetuated (*sic*) against the Jews for years under the Nazi regime and its accomplices and satellites were to be considered as *fait accompli*.[15]

Accordingly, the Council of Jews from Germany requested that the United Nations recognize their claims for indemnification of individuals and a share of the reparations to be allocated for rehabilitation and resettlement.

Eleven delegations from the Western bloc arrived in Paris in the summer of 1946 to promote the Jewish cause. Representatives of organizations from the United States, the United Kingdom, France, Canada, South Africa, and Palestine discussed amendments to the proposed peace treaties. Their proposals covered a broad range of subjects including full restitution and indemnification for all losses not compensated by restitution. The 1944 essays by Moses and Robinson provided the legal justification for these demands. Discussions between the Jewish organizations resulted in an agreement on over forty proposed amendments to the peace treaties drafted with the aid of Hersch Lauterpacht, the renowned expert on international law. On August 20, 1946, the organizations sent a document listing their amendments to the twenty-one governments participating in the Peace Paris Conference. When the draft treaties emerged from the closed sessions of the Council of Foreign Ministers, the Jewish groups found that their interests had been totally disregarded. Instead, vague clauses required the former allies of Germany to respect human rights and fundamental freedoms. Israel Cohen, a representative of the Board of Deputies of British Jews at the conference, described the experiences of the Jewish delegations in 1946 as a depressing contrast to those of their predecessors in 1919.[16] Jacob Robinson, brother of Nehemiah and a delegate at the conference, complained that "Not only is the word 'Jew' taboo, but even camouflaged provisions . . . are missing."[17]

The Allied states made one concession to Jewish demands for reparations. Article 8 in the Final Act of the Paris Conference on Reparation awarded a payment of 25 million US dollars derived from German assets in neutral countries and all non-monetary gold in Germany for the benefit of stateless and other non-repatriable victims of Nazism. The term "non-repatriable" refers to individuals who "cannot be returned to their countries within a reasonable time because of prevailing conditions."[18] Again, the article contained no specific mention of Jews, but the Allied representatives agreed that ninety percent of the sum stipulated in the article would be used to assist Jewish survivors. According to Cohen, the Jewish delegations were told that the injuries suffered by Jews in the Second World War must be regarded as their share in the national war effort or war misfortunes of their respective countries.[19] The law professor, Richard Buxbaum, later described Article 8 as "no more than an embarrassing sop to conciliate the demands of the Displaced Persons' community and its representatives."[20]

The omission of any reference to Jews in the 1946 peace treaties and disregard of claims for restitution and reparations to Holocaust victims require an explanation. Clearly, the prime concern of the Allied nations was to further state interests. In 1919, the Soviet Union did not attend the peace talks. The absence of a Soviet delegation at Versailles left the floor open to lobbying by communities and organizations. Twenty-seven years later, Stalin had destroyed all opposition at home and controlled most governments in Eastern Europe. The participation of the Soviet Union in the Paris Peace Conference added tension to the already difficult negotiations between victors and defeated parties. Each participant sought to maximize its gains. The focus on state interests came at the expense of demands of non-state actors such as Jewish organizations and their claim for reparations.

The United Kingdom had an ulterior motive for disregarding Jewish demands at the Paris Peace Conference. The conference coincided with the bombing of the King David Hotel by a Jewish underground movement (*Etzel*) that sought to end British control of Palestine. British Foreign Minister Anthony Eden advised Churchill to keep the Zionist leader Chaim Weizmann away from Soviet officials in order to prevent the latter's support of Jewish emigration to Palestine.[21] The intention was to avoid highlighting the plight of Jewish survivors stranded in displaced person camps across Europe due to British restrictions on immigration to Palestine.

Antisemitism also contributed to the rejection of Jewish demands. Stalin and his inner circle were notoriously antisemitic.[22] The US Secretary of War Henry Stimson and British diplomats had similar views on Jews.[23] This antisemitism blinded politicians and diplomats of the Allied countries to the nature of Germany's war against Jews. It also prevented a discussion of Jewish demands for reparations or the inclusion of specific arrangements relating to Holocaust victims in the Paris Peace Treaties.

JEWISH INTERNATIONALISM

The transformation of cross-border activism was a vital step in the evolution of the Claims Conference. The postwar era witnessed an exponential increase in the activities of governments and non-state actors in the international scene. Britain, the United States, and even the Soviet Union (for a limited period) joined forces to alter international relations for the promotion of global cooperation. Non-state actors including religious groups, members of professions, and proponents of different ideologies also established institutions to provide aid to kinsmen in Europe and influence public policy. Jewish activists adopted the structure and mode of the operations of the postwar generation of institutions, the precursors to the Claims Conference.

Origins of Cross-Border Activities

The mid-nineteenth century marked the beginning of transnational activities by individuals and communities. Bob Reinalda, the author of a comprehensive book on international organizations, links the birth of transnationalism to the anti-slavery movement in Britain and America. Transatlantic ties between British and American abolitionist societies formed the background and precedent for the emergence of a "transnational network of citizens."[24] Methodists, Presbyterians, Quakers, and Unitarians exchanged information and convened an international anti-slavery conference in 1840. The conference took place in London and was attended by delegations from Britain, France, and North America. The exclusion of women from the anti-slavery movement led to the creation of all-women transnational networks to advance national suffrage and an end to sex trafficking.[25]

Communities adopted this form of activism to address a broad range of issues. The Napoleonic Wars motivated Quakers to set up a network of peace societies in Britain and North America for the promotion of arbitration as a means for settling controversies between nations. Other cross-border activities included the Young Men's Christian Association (founded in London in 1844), the International Committee of the Red Cross (founded in Geneva in 1863), and the Socialist First International (founded in London in 1864).

Early Jewish Transnational Organizations

Jewish groups also created institutions to operate across borders. Modern communications and the press drew attention to the misfortunes of Jews in the Ottoman and Russian Empires as well as in Romania. A chart portraying the timeline of Jewish transnational organizations appears in figure 1.1. It depicts the evolution of organizations that differed greatly in size and scope of operations. Many of these organizations were members of the Claims Conference and participated in negotiating and distributing German reparation funds.

The first Jewish transnational organization was *Alliance Israélite Universelle* (*Alliance*). In 1860, a group of young liberal Jews in Paris set up the *Alliance* for the specific purpose of helping Jews around the world obtain citizenship, material security, and "moral progress."[26] The organization focused on establishing schools in North Africa and the Near East

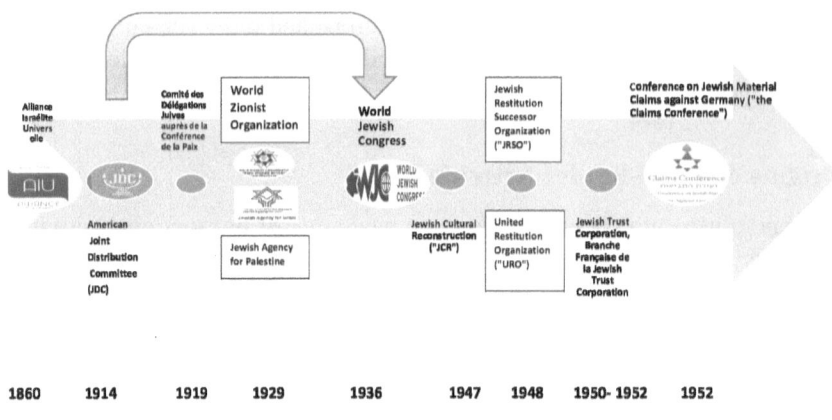

Figure 1.1 Timeline of Evolution of Jewish Transnational Organizations. *Source*: By the author.

and improving the image of Jews. It was the forerunner of a vast range of Jewish transnational organizations as well as a member of the Claims Conference.

The turn of the century marked the beginning of the migration of the center of transnational activism and leading Jewish organizations from Europe to the United States. The Joint Distribution Committee, also known as the Joint (JDC), is an example of an organization based in the New World operating on a global basis. In 1914, on the eve of the First World War, two American Jewish committees, one Orthodox, the Central Committee for the Relief of Jews, and one chiefly Reform, the American Jewish Relief Committee, agreed to set up a "joint" committee to facilitate the distribution of funds raised by them from their congregants. In 1915, the People's Relief Committee joined the JDC. The object of the joint committee was to assist "our less fortunate brethren." Between 1914 to 1929, the JDC collected $78.7 million (in present-day terms, over $1 billion) from American Jews to help their coreligionists in the Russian, Austrian, and Ottoman Empires, who were made homeless by the war and suffered persecution and poverty.[27] The JDC is a key member of the Claims Conference and a major beneficiary of reparation funds.

The Zionist Congress convened by Theodore Herzl in 1897 created transnational organizations to promote the building of a homeland in Palestine. These organizations included the World Zionist Organization (WZO) set up by the first Zionist Congress and the Jewish Agency for Palestine established by the sixteenth Zionist Congress in 1929 in Basel. The Jewish Agency acted as a government without a state during the British Mandate rule of Palestine and was another founding member of the Claims Conference.

Attempts to Create a United Jewish Front

Jewish transnational organizations represented (and represent) individuals from a broad range of countries with differing religious outlooks and ideologies. Leaders and activists established innumerable organizations, local and international. Many of these organizations operated in the same fields, sometimes competing with one another. The *Alliance* and the committee established to represent Jewish interests at the 1919 peace talks illustrate attempts to present a united Jewish front vis-à-vis communities and nations. Neither entity spoke in the name of broad sectors of Jewish communities worldwide.

As the name indicates, the founders of the *Alliance* intended to create a universal organization with a global membership. To further this end, they set up chapters throughout Europe, North Africa, and the Middle East to send donations for projects approved by the Central Committee. In 1881, of the 24,000 members of the organization, only 23.6 percent were French.[28] Nevertheless the Central Committee in Paris took all major decisions. Furthermore, *Alliance* was a modernist and secular movement opposed to Jewish nationalism. It was committed to the progress of "civilization" and French civic virtues. The French and secular nature of the movement limited the appeal of the organization and prevented it from becoming a united front for Jews worldwide.

A new opportunity to form a broad coalition promoting Jewish causes arose at the end of the Great War. The first Paris Peace Conference offered the "greatest opportunity of all in modern times to construct a common front."[29] After a series of attempts, the American Jewish Congress and Zionist activists established the *Comité des Délégations Juives auprès de la Conférence de la Paix* (*Comité des Délégations Juives,* or the Committee) in March 1919. They invited delegations from thirteen countries including Palestine, the United States, Canada, Russia, Poland, Romania, Czechoslovakia, Italy, Yugoslavia, and Greece to join the Committee. Two delegations from Britain and France rejected the offer, and the founders did not invite delegations from the defeated countries—Germany and Austria—to participate in the coalition. The Committee's efforts led to the signing of the Minorities Treaties between the League of Nations and Poland, Yugoslavia, and Czechoslovakia. Similar treaties were imposed on Greece and Romania. Their object was to guarantee group rights to citizens who differed from the majority of the population of new and enlarged states in religion, language, education and culture.

The success of the Committee was short-lived. It operated as a formally recognized lobby representing Jewish interests at the League of Nations in Geneva. The Committee filed complaints against discriminatory practices directed against Jews in Romania and Poland, but the League of Nations refused to intervene. In the long run, the minority protection clauses "were erratic and futile."[30] Different Jewish groups and organizations attacked the Committee and its policy. In the words of the historian Carole Fink, rivalry was inherent between "two kindred movements, one based on the removal of a massive number of Jews to Palestine, the other on securing a robust national life for the Jewish masses in Eastern Europe."[31]

In 1936, after Hitler came to power, Goldmann and Rabbi Stephen Wise convened the World Jewish Congress (WJC)—the Committee under a new name—in Geneva.[32] The intention was to reach a broad consensus on steps to protect Jews in Germany and Eastern Europe. For many decades Goldmann (see figure 1.2 below) was a leading figure in the Jewish world. He played an instrumental role in the WJC, the Zionist movement, and other organizations. Born in Visznewo, a townlet in Lithuania and part of the Russian Empire, to a Jewish religious family in 1895, he grew up in Frankfurt and studied law and philosophy in the University of Heidelberg.[33]

Goldmann was an accomplished diplomat. He headed the Committee after 1933 and represented the Jewish Agency at the League of Nations in 1935. Goldmann viewed himself as representing both the Zionist movement and diaspora Jews and would play a central role in setting up and directing the Claims Conference. Wise acted on behalf of American Jewry. He was a leading Reform rabbi in the United States who organized mass anti-Nazi rallies in New York in the 1930s, calling for a boycott of German goods.

Members of the WJC represented the Jews of thirty-two countries but not all Jewish organizations accepted the proposal to participate in the alliance. In addition, Goldmann and Wise did not invite the Jews of Germany and the

Figure 1.2   Nahum Goldmann. *Source*: Courtesy of the Claims Conference Archives.

Soviet Union to join the WJC.[34] The object was to "assure the survival, and to foster the unity of the Jewish people."[35] The WJC protested against the 1935 Nuremberg laws enacted by Germany, called for equal rights for Jews of Eastern Europe, and pleaded for League of Nations support for Jewish refugees. None of these activities succeeded. Aryeh Leon Kubowitzki, who was commissioned by the WJC to write the first history of the organization in 1948, stated that "In no other field have the victories of the Congress been so complete as in the ideological."[36] The tragedy is that the needs of the Jews at this time were not ideological but practical: refuge and protection from hostile regimes.

PRECURSORS OF THE CLAIMS CONFERENCE

The end of the Second World War generated a wave of activism in the Jewish world. In the eyes of Jewish leaders, the Holocaust illuminated the abandonment of the Jews by their countries and by their fellow citizens. The solution was for Jewish leaders and organizations to act and not to rely on foreign powers. According to Goldmann:

> The more obvious it became that the bulk of European Jewry was irretrievably lost, the more necessary it was to draw the conclusions from this tragedy and create a basis for the continued existence of the Jewish people. . . . This work had two goals. One was to rehabilitate the European survivors and obtain restitution from Germany, the other to seek a definitive solution to the problem of Palestine.[37]

The result was a great increase in the scope of Jewish transnational activities in the war's aftermath.

After the Paris Peace Conference, Jewish leaders and organizations concentrated their efforts on promoting the restitution of property. The Jewish Cultural Reconstruction, Inc. (JCR), incorporated in 1947, was the first postwar institution seeking restitution in occupied Germany. It evolved out of the Commission on European Jewish Cultural Reconstruction established by Salo Baron, a professor of Jewish literature and history at Columbia University, together with Theodor H. Gaster, the head of the Hebraic Section at the Library of Congress. Hannah Arendt served as the JCR executive secretary. The mission of the organization was to reclaim heirless books and ritual objects in the US zone of occupied Germany.

On February 15, 1949, the JCR signed a memorandum of agreement with the Office of Military Government of the United States. This agreement stated that Jewish cultural properties "separated from owning individuals and organizations in Europe during the period of Nazi rule" would be transferred to the JCR and held on a "custody basis only."[38] The JCR would seek rightful owners and deliver the property to them. By the end of its operations in 1952, the JCR had redistributed hundreds of thousands of books and thousands of *Torah* scrolls and other ritual objects to major libraries and museums, including the Library of Congress, the Bezalel School of Art in Jerusalem, the Jewish Theological Seminary, and other higher education institutions.

The next postwar institution was the Jewish Restitution Successor Organization (the JRSO) founded in 1948. The prime mover behind the establishment of the JRSO was the JDC, whose representatives distributed food, clothes and equipment to camps for Jewish displaced persons. The JDC was therefore well-acquainted with the conditions in occupied Germany. It invited societies and organizations representing Jewish communities from different countries and religious denominations to join the JRSO. The new alliance offered members an opportunity to work together for a common end. The object was to trace and retrieve unclaimed and therefore, presumably heirless properties in the American zone of occupied Germany. At the end of 1947, the US government enacted a law for the restitution of identifiable property. All potential heirs, no matter how remote the relationship to the original owner, were authorized to present claims. In the case of property owned by Jews before confiscation by the German government, many owners and their immediate heirs had been murdered and no legal heir could be easily located. The solution put forward by Jewish organizations in occupied Germany was to establish an entity that would stand in for the murdered owners and their heirs. The director general of the JRSO, Benjamin Ferencz, explained that the possessions of those who perished in the Nazi infernos should not be allowed to rest in German hands, but instead, be retrieved to reconstruct the shattered lives of those who survived.[39]

Cooperation in the JRSO proved successful and the JDC, the Jewish Agency, and the CBF created similar organizations in the British zone of occupied Germany (the Jewish Trust Corporation) and the French Zone (*Branche Française de la Jewish Trust Corporation*). These three organizations acting in each zone under Western control are known as the successor organizations. They opened a joint office for the three sectors of West Berlin.

To enable individual claimants to exercise their rights under local restitution legislation, the Council of Jews from Germany established the United Restitution Organization (URO). Incorporated in England in 1948, this body worked closely with the JRSO. Its object was to enable "poorer Jewish victims of Nazi oppression to obtain what was their due" and protect them from "rapacious lawyers."[40] The British barrister Norman Bentwich served as its first chairman. URO set up legal aid offices in London, Israel, the United States, France, and Germany. From 1948 to 1953, the JDC funded its activities.[41]

The successor organizations, together with URO, procured the restitution of many thousands of private and communal assets. In the US zone alone, the JRSO filed over 163,000 claims.[42] In the course of five years, it restored assets valued at DM 800 million (currently equivalent to approx. $1.7 billion) to 50,000 original owners or their heirs and located and claimed heirless assets valued at DM 91 million (currently equivalent to approximately $800 million).[43] Members of the organizations reached (mainly amicable) agreements on the distribution of heirless assets recovered by them. In addition, individual claimants aided by URO recovered a total sum of $12.5 million between 1948 and 1953.[44]

CHANGES IN JEWISH TRANSNATIONALISM

The postwar generation of Jewish global organizations differed from their predecessors. Internal and external factors altered the structure of Jewish coalitions and their administration. The successor organizations served as a model for the Claims Conference. Their experience of negotiating with governments and allocating funds between members provided the tools for the establishment of an alliance to demand and distribute reparations.

The successor organizations demonstrated a new spirit of cooperation that constituted a break with the past. Divisions between groups with rival ideologies did not cease upon the outbreak of the Second World War. Mark Wyman, in his book on displaced persons, writes that "Even in wartime, in the face of Nazi attacks, the different groups within Judaism had trouble working together."[45] Antagonism between Zionist and non-Zionist organizations declined after the mass murder of European Jewry. The originally non-Zionist JDC and the Jewish Agency joined forces to enable the rehabilitation of survivors and refugees. According to a JDC representative, the Zionists "were the only ones that had a program that seemed to make sense after this catastrophe."[46] This new perspective led the JDC to provide financial assistance for the immigration of refugees to Palestine. JDC representatives in camps for displaced persons also donated funds for the clandestine immigration of refugees to Palestine, without the permission of leaders at the head office in New York.[47]

Zionist and non-Zionist members of the successor organizations agreed on the division of proceeds from the sale of heirless assets. The JRSO allocated the sum of DM 38,157,190 to the Jewish Agency for relief purposes in Israel and the sum of DM 18 million to the JDC.[48] The successor organization in the British zone of occupied Germany, the Jewish Trust Corporation for Germany, also divided proceeds between Zionist and non-Zionist causes.[49]

The Jewish Agency used the funds allocated by the JRSO to purchase German prefabricated houses for newly arrived refugees in Palestine, agricultural machinery, and construction equipment.[50] The JDC used its share of the proceeds to support its relief work in Germany. This included grants to aged and sick survivors, "hardcore" medical cases (mainly suffering from tuberculosis and mental health problems) and refugees from Eastern Europe.

The Impact of Postwar Organizing on Jewish Institutions

Jewish postwar institutions modeled themselves on their non-Jewish counterparts. Cross-border activism in this era was originally and primarily an American movement. The United States led the drive to build new institutions for global governance.[51] Examples of these institutions are, first and foremost, the United Nations Organization, the North Atlantic Treaty Organization (NATO), the UN Relief and Rehabilitation Administration (UNRRA), the United Nations Children Fund (UNICEF), and the United Nations Scientific Educational and Cultural Organization (UNESCO). All these organizations had their headquarters in the United States, and American individuals served in senior management positions. Similarly, American citizens and communities contributed to the proliferation of transnational nongovernmental organizations. They set up institutions to perform tasks in response to the humanitarian catastrophe resulting from the Second World War. Two examples are Catholic Relief Services (CRS) and Lutheran World Relief (LWR). In 1943 Roman Catholic bishops of the United States established the CRS to assist Polish refugees in Mexico, Palestine, and other Catholic refugees and prisoners of war.[52] American Lutherans established the LWR in 1945 to assist their kin in Europe.[53]

Americans, not Europeans, established, funded, and served as executives in the successor organizations. American citizens initiated the JCR project. Baron and Gaster were both born in Europe but lived in the United States and worked in American institutions (Columbia University and the Library of Congress, respectively) prior to establishing the JCR, a New York corporation. Similarly, the American JDC initiated the creation of the JRSO and the other successor organizations and funded the URO in its first years. Moreover, American executives played a leading role in the management of the successor organizations.

No organization or individual from the Soviet Union or any other East European country joined the Jewish organizations engaged in restitution. Again, the absence of members from these countries characterized the postwar generation of international and transnational institutions. The Soviet Union cooperated with the United States in forming interstate organizations during their "political honeymoon," which lasted four (difficult) years

(1941–1945).⁵⁴ Unity between the Great Powers broke down at the end of the war when tensions, hostility, competition, and conflict emerged between the Soviet Union and the West, first and foremost the United States.⁵⁵ The Cold War marked the end of Soviet involvement in the drive to set up intergovernmental organizations. As Soviet influence spread, the Kremlin put pressure on East European countries to quit international organizations they had joined prior to Sovietization.⁵⁶ The nature of the Soviet regime and Cold War politics explain the absence of East Europeans from nongovernmental transnational activism. Centralist government in the Soviet Union prevented the formation of this type of organization. Moreover, the isolation of citizens by Eastern European governments behind the Iron Curtain and the danger of contacts with Westerners precluded their participation in international nongovernmental organizations.

Jewish communities from Eastern Europe did not participate in the successor organizations, despite the persecution that almost all their members suffered during the Second World War. The number of Jews in Eastern Europe after the war was 2.85 million, with over 1,760,000 in the Soviet Union (860,000 in Russia and 900,000 in Ukraine and Moldova) and 430,000 Jews in Romania.⁵⁷ No Jewish successor organization was created in the Soviet zone of occupied Germany.⁵⁸ Furthermore, no person or organization represented the Jews of Eastern Europe in the distribution of cultural assets and proceeds from the restitution of heirless property. In this context, it is interesting to note the position of Jerome Michael, acting chairman of the Commission on European Jewish Cultural Reconstruction, on claims of Jewish communities scattered throughout Europe (many in the East). In his view, returning objects and books looted from a community, when most of its former citizens were killed or had emigrated would be

> most unwise and unfair . . . unwise because the almost certain result would be their dissipation, and unfair because the interests of the much larger numbers of members of the old communities who now live abroad and of the Jewish people would be sacrificed on the altar of legal title.⁵⁹

The absence of representatives from Eastern European communities in the JCR resulted in the distribution of books and proceeds first and foremost to Jewish communities in the United States and Palestine. Of the 7,867 religious objects distributed by the JCR by 1952, Israel received 3,261 and the United States received 3,250.⁶⁰ Not a single object was returned to Eastern Europe.

The postwar generation of Jewish transnational organizations engaged in legal work, unlike its predecessors. Earlier cross-border initiatives such as the *Alliance*, the JDC, and other global Jewish organizations centered on philanthropy. They employed educators to set up schools and welfare workers to provide relief and assistance to destitute communities and individuals. The successor organizations and the URO performed legal services. They hired teams of multilingual legal experts from Israel, England, France, and the United States.[61] Lawyers traced plundered property through local registries, official bodies, and local courts and filed claims for restitution.

The tasks imposed on the successor organizations required a new cadre of administrators. Full-time managers replaced part-time volunteers. They implemented administrative practices adopted by the new governmental and nongovernmental institutions. The postwar generation of organizations attached great importance to the employment of qualified and competent staff. Founders and staff projected the ideas of experts and specialists who directed operations. International bureaucrats purportedly based their actions on scientific, rational considerations devoid of political content. The emphasis on professionalism was intended to enable administrators to mediate between governments and mobilize domestic groups.[62] They conducted their international work far from the public's gaze.[63] In the decades following the Second World War, a culture of secrecy characterized organizations of all types.

The successor organizations served as a training ground for members and directors who subsequently used their skills for the management of the Claims Conference. Individuals who had acquired their training in the US Army or American institutions entered Jewish organizational life and like the international bureaucrats, advocated improved scientific management. Ferencz and Saul Kagan, both ex-servicemen, are prime examples. Ferencz was born in Transylvania in 1920, immigrated to America, studied at Harvard Law School, and enlisted in the US Army. After fighting in an antiaircraft artillery battalion in Europe, the United States government recruited the talented multilingual lawyer to investigate and prosecute Nazi criminals at the Nuremberg war crimes trials.[64] At the end of the trials, representatives of the JDC approached Ferencz and asked him to set up the JRSO.[65] Ferencz was assisted by Kagan who served as corporate secretary. Kagan was born in Vilna in 1920, fled Lithuania and arrived in America in 1940. He joined the US Air Force and landed at Normandy in 1944. The two men met in Berlin in 1946 and subsequently worked together, first in the JRSO and later as advocates for reparations.[66] They developed and administered an efficient system for the collection and distribution of assets on a worldwide basis. The skills acquired by Ferencz and Kagan from their military training and their knowledge of American institutions, contributed to the organizations they directed.

Members and directors of the successor organizations engaged in diplomacy with military forces in occupied Germany. The JCR signed a memorandum of agreement with the Office of Military Government of the United States on the transfer of looted Jewish cultural properties to the JCR and restoration to their owners.[67] Similarly, the US Military Government in occupied Germany recognized the JRSO as the entity authorized to recover heirless property.[68] The Claims Conference benefited from this experience in the subsequent conduct of negotiations with West Germany.

Principles of Allocations by the Successor Organizations

In the field of allocations, the successor organizations applied a number of principles that had considerable influence on the allocation of reparations by the Claims Conference. The first principle was that funds and assets would be distributed for the benefit of the entire Jewish people. In the words of Georg Landauer of the Jewish Agency, explaining how the JRSO was created, "there was a conscious intention to make, so to say, world Jewry the successor and the inheritor of a quasi-annihilated and plundered [Jewish] group. This is repeatedly emphasized in the documents of the State Department."[69] Consequently, the organizations did not restrict the allocation of funds and assets to communities that had suffered from German persecution.

The second principle of allocation was that the JCR and successor organizations distributed funds to organizations, usually member organizations of the allocating entities, not individuals. In addition, the successor organizations granted the Jewish Agency and the JDC special standing as "operating agents."[70] As a result, the Jewish state and American Jewish organizations were the main beneficiaries of the proceeds. Of the total sum of DM 91 million recovered by the JRSO from unclaimed or heirless properties in the first five years of its operations, over DM 38 million went to the Jewish Agency and over DM 18 million to the JDC.[71] Similarly, in 1952, the JCR distributed 3,261 ritual objects to Israel, 3,250 ritual objects to the United States, and the remaining 1,356 objects to South Africa, Canada, Argentina, Peru, and Western Europe.[72]

A third principle was that Jews from Germany and in Germany were not entitled to a special status or a fixed share of restituted funds and assets recovered in Germany. The Council of Jews from Germany objected to this policy on the grounds that "the monies in question were derived on the basis of alienations of the property of the Jews in Germany."[73] Consequently, they argued, a part of the funds should be used for the benefit of Jewish refugees from Germany. Similarly, Dr. Hendrik G. van Dam of the *Zentralrat der Juden in Deutschland* (the Central Committee of Jews in Germany, or *Zentralrat*) argued that since the property was German Jewish, the survivors should receive a fair share to meet present needs.[74] The Jewish Trust Corporation accepted the Council's claim and granted one-third of the funds generated by the restitution of Jewish property in the British zone of occupied Germany to the CBF. However, the JRSO rejected the demands of the Council and the

Zentralrat and refused to allocate funds to German refugees. Both successor organizations also dismissed the claims of Jews living in postwar Germany for preferential treatment. According to the JRSO, the newly formed communities were "small and often irresponsible groups."[75] Consequently, of the total funds realized from the sale of heirless assets in the first five years of operations (DM 91 million), the JRSO granted local Jewish communities in Germany only DM 3.76 million.[76] Similarly, the JCR distributed only 120 of the 7,687 religious objects located to Jewish communities in Germany. The primary goal of the organization was "to get as many objects out of Germany as possible."[77]

CONCLUSION

The quest for restitution of looted Jewish property transcended ideological differences. Jewish organizations with conflicting ideologies created new institutions to locate and claim assets in occupied Germany. Their efforts resulted in the restoration of assets to individuals and, in the case of heirless objects, to communities. They succeeded mainly in the US zone of occupied Germany, where the military government promoted regional legislation (by *Länder*) on restitution. The value of the restored assets paled in comparison to the scope of the property expropriated from Jewish owners during the twelve-year reign of the Third Reich. Moreover, plunder was only one of many forms of persecution perpetrated against Jews. The occupation of Germany and the absence of an entity recognized as a spokesman on behalf of Jewish Holocaust victims prevented a breakthrough in the campaign for reparations.[78] In the meantime, only survivors who had owned assets in a limited number of regions of Germany received compensation for material losses. The recipients constituted a small fraction of the total number of Holocaust survivors.

NOTES

1. James Crawford, *Brownlie's Principles of Public International Law* – Eighth Edition (Oxford: Oxford University Press, 2012), 567.

2. Permanent Court of International Justice, Case Concerning the Factory at Chorzów, issued July 26, 1927, 21.

3. Larry May, *After the War: A Philosophical Perspective* (Cambridge: Cambridge University Press, 2012), 204. See also Dinah Shelton, "Righting Wrongs: Reparations in the Articles on State Responsibility," *The American Journal of International Law* 96, no. 4 (2002): 833–856. https://doi.org/10.2307/3070681; Richard M. Buxbaum, "A Legal History of International Reparations,"

Berkeley Journal of International Law 23 (2005): 315–316. DOI: 10.15779/ Z38J936.

4. Sagi, *German Reparations*, 15.

5. Robinson, *Indemnification and Reparations*, 7–8.

6. Siegfried Moses, *Jewish Post-War Claims* (Irgun Olej Merkaz Europa: Tel-Aviv, 1944), 15–16.

7. Bruno Weil, "Review," *The American Journal of International Law* 39 (1945): 364. See also Bruno Weil, "Review," *The American Journal of International Law* 40 (1946): 221–227.

8. Emilio von Hofmannsthal, *Draft of a Restoration Law for Axis and Axis occupied countries*, trans. Ferdinand W. Coudert (Baltimore, MD: University of Maryland, 1944).

9. *Draft of an Indemnification Law for Germany* submitted by the Council for the Protection of the Rights and Interests of Jews from Germany (London: n.p., 1947).

10. *Foreign Relations of the United States: Diplomatic Papers, 1943, General, Volume 1*, Document 456. See "Inter-Allied Declaration Against Acts of Dispossession Committed in Territories Under Enemy Occupation or Control," *U.S. Department of State Office of the Historian*, n. d., accessed on October 20, 2019, https://history.state.gov/historicaldocuments/frus1943v01/d456.

11. Article V of the Yalta Conference Agreement, Declaration of a Liberated Europe, dated February 11, 1945.

12. Article III of the Potsdam Agreement – Protocol of the Proceedings, dated August 1, 1945.

13. Michael Neiberg, *Potsdam: The End of World War II and the Remaking of Europe* (New York: Basic Books, 2015), 252.

14. Neiberg, *Potsdam*, 255.

15. *Memorandum Submitted by the Council for the Protection of the Rights and Interests of Jews from Germany to the Signatory Powers of the Final Act of the Paris Conference on Reparations*, (London: n.p., March 1946). On the experience of lobbying after the Great War see, David Vital, *A People Apart: A Political History of the Jews in Europe 1789–1939* (Oxford: Oxford University Press, 2000), 729–761.

16. Israel Cohen, "Jewish Interests in the Peace Treaties," *Jewish Social Studies* 11 (1949): 108. On the achievements of Jewish lobbying at the end of the Great War see p. 27–28 below.

17. Cited in Nathan Kurz, "In the Shadow of Versailles: Jewish Minority Rights at the 1946 Paris Peace Conference," *Simon Dubnow Institute Yearbook* (2017): 199–200.

18. Article 8 of the Final Act of the Paris Conference on Reparation (Paris, December 21, 1945).

19. Cohen, "Jewish Interests in the Peace Treaties," 108.

20. Buxbaum, "A Legal History of International Reparations," 335.

21. Neiberg, *Potsdam*, 253.

22. Amir Weiner, *Making Sense of War: The Second World War and the Fate of the Bolshevik Revolution* (Princeton, NJ: Princeton University Press, 2001), chap. 6;

Benjamin Pinkus, *The Soviet Government and the Jews, 1948-1967: A Documented Study* (Cambridge: Cambridge University Press, 1984), chap. 3.

23. Harvey Strum, "Henry Stimson's Opposition to American Jews and Zionism," *Patterns of Prejudice* 18, no. 4 (1984): 17–24. https://doi.org/10.1080/0031322X.19 84.9969780; On the attitude of the British Foreign Office to Jews see Miriam Haron, "Britain and Israel, 1948–1950," *Modern Judaism* 3, no. 2 (1983): 217–223. https://www.jstor.org/stable/i260689.

24. Bob Reinalda, *Routledge History of International Organizations: From 1815 to the Present Day* (Oxford: Routledge, 2009), 35–40.

25. Margaret McFadden, *Golden Cables of Sympathy: The Transatlantic Sources of Nineteenth-Century Feminism* (Lexington, KY: University Press of Kentucky, 1999), 176; Nitza Berkovitch, "The Emergence and Transformation of the International Women's Movement," in John Boli and George M. Thomas, eds., *Constructing World Culture: International Nongovernmental Organizations since 1875* (Stanford: Stanford University Press, 1999), 100–126.

26. Leff, *Sacred Bonds of Solidarity*, 159.

27. Yehuda Bauer, *American Jewry and the Holocaust: The American Jewish Joint Distribution Committee, 1939–1945* (Detroit: Wayne State University Press, 1981), 22.

28. Leff, *Sacred Bonds of Solidarity*, 164.

29. Vital, *A People Apart*, 842.

30. Regula Ludi, "The Vectors of Postwar Victim Reparations: Relief, Redress and Memory Politics," *Journal of Contemporary History* 41, no. 3 (2006): 430. https://doi.org/10.1177%2F0022009406064654.

31. Fink, *Defending the Rights of Others*, 127.

32. On the creation of the organization see Zohar Segev, *The World Jewish Congress During the Holocaust: Between Activism and Restraint* (Berlin and Boston: De Gruyter Oldenbourg, 2014), 1–22.

33. Reinharz and Friesel, "Nahum Goldmann, Jewish and Zionist Statesman - An Overview," in Raider, ed., *Nahum Goldmann: Statesman without a State*, 5–9.

34. Aryeh Leon Kubowitzki, *Unity in Dispersion: A History of the World Jewish Congress*, 2nd rev. ed. (New York: Institute of Jewish Affairs of the WJC, 1948), 32.

35. Articles 1 and 2 of the WJC constitution. See World Jewish Congress in *Encyclopedia Judaica*, 2nd ed., vol. 16 (Jerusalem: Keter Publishing House, 1973), 637.

36. Foreword to Kubowitzki, *Unity in Dispersion,* ii.

37. Nahum Goldmann, *Memories: The Autobiography of Nahum Goldmann: The Story of a Lifelong Battle by World Jewry's Ambassador at Large*, trans. Helen Sabba (London: Weidenfeld and Nicolson, 1970), 215.

38. Robert G. Waite, "Returning Jewish Cultural Property: The Handling of Books Looted by the Nazis in the American Zone of Occupation, 1945 to 1952," *Libraries & Culture* 37, no. 3 (2002): 222. https://www.jstor.org/stable/25549010.

39. *After Five Years 1948–1953: A Report of the Jewish Restitution Successor Organization on the Restitution of Identifiable Property in the US Zone of Germany* (Nurnberg: The Organization, 1953), 1.

40. Norman Bentwich, *Siegfried Moses and the United Restitution Organization* (Tel-Aviv: Irgun Olej Merkas Europa, 1962), 195.

41. Hans Günter Hockerts, "Anwälte der Verfolgten, Die URO" (Representatives of the Victims: The URO) in Ludolf Herbst and Constantin Goschler, eds., *Wiedergutmachung in der Bundesrepublik Deutschland* (Reparations in the Federal Republic of Germany) (Munich: Oldenbourg, 1989): 252. Subsequently, the Claims Conference financed the activities of URO. See the Study Committee Report of September 1958, American Jewish Historical Society (AJHS), Center for Jewish History (CJH), Conference on Jewish Material Claims against Germany Collection 1955–1972, Call 1–319, Folder 4.

42. *After Five Years*, 5.

43. *After Five Years*, 29.

44. Bentwich, *Siegfried Moses and the United Restitution Organization*, 198.

45. Wyman, *Displaced Persons*, 140. On internal disputes between different groups in the Warsaw ghetto, see Havi Dreifuss, "The Leadership of the Jewish Combat Organization during the Warsaw Ghetto: A Reassessment," *Holocaust and Genocide Studies* 31, no. 1 (2017): 24–48.

46. Koppel S. Pinson, "Jewish Life in Liberated Germany – A Study of Jewish DPs," *Jewish Social Studies* 9 (April 1947): 117.

47. Menahem Kaufman, *An Ambiguous Relationship: Non-Zionists and Zionists in America, 1939–1948* (Jerusalem: Magnes Press, 1991), 201–202; Ephraim Dekel, *B'riha: Flight to the Homeland*, trans. Dina Ettinger (New York: Herzl Press, 1972), 92–94.

48. *After Five Years*, 19–21.

49. C. I. Kapralik, *Reclaiming the Nazi Loot: The History of the Work of the Jewish Trust Corporation for Germany* (London: The Sidney Press Ltd. 1962), 69.

50. *After Five Years*, 19.

51. Patricia Clavin, "International Organizations," in Richard Bosworth and Joseph Maiolo, eds., *The Cambridge History of the Second World War*, vol. II, *Politics and Ideology* (Cambridge: Cambridge University Press, 2015), 141.

52. Christopher J. Kauffman, "Politics, Programs, and Protests: Catholic Relief Services in Vietnam, 1954–1975," *The Catholic Historical Review* 91, no. 2 (2005): 223–250.

53. Brian H. Smith, *More than Altruism: The Politics of Private Foreign Aid* (Princeton, NJ: Princeton University Press, 2014), 51.

54. The term "political honeymoon" appears in Henry Heller, *The Cold War and the New Imperialism: A Global History, 1945–2005* (New York: Monthly Review Press, 2006), 25.

55. Klaus Larres and Ann Lane, eds., *The Cold War: The Essential Readings* (Oxford, UK: Blackwell Publishers, 2001), 1.

56. Alvin Z. Rubinstein, *The Soviets in International Organizations: Changing Policy Toward Developing Countries, 1953–1963* (Princeton, NJ: Princeton University Press, 1964), 30.

57. Sergio DellaPergola, "Reflections on the Multinational Geography of Jews After World War II," in Françoise S. Ouzan and Manfred Gerstenfeld, eds., *Postwar*

Jewish Displacement and Rebirth, 1945–1967 (Leiden, Boston: Brill, 2014), Table 1 on p. 16.

58. Ayaka Takei, "The 'Gemeinde Problem': the JRSO and the Postwar Jewish Communities in Germany, 1947–54," *Holocaust and Genocide Studies* 16, no. 2 (2002): 268.

59. Waite, "Returning Jewish Cultural Property," 219.

60. Katharina Rauschenberger, "The Restitution of Jewish Cultural Objects and the Activities of Jewish Cultural Reconstruction, Inc.," *Leo Baeck Institute Year Book* 53 (2008): 222. https://doi.org/10.1093/leobaeck/53.1.191.

61. *After Five Years,* 21.

62. Andrew Moravcsik, "A New Statecraft? Supranational Entrepreneurs and International Cooperation," *International Organization* 53, no. 2 (1999): 267. https://doi.org/10.1162/002081899550887. Moravcsik himself disputes the importance of supranational entrepreneurs.

63. Clavin, "International Organizations," 160.

64. See "Benjamin Ferencz: A Former Prosecutor at the Nuremberg War Crimes Trials," *BenFerencz.org*, n. d., accessed on October 20, 2019, https://benferencz.org/biography/.

65. This information is based on correspondence between the author and Benjamin Ferencz dated May 25, 2014.

66. Benjamin B. Ferencz, *Less than Slaves: Jewish Forced Labor and the Quest for Compensation* (Cambridge, MA: Harvard University Press, 1979), 39.

67. Waite, "Returning Jewish Cultural Property," 10.

68. *After Five Years,* 2.

69. Cited in Takei, "The 'Gemeinde Problem,'" 271.

70. Takei, "The 'Gemeinde Problem,'" 273.

71. *After Five Years,* 19–20.

72. Rauschenberger, "Restitution of Jewish Cultural Objects," 200.

73. Dr. W. Breslauer and Dr. F. Goldschmidt, *The Work of the Council of Jews from Germany in the Sphere of Indemnification: Report* (London: The Organization, 1966).

74. Hal Lehrman, "The New Germany and the Remaining Jews," *Commentary,* December 1953, accessed on October 20, 2019, https://www.commentarymagazine.com/articles/the-new-germany-and-her-remaining-jewsa-reporters-notebook/.

75. *After Five Years,* 12.

76. *After Five Years,* 20 and 29.

77. Rauschenberger, "Restitution of Jewish Cultural Objects," 200.

78. Throughout this book I refer to the Claims Conference as "spokesman" and not "spokesperson" because it consisted almost only of men.

Chapter 2

Who Speaks for the Jews on Reparations?

The Genesis of the Claims Conference

In 1952, negotiations commenced with West Germany on reparations. Not one but two parties claimed to speak on behalf of Hitler's Jewish victims: Israel and a previously unknown entity: the Claims Conference. Israel was a sovereign state with a democratically elected government, recognized under international law. According to the principles of international law, Israel had no claim to reparations due to its establishment after the end of the Second World War. The Claims Conference, which spoke "in the name of the most important Jewish organizations in the world," was a recently formed and non-elected body.[1] It purported to represent the Jewish people but had no legal status at the time of the execution of the Luxembourg Agreement.[2]

Examining the genesis of the Claims Conference illustrates the emergence of leadership from a group of individuals seeking reparations. The issue of representation of Jewish victims and survivors came at a critical time. The wartime destruction of communities in Central and Western Europe put an end to leadership roles for representatives from both regions. In addition, the establishment of Israel altered the balance of power between citizens of the ancestral homeland and diaspora communities. Israeli politicians claimed that the state was the sole legitimate representative of Jews worldwide. Rejection of this view by American communal leaders set the scene for a confrontation.

An extensive literature exists on the course of events that resulted in the signing of the Luxembourg Agreement on September 10, 1952. Figure 2.1 lists the main developments leading up to the execution of the Luxembourg Agreement between West Germany, the state of Israel, and the Claims Conference.[3] On the other hand, little has been written on why and how the Claims Conference came into existence. The proceedings surrounding the initiation of negotiations on compensation indicate that three parties contributed to the creation of the Claims Conference: diaspora organizations, West

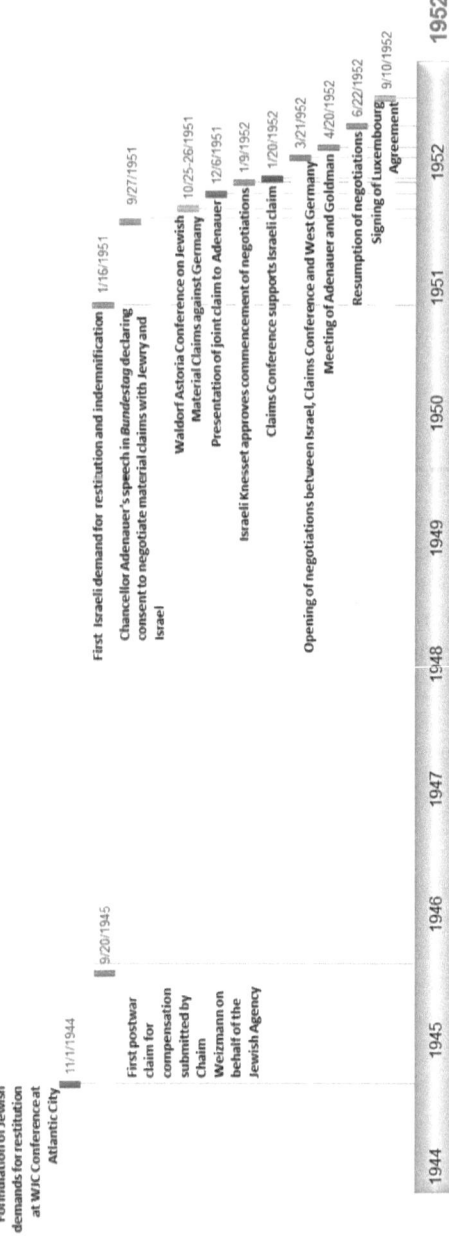

Figure 2.1 Chronology of Events Leading up to the Luxembourg Agreement. *Source:* By the author.

Germany, and Israel. One individual, Goldmann, acted as godfather to the conference. The different contributions are discussed below. Ironically, the conference convened by Goldmann to approve and support the Israeli claim for reparations resulted in the formation of a separate delegation to represent the claims of diaspora Jews against Germany.

JEWISH DIASPORA ORGANIZATIONS AND NEGOTIATIONS ON REPARATIONS

Demands made by diaspora organizations for separate representation on the issue of reparations were a natural continuation of their involvement in drafting claims for compensation and seeking restitution. Their presence in occupied Germany and the contacts they formed with local officials triggered the opening of negotiations on reparations. Furthermore, the insistence on a separate delegation to put forward diaspora claims was part of the ongoing struggle between Israel and mainly American organizations on "who speaks for the Jews."[4]

The WJC began to plan demands for compensation for crimes perpetrated by Germany against Jews in the early 1940s. At that time and based on the precedent of the Versailles Treaty, WJC president Goldmann and his colleagues believed that the Allied Powers would impose reparations on Germany after its defeat. WJC calls for compensation of Jewish victims were aimed at the Allies and intended to influence their demands from a conquered Germany. Goldmann feared that since under international law, the Jewish people were not at war with Germany, the Allies would not recognize a claim for their compensation. Therefore, during the war the WJC directed its efforts to ensuring that Jewish victims were not left out of a future peace treaty.

At the 1941 conference, Goldmann declared that if reparations were to be paid, "we are the first who have a claim to them."[5] He did not specify who "we" meant. In his autobiography he wrote that leaders of the organization (in other words, he and his associates) "worked out a program" on compensation from a conquered Germany in 1942 and 1943. The 1944 WJC conference at Atlantic City recognized that "the Jewish people has a right to collective compensation for the material and moral losses sustained" by the people, its institutions, and individual Jews who (or whose heirs) cannot make their own claims.[6] The resolution was adopted before the end of the war and four years prior to the establishment of Israel. Goldmann did not specify who would represent the Jewish people. Based on his lengthy involvement in Jewish organizational life and the declarations he made in WJC conferences, it may be assumed that Goldmann had the WJC in mind.

At the same time, Jewish lawyers conceived the idea of forming a new entity to present Jewish claims against Germany. Moses, in his discussion of postwar claims, advocated for the establishment of a representative body "capable of action on behalf of the Jewish People."[7] He proposed the formation of a representative body by the Jewish Agency together with world Jewry organizations and central associations of Jews from Germany and other countries. Its purpose was to present the Jewish collective claim. That same year, Nehemiah Robinson of the WJC suggested establishing a Jewish Agency for Reconstruction. This entity would claim the assets of individuals and communities that belonged to the category of "disappeared persons" and "dispose of them in a manner ensuring their proper use."[8] Robinson added that the agency could not be created simply by constituting it on the model of other Jewish organizations of international scope and it had to have a legal status enabling it to make deals with governments and effect a settlement of claims.[9] Robinson subsequently participated in negotiations with West Germany as a member of the Claims Conference delegation. Hugo Marx, a former German judge, put forward a different solution. He advocated for the establishment of a special agency by foreign governments to engage in reparations on behalf of the Jews of Germany.[10]

At the end of the war, Jewish transnational organizations maintained a presence in occupied Germany for the dual purposes of welfare work in displaced persons camps and restitution of Jewish property. In 1946, there were between 220,000 and 260,000 homeless Jews in Central Europe.[11] Immediately after the war, the Allied Powers forcibly repatriated more than six million non-German nationals situated on German soil, including prisoners of war and forced laborers. However, they allowed Jews to remain in Germany and Austria. Moreover, the Allies did not prevent East European Jews fleeing pogroms and the descending Iron Curtain from crossing borders into occupied Germany, Austria, and Italy. Military governors housed homeless Jews in camps for displaced persons administered by UNRRA and other civil relief organizations.

Welfare work in the camps brought delegations of Jewish organizations to occupied Germany. Dr. Noah Barou was a member of one delegation. Born in the central Ukrainian town of Poltava, he moved to London as director of the Cooperative Moscow Narodny Bank in 1925. Barou was one of the architects of the WJC and the president of its European executive.[12] Barou first visited Bergen-Belsen shortly after its liberation by the British army and subsequently came so often that "he was treated by the survivors as one of their own."[13] These visits brought him into contact with Germans and formed the basis of his intimate understanding of the circumstances in Germany. Barou lobbied for reparations and initiated contacts with the German Ministry of Foreign Affairs.

The JDC provided food, clothing, and medicines to Jewish displaced persons in camps. Representatives of the organization, including its European director, Dr. Joseph Schwartz, operated welfare, educational, and religious services in the camps and cooperated with the occupying forces and UNRRA.[14] The scope of expenses incurred by the JDC and other Jewish organizations on victims of National Socialist persecution was enormous. The organizations estimated that they had spent $1.1 billion on aid and rehabilitation for refugees and survivors between 1933 and 1951.[15] Moreover, they planned to continue assisting victims outside Israel including 22,000 ill, mentally and physically disabled, as well as 150,000 less serious cases. The need to ensure future funding for care of victims strengthened the call of communal leaders for separate representation in claims for reparations.

Restitution work initiated by diaspora alliances set in motion negotiations on reparations. Lawyers hired by the successor organizations and URO came into daily contact with Germans. They were well acquainted with local conditions, German legislation, and bureaucracy. This knowledge assisted them in drawing up claims for the compensation of survivors.

Zionist organizations played a relatively minor role in restitution work in occupied Germany. They concentrated on facilitating the legal and illegal emigration of survivors to Palestine and avoided direct contact with local officials. Before the start of negotiations on reparations at Wassenaar, Israel did not have diplomatic ties with West Germany. An Israeli consulate operated in Munich in connection with displaced persons and UNRRA but had no connection with German institutions.[16] It was not until Israel decided to seek reparations in April 1951 that representatives of the state first met the German chancellor and then behind a thick veil of secrecy.[17]

Goldmann, in his capacity as joint chairman of the Jewish Agency, was the only official representative of the Jewish community of Palestine, and subsequently the state of Israel, in direct and open contact with Germans. He was a member of the Board of Directors of JRSO and understood at an early stage the need for direct negotiations with Germans on reparations. Unlike Israeli politicians, Goldmann had no qualms on this issue. Ferencz, the director general of JRSO who was subsequently appointed by Goldmann to advise the Claims Conference delegation, explained the different attitudes Israel and diaspora organizations held regarding direct negotiations with Germany:

> I had been demanding restitution for a long time. I didn't know what all this fuss was about dealing with the Germans. I had received millions of dollars from the Germans already. It was Jewish money, so I had no hesitation at all about taking it. On the contrary, I regretted that I couldn't recover more.[18]

The diaspora organizations took it for granted that they would participate in negotiations with Germany, and not under the leadership of an Israeli delegation. In an oral testimony given in 1961, Goldmann stated that after the war, "we" (again, he does not specify who "we" was) began to discuss demands for indemnification with Jewish organizations and governments at a time when "we didn't know if there would be [a] Jewish state."[19] It is hard to reconcile the intensive involvement of organizations in discussions on reparations and their operations in Germany with the claim that Israel initiated the establishment of the Claims Conference.[20]

The relationship between diaspora leaders and Israel in the early years after its establishment also contributed to the creation of the Claims Conference. Negotiations on reparations began during a period of tension between the state and predominantly American, transnational organizations. Non-Zionist organizations feared that the domestic and foreign policies of Israel would lead to accusations of dual loyalties. This friction reinforced the will of diaspora leaders for separate representation in negotiations on reparations.

In the first years of the state, Israeli politicians condemned diaspora life and called for an ingathering of exiles. American organizations objected to the description of Jews as a nation and of those living in the diaspora as exiles. For them, Judaism was a religion. Therefore, there was no contradiction between their American nationality and Jewish identity. For example, Chaim Weizmann, the first president of Israel, declared in a speech on February 14, 1949, on the occasion of opening the Israeli Parliament, that the establishment of the state had been earned "by all the hardships . . . *when one third of our nation was annihilated.*"[21] Jacob Blaustein, co-founder of American Oil Company (Amoco) and president of the American Jewish Committee (AJC), the global advocacy organization, took offense to the term "the Jewish nation," which he described as "abhorrent, implying that all Jews *ipso facto* were citizens of a foreign state (Israel) and casting aspersions on their American nationality and citizenship."[22]

A few months later, Ben-Gurion, the first prime minister of Israel, called for mass immigration. In an address to an American Trade Union delegation visiting the country, he appealed "chiefly to the youth of the United States and in other countries to help us achieve this big mission."[23] A headline published by the Jewish Telegraphic Agency following the visit stated: "Ben-Gurion urges American Parents to send their children to Israel for permanent settlement."[24] Lessing Rosenwald protested to Secretary of State Dean Acheson and warned that the statement "threatens to undermine the stability of American Jews."[25] Rosenwald, son of the successful businessman Julius Rosenwald who was also one of the leading philanthropists of his time, succeeded his father as the chairman of Sears, Roebuck and Company. From 1943 to 1955, Lessing Rosenwald served as president of the American Council for Judaism, an organization that advocated that Jews were a religious group and not a nationality. The timing of these altercations coincided with preliminary Jewish contacts with West Germany on reparations.

Eventually an understanding was reached to defuse the tension. Prime Minister Ben-Gurion hosted an official luncheon in honor of Blaustein on August 23, 1950. In his speech, the prime minister clarified that American Jews had only one political attachment, to the United States, and did not owe political allegiance to Israel. Blaustein responded by explaining that Israel means much to Jews of the diaspora but added "to American Jews, America is home."[26] Reactions in Israel and the United States were mixed but the understanding reduced heated disputes. This context contributed to the desire of American Jewish organizations for a separate delegation to participate alongside Israel in negotiations on German reparations.

WEST GERMANY AND REPRESENTATIVES OF WORLD JEWRY

West Germany advocated for negotiations with two parties on compensation for Jewish victims of the Third Reich: world Jewry and Israel. The newly founded republic had a strong interest in the participation of American Jewry in talks alongside Israel. As a result, German policy made an indirect but significant contribution to the formation of the Claims Conference.

Many countries participated in the mass murder of Jews and plunder of their property before and during the Second World War. In the early 1950s, West Germany was the only country willing to negotiate reparations for crimes perpetrated against Jews. East Germany, whose citizens had also plundered and murdered Jews, denied continuity with the National Socialist regime.[27] This state, officially the German Democratic Republic, was established in the territory occupied by Soviet forces at the end of the Second World War. In accordance with the Soviet policy of non-recognition of the Holocaust, East German politicians refused to admit German responsibility for the persecution of Jews throughout Europe and North Africa. They claimed that many of their citizens were among the "antifascist resistance fighters."[28] Consequently, the Soviet proxy state did not enter into negotiations on reparations. Austria based its refusal to pay compensation or reparations on the contention that it had been the first victim of the Third Reich. The Allied Moscow Declaration of October 1943 formed the basis of the claim that Austria had also been a victim of Hitler. Against the background of the Cold War, few questioned this proposition.[29] Other countries such as France, Holland, and Switzerland continued to deny their complicity in the persecution for decades.

The Federal Republic of Germany, West Germany, arose out of the ashes on May 23, 1949, following the collapse of the Third Reich and four years of occupation by the Allied Powers. Its new constitution declared that the state was required to respect and protect human dignity. In this manner, and without explicit reference to the former regime, the drafters wished to clarify that a new era had arrived and that West Germany had severed its links with the past. The Allied nations and the German public shared the desire to view West Germany as a new entity, a tabula rasa.[30] The state could not, however, escape from its past and from the crimes carried out by its citizens.

German citizens, inside and outside the country, demanded redress of losses resulting from National Socialist persecution. In the words of the German historian Constantin Goschler, "at the end of the Second World War, and for a long time thereafter the racial persecution of Jews, which culminated in the Holocaust, was considered only one aspect of the vast array of human and material destruction caused by Nazi Germany."[31]

German discussions on compensation began before the war. Communists, socialists, and other political opponents of National Socialism were the first group to demand compensation for crimes perpetrated against them. Hermann Brill, a Social Democratic politician, wrote a manifesto in 1936 calling for the release of political prisoners and *"Wiedergutmachung"* for injustices perpetrated.[32] The literal meaning of the word *"Wiedergutmachung"* is to make good again, to return to a former condition and in a broader sense, to a former state of co-existence.[33] After the war, Germans used the term to refer to reparations for Jewish victims of the Third Reich, although as pointed out by the German political scientist Axel Frohn, the idea of monetary compensation as a means of restoration, in the context of the Holocaust, sounds helplessly naïve and out of place.[34]

At the end of the war, two main groups inside and outside Germany demanded payment of compensation: Jews and individuals who had suffered persecution on political grounds. The Union of Persecutees of the Nazi Regime, an association created in June 1945, represented political opponents of the regime.[35] Conditions for negotiations on Jewish demands ripened seven years after the end of the war. Other victims, such as Sinti and Roma, had to wait until the reunification of West and East Germany in 1990.

The West German government initially refused to recognize the persecution of Jews by the former regime. Konrad Adenauer, in his inaugural speech to the German Parliament, the *Bundestag*, as chancellor, made no mention of German-Jewish relations. In the words of Goschler, West Germany "did not regard the compensation of Nazi victims—Jewish as well as others—as a debt for which they should actively seek a solution. Instead they showed a strong tendency to wait for claims first and then to try to beat down the price."[36]

Jewish diaspora organizations played a crucial role in bringing West Germany to the negotiating table. Their representatives approached German officials and started the process that ultimately led to the payment of reparations. Barou of the WJC frequently traveled to Germany to raise the issue of reparations with German civil servants. He first met lower echelon officials and gradually worked his way up the ladder to more influential figures.[37] In June 1951, Barou met Herbert Blankenhorn, a senior official in the German Ministry of Foreign Affairs.[38] Blankenhorn suggested, to break the ice, that the chancellor make a speech in the *Bundestag* acknowledging Germany's national responsibilities for atrocities perpetrated against the Jews of Europe and expressing willingness to compensate them for material losses.[39] Following the approaches of the organizations and a meeting with Israeli representatives in April, the chancellor prepared a draft speech. He sent it to Goldmann in advance for his approval.[40]

On September 27, 1951, Adenauer addressed the German Parliament on the occasion of the Jewish New Year. In his speech, the chancellor declared that the federal government was willing to pay reparations for the crimes of the Third Reich and proposed negotiations with representatives of two parties: world Jewry and the state of Israel. He not only distinguished between the two advocates but placed world Jewry first. This speech strengthened the demand of diaspora organizations for their own representative in negotiations on reparations.

Historians have put forward different explanations for West German support of separate representation for diaspora Jews on the issue of reparations. According to Rolf Vogel, the chancellor was motivated by a desire to please American Jewry. Adenauer's representatives had met members of the AJC one day before the speech. The organization repeatedly expressed misgivings about Israel's claims that it spoke in the name of all Jews.[41] Therefore, the chancellor referred in his speech to "representatives of world Jewry and the state of Israel."[42]

The historian Yeshayahu Jelinek also attributed German support for separate representation to the desire of German politicians to foster close relations with American Jewish leaders. This desire was part of the belief of German politicians and the press that placating the Jews of America would facilitate Germany's return to the family of nations.[43] In an interview given in 1956, in response to a question on reconciliation between West Germany and the US government, Adenauer said: "One should not underestimate, therefore, the power of the Jews, particularly in America."[44] According to this view, West Germany "placated the Jews" by supporting the participation of American Jewish organizations in the framework of the Claims Conference in negotiations on reparations.

Ronald Zweig, the author of a book and articles on German reparations, described the appeal of a diaspora entity to the German successor state. West Germany hoped that the organization would handle "hard-core Jewish DPs still in West Germany."⁴⁵ Another possible explanation was the German desire to reach one agreement on all issues relating to Jewish victims. Any agreement between two parties only, West Germany and Israel, was open to attack by diaspora Jews on the grounds that they had not been represented in the negotiations and were not bound by bilateral undertakings. German support contributed to the participation of a separate negotiating party, the Claims Conference, acting on behalf of diaspora organizations on the issue of reparations.

ISRAEL AND ITS SHIFTING POSITION ON REPRESENTATION OF A COMMUNITY

Israel was the third party involved in the creation of the Claims Conference delegation. The attitude of Israeli politicians toward the question of separate representation of diaspora Jews underwent a transformation. Initially, the state argued that it was the sole authorized spokesman of the Jewish people on all matters, including compensation for the Holocaust. Accordingly, it objected to tripartite negotiations. Shortly before the beginning of talks with West Germany, Israel withdrew its objection to shared representation of Holocaust victims and assisted in convening the conference that led to the establishment of a separate delegation. At the same time, Israel intended for the diaspora delegation to play a narrow role limited to the support of Israeli claims for compensation.

The question of who represented Jewish victims of the Third Reich was an integral part of discussions in Israel among politicians on negotiations for reparations. Weizmann, future Israeli president, made the first claim for compensation at the end of the war. In a letter to the Allied nations dated September 20, 1945, he demanded, on behalf of the Jewish Agency, the restoration of heirless Jewish property in Axis and neutral countries to "representatives of the Jewish people" for "use in Palestine."⁴⁶ In addition, the letter contained the following demand: "That the Jewish people should be allotted a proper percentage of reparations, to be entrusted to the Jewish Agency for Palestine for the rehabilitation and resettlement in Palestine of Jewish victims of racial and religious persecution."⁴⁷ In other words, Weizmann requested the payment of compensation to the Jewish Agency for use in the Jewish homeland and ignored the claims of diaspora organizations and individual victims. The Allies did not respond to this demand, and for the next three years, the Jews of Palestine and Zionist organizations worldwide concentrated their efforts on the struggle to end the British Mandate. The establishment of the state followed by the War of Independence again postponed the issue of reparations and who would put forward claims on behalf of the survivors.

In 1950, the Israeli government began to examine how to obtain compensation for atrocities perpetrated by Germany against Jews. Consent to negotiate with West Germany resulted from a combination of economic and political considerations. Three factors influenced Israeli policy: the country's dire economy, global politics, and the fear of missing a window of opportunity for reaching a favorable settlement on reparations.

Israel experienced an economic crisis commencing in the last months of 1950. Mass immigration followed the establishment of the state. From May 1948 to the end of 1951, Israel's Jewish population more than doubled from 650,000 to 1,324,000. The state had to provide food, clothing, and shelter (initially in the form of tents) to impoverished immigrants from Europe, North Africa, and Asia. To meet this challenge, the government introduced an austerity program with price controls and rationing of food and raw materials to ensure minimum standards of consumption for the entire population. Imports in 1950 totaled $327.6 million while exports amounted to the "miniscule" sum of $45.8 million.[48] Official figures put unemployment at 11.5 percent. A drought in the winter of 1950–1951 put further pressure on the country's economy and led to stricter measures. Israel desperately needed foreign investments to build infrastructure and provide employment opportunities for new immigrants.

The developing Cold War also contributed to the Israeli decision to seek reparations. Israel originally sought financial redress from both East Germany and West Germany and avoided taking sides in the hostilities between the Soviet Union and the West. Against the backdrop of the Korean War and the increasing bipolarity of world politics, the Allies prepared to grant West Germany full sovereignty. This change in world politics forced Israel to abandon its policy of non-identification and seek reparations from the only country willing to negotiate reparations, namely West Germany.[49]

Furthermore, Israel feared that Jewish organizations might assume control of negotiations with the German authorities. According to Jelinek, Jerusalem did not trust German leaders. Israel suspected that Adenauer's emphasis in his *Bundestag* speech on the Jewish people concealed an intention to pay indemnification to individual victims at the expense of the collective claim of the state of Israel.[50] This concern contributed to a change in policy.

The Israeli government planned to commence negotiations on reparations against a backdrop of widespread public opposition to contacts with Germany. In the first years after the establishment of the Jewish state, no other issue was as explosive as relations with Germany. Menachem Begin, the head of the Revisionist *Herut* party, made inflammatory speeches at public rallies and in the *Knesset* comparing negotiations on reparations to trading in blood.[51] His party newspaper stated that "the reparations money is dipped in Jewish blood."[52] Begin denounced direct negotiations on the grounds that they were a step in the direction of the murderers' rehabilitation. The left-wing party *Mapam* also strongly opposed negotiations with Germans. Nevertheless, pragmatic considerations prevailed.

On March 12, 1951, Israel sent notes to the four Allies stipulating its claim against Germany. The state emphasized that it alone was entitled to reparations owed to the Jewish people:

> Israel is the only state which can speak on behalf of the Jewish people . . . Israel has been built up for the specific purpose of providing a refuge for all persecuted and homeless Jews . . . Israel has made itself responsible for the absorption and rehabilitation of the survivors of that catastrophe. For all these reasons, the state of Israel regards itself as entitled to claim reparations from Germany by way of indemnity to the Jewish people.[53]

The notes make no mention of the claims of individual survivors or diaspora organizations.

Documents of the Israeli Ministry of Foreign Affairs from this time also stress that only a sovereign state was entitled to reparations. This view was supported by international law but ignored that Israel had not existed at the time of the plunder and murder. After returning from an unofficial visit to Germany, Boris Guriel, director of the political department of the Ministry, wrote in a memorandum on June 12, 1950, that Israel, as a member of the United Nations, should be the sole representative of the Jewish people in matters pertaining to Germany.[54] A few months later, a consultation at the Ministry included a discussion of Israel's right to represent Jewish demands for reparations. The participants agreed that in the United States there were five times the number of Jews in Israel and in the USSR, there were 2 million Jews. These numbers did not detract from the exclusive right of Israel to demand reparations since neither President Truman nor General Secretary Stalin claimed to represent the Jewish people. The conclusion of the consultation was that Israel should monopolize Jewish demands against Germany.[55]

In September 1950, an internal document addressed to Israel's foreign minister proposed that Israel and the Jewish Agency set up a "High Jewish Commission" to handle all matters relating to restitution and reparations. The founders of the Commission should invite several Jewish organizations to join them, including the JDC, CBF, JRSO, the Jewish Trust Corporation, and URO. The Commission would have an advisory status but the Israeli delegation would be the sole representative of the victims in negotiations with Germany.[56] From these documents, it appears that until September 1951, Israel rejected the idea of a third party in negotiations on reparations. It therefore opposed the formation of a delegation representing organizations from outside the state.

The transition in Israeli policy occurred in October 1951. Goldmann, in the name of the Jewish Agency and after discussions with the Israeli Foreign Ministry, convened a conference on Jewish material claims against Germany in New York. The creation of a separate negotiating party was the outcome of this meeting. Official documents do not explain the change in Israeli policy. Two events, which occurred shortly before the convening of the meeting in New York, shed light on this development. First, in his speech to the German Parliament at the end of September, Adenauer made explicit reference to two partners to negotiations: Israel and representatives of world Jewry. Second, Israeli leaders held discussions with Goldmann in October on coordinating claims for reparations. In these discussions, Dr. Felix Shinnar, Israeli diplomat and adviser to the foreign minister who subsequently led the Israeli delegation to negotiations with Germany, submitted a proposal on the form that coordination between the Israeli government and diaspora organizations would take. Goldmann objected to the proposal for failing to acknowledge the right of the latter to represent the Jewish people.[57] According to Shinnar, the discussions ended with a suggestion by Goldmann to set up an entity composed of all the important Jewish organizations in the world. The object of this entity was to file individual claims on behalf of Nazi victims.[58] Israel accepted the proposal.

In conclusion, German insistence on tripartite negotiations and Goldmann's refusal to take orders from the Israeli government resulted in a shift in Israeli policy. Foreign Minister Moshe Sharett asked Goldmann to invite Jewish organizations to a conference "to express support for Israel's demands and thereby present a united Jewish front."[59] Goldmann duly convened the meeting.

CREATION OF THE CLAIMS CONFERENCE

The founding meeting of the Claims Conference took place at the Waldorf-Astoria Hotel in New York on October 25 and 26, 1951. Goldmann invited twenty-two Jewish organizations to the conference, where he presided as self-elected chairman. In his opening statement, Goldmann emphasized the informal nature of the meeting and added that the conference was not in any way a parliament or elected and could not bind anyone. He added that the limited purpose of the conference was Jewish claims against Germany.[60]

Discussions at the conference centered on two issues: direct negotiations with West Germany and separate representation of diaspora organizations. On the first question, all participants except for one approved the acceptance of Adenauer's proposal to seek a solution for material claims. The sole opponent, *Agudas Israel World Organization (Aguda)*, a society established in 1912 in Katowice, Poland, to represent Orthodox Jews worldwide, stated that accepting the chancellor's offer amounted to "moral suicide."[61] The second question was whether to accept the Israeli position that the state alone represented Jewish claims against Germany.

At the conference, Israel called on the diaspora organizations to limit their participation in negotiations to support for the payment of collective reparations to the state. The Israeli representative to the conference, Abba Eban, ambassador to the United States and Permanent Representative to the United Nations, declared that

> the Government of Israel regards the state of Israel as the collective expression of the Jewish will for survival and for equality. Moreover, the state of Israel alone amongst the countries of the world became the refuge and the repository of the great mass of those who managed to survive the Holocaust of Nazism, therefore the primacy of this claim above all others, both in moral and in practical terms.[62]

He added that in his view, the purpose of the conference was to "align the Jewish people everywhere in support of the Israel claim."[63] Blaustein of the AJC rejected this position. In his words:

> The claim of course is preponderantly that of Israel, but it is not only an Israeli claim, and that is where I have the one partial exception perhaps from what the Ambassador said. I do not believe that they can come out with a monopoly for the Israel claim. I think that Israel should be greatly emphasized but it should not be in the category of monopoly.[64]

Another participant representing the American Jewish Congress clarified "that it is our view that Germany's debt is not only to Israel, but to all Jewry."[65]

Ambassador Eban took issue with these views. In his response to the speeches by American delegates, he emphasized "a complete distinction between the clear-cut character" of the Israeli claim and the "inchoate, unagreed (*sic*) character of other Jewish claims."[66] The former was based on the cost of absorbing 500,000 Holocaust survivors, amounting to a total of $1.5 billion whereas the latter claims were plunged in deep obscurity. Eban argued that the presentation of a separate Jewish claim by the organizations will "infect our clarity with your obscurity."[67] Goldmann, who presided over the proceedings, did not express an opinion on the matter in dispute and no vote was taken on the Israeli proposal. At the end of the conference, representatives of the organizations adopted a resolution recording "wholehearted support" for the Israeli claim for rehabilitation of Nazi victims in Israel and demanding satisfaction of "all other Jewish claims against Germany."[68] In addition, the conference decided to create two committees to take such practical steps as developments necessitated. These committees were named after the meeting that authorized their creation: the Claims Conference. No mention of the committees appears in the formal resolution adopted by the conference.

The minutes of an Israeli government meeting present a different account of the creation of the Claims Conference. The meeting, which took place on the same day as the proceedings at the Waldorf-Astoria, reviewed the issue of reparations.[69] Foreign Minister Sharett described contacts held with the Jewish Agency and other associations on the question of who would present claims to West Germany on behalf of Jewish victims. He argued that ideally, there would be only one Jewish delegation to the talks, namely Israel. A joint delegation on behalf of the state and Jewish organizations was out of the question. Goldmann had rejected another Israeli proposal for bilateral negotiations with an advisory committee liaising between Israel and the organizations. Sharett explained that the organizations had refused to accept his proposal for Israel alone to represent all Jewish claims. Goldmann insisted on separate representation for diaspora Jews. The finance minister asked if the organizations intended to claim monetary compensation. Sharett replied in the affirmative and added that the money would go to Israel but not necessarily to the Israeli government. He concluded that an entity would be set up to operate on behalf of the organizations in coordination with Israel.

After the New York meeting, Goldmann proceeded with the creation of the Claims Conference. He appointed himself president and nominated the first executive committee, a committee of experts on reparations and Kagan as secretary.[70] At this stage, the Claims Conference was no more than two committees with a small administrative staff occupying offices on the premises of the JDC.

Israel allowed the new alliance to lead the way to negotiations with West Germany. The *Knesset* debated entry into direct contacts with Germans on reparations in January 1952. Violent mass demonstrations formed a background to the debate (see figure 2.2). Demonstrators threw grenades and rocks that shattered windows of the building where the session was held.[71]

In his opening speech in the *Knesset*, Ben-Gurion cited the convening of Jewish organizations in New York and their full support of Israeli demands as justification for the government decision to negotiate directly with Germans. He added that the organizations further sought restitution and compensation for victims and their heirs.[72] Ben-Gurion made no mention of the state's initial opposition to separate representation for Jews of the diaspora or the leading role played by non-Israelis in initiating discussions with West Germany on reparations. Partial disclosure, together with the concealment of relevant facts, presented a distorted picture to the *Knesset* and the public. This was part of the "obfuscation tactics" practiced by the government on

Figure 2.2 Demonstration in Israel against Direct Negotiations with West Germany on Reparations. *Source*: Courtesy of Hans Pinn, photographer, Israel Government Press Office.

the extremely sensitive topic of compensation for crimes perpetrated against Jews during the Second World War.[73] The *Knesset* approved the government motion by a narrow majority.

Why did Goldmann form the Claims Conference to represent Jewish diaspora organizations in negotiations on German reparations instead of using the existing WJC where he too served as president? Goldmann, in his many testimonies, biographies, and personal files, did not refer to this question. Documents indicate that the decision to create a new entity was made by Goldmann without first consulting executives of the WJC. In April 1951, Alex Easterman, Scottish lawyer and senior European WJC executive, wrote a letter berating the convening of a conference of Jewish organizations:

> The Congress [the WJC] breaks its neck formulating the whole business, representations, heirless property etc., works it out in technical details and makes numerous presentations and representations. . . . Then lo and behold, somebody decides to set up a lovely thing called "a consortium" of Jewish organizations. Next. . . someone decides to call a conference of Jewish organizations, international, local, political relief, charitable and what not. Does the WJC know about these things?[74]

A possible reason for the creation of the delegation was the desire to prevent friction with American Jewish leaders who viewed the WJC as Goldmann's own organization. Goldmann, in the name of the Jewish Agency, sent invitations to the New York conference without prior consultation with the participants. This caused resentment, and three weeks before it commenced, the head of the JDC office in Berlin questioned the wisdom of attending the conference.[75] The need for cooperation with the JDC and the AJC is one explanation for the creation of a new entity. According to this proposition, the intention was to bypass criticism and promote cooperation between diaspora representatives. The Claims Conference delegation was not overtly identified with Goldmann and granted equal status to all its members.

Another explanation for the creation of a new lobby group was Goldmann's recognition of the limitations of the WJC. The WJC served as a forum for speeches and debates but had no executive powers. Goldmann himself acknowledged its shortcomings when he wrote that its "only conspicuous success" came in 1938 in the campaign conducted against Romania's antisemitic policy.[76] Even in this case, the steps taken by the WJC had limited practical effect on the lives of Romanian Jews. The successor organizations created after the Second World War provided a new model. Broad administrative powers enabled them to operate in an efficient manner. They achieved a specific task—restitution—on a tight schedule. For this purpose, they recruited teams of experts, mainly lawyers, to locate properties, search for their owners or heirs, and file claims with German states (*Länder*). In addition, the successor organizations with their small and professional staff reacted quickly to changed circumstances. Goldmann was well acquainted with these organizations and their mode of operations. It may be assumed that he sought to create an entity based on the model of the JRSO. Ferencz, who was involved in early operations of the Claims Conference, replied when asked on the matter:

> I was not there when the Claims Conference was set up and was informed of discussions ... I'm only guessing ... It was a conference convened at the initiative of Nahum Goldmann, chairman of the WJC. He wanted to give himself greater importance, because the WJC didn't represent any congress and didn't represent the world. It didn't even represent the Jews.[77]

In December 1951, Goldmann met Adenauer in London. After the meeting, Adenauer sent a letter to "Dr. Nahum Goldmann, Chairman of the Conference on Jewish Claims (*sic*) Against Germany," affirming the consent of the Federal Government to treat the demands stipulated by Israel in the notes of March 1951 as the basis for discussions.[78] All three parties were now ready to negotiate.

CONCLUSION

The genesis of the Claims Conference indicates the impromptu nature of the emergence of a community spokesman. The delegation answered the political needs of three parties: Jewish diaspora organizations, West Germany, and the state of Israel. Israel initially opposed separate representation. At a later stage, following the German call to negotiate with "representatives of world Jewry" and in view of Goldmann's persistence, the state supported the formation of a separate delegation for the limited purpose of strengthening its claim to reparations.

There is no evidence of a formal Israeli resolution authorizing the creation of a separate delegation to represent Jews of the diaspora. The *Knesset* approval was limited to the government's entry into negotiations with West Germany on reparations. Participants at the meeting convened by Goldmann in New York did not pass a resolution on the appointment of a separate delegation on their behalf to negotiations with West Germany. They agreed to appoint two committees on a temporary basis. Subsequently, Goldmann created organs and appointed functionaries. In the words of the general counsel of the JDC at the time: "It appears that Nahum Goldmann has grabbed the ball and is running with it."[79]

In all his testimonies and biographies, Goldmann credited Israel with initiating the creation of the Claims Conference. The only exception was an article published in the German weekly magazine, *Weltwoche*, in September 1966, where Goldmann wrote that he set up the Claims Conference, offering evidence of the difficulty of relying on his testimony.[80] Clearly, the state played a role in the timing of the creation of the delegation. Israel's willingness to conduct direct negotiations with West Germany prompted the meeting of diaspora organizations in New York. The state also provided technical support for the convening of the conference. Goldmann sent out invitations to the organizations in the name of the Jewish Agency. Nevertheless, the moving spirit behind the new entity was Goldmann. This fact clearly emerges from documents of the Foreign Ministry and the JDC as well as the description of the events in a book written by Shinnar, the Israeli diplomat who negotiated the convening of the New York conference with Goldmann. In his book, Shinnar wrote that following their talks "and at the suggestion of Dr. Goldmann, the Claims Conference was set up."[81] The only evidence of an Israeli desire to create a new alliance of transnational organizations representing Jews from the diaspora is the testimony of Goldmann.

Goldmann's version of the creation of the Claims Conference that omitted any reference to Israeli opposition to separate representation and concealed his central role is puzzling. Goldmann had been negotiating with states and international organizations in the name of the Jewish people for three decades and was not known for his reticence. From his writing, it appears that he was driven by the prevailing view that under international law only states were entitled to reparations.[82] Consequently, he emphasized Israel's role and approval of the formation of the Claims Conference. Furthermore, the establishment of a sovereign state undermined Goldmann's claim that he and his organizations represented the Jewish people vis-à-vis foreign governments. In view of the changed circumstances, he searched for and found a legal basis for his actions. Attributing the credit for the creation of the Claims Conference to Israel provided the justification and authorization he sought.

The course of the negotiations with West Germany on reparations and their outcome are discussed in the following chapter.

NOTES

1. See the document headed "Erklärung der 'Conference on Jewish Material Claims Against Germany' zur Eröffnung der Verhandlungen mit den Vertretern der Deutschen Bundesrepublik," CAHJP, Claims Conference file 8132.

2. The Claims Conference was incorporated in New York on November 21, 1952, two and a half months after the execution of the Luxembourg Agreement. See "Corporation and Business Entity Database," *NYS Division of Corporations, State Records and UCC*, n.d., accessed on October 20,2019, https://www.dos.ny.gov/corps/bus_entity_search.html.

3. See for example, Vogel, *The German Path to Israel*; Balabkins, *West German Reparations to Israel*; Sagi, *German Reparations*; Weitz, "HaDerech LeWassenaar," 247–275.

4. David Vital discusses this question in the context of the Paris Peace Conference. See Vital, *A People Apart*, 728.

5. Goldmann, *Memories*, 250.

6. Goldmann, *Memories*, 251.

7. Moses, *Jewish Post-War Claims*, 57.

8. Robinson, *Indemnification and Reparations*, 257–258.

9. Robinson, *Indemnifications and Reparations*, 259–260.

10. Hugo Marx, *The Case of the German Jews vs. Germany: A Legal Basis for the Claims of the German Jews Against Germany* (New York: Egmont Press, 1944), 115.

11. Michael L. Meng, "Review: After the Holocaust: The History of Jewish Life in West Germany," *Contemporary European History* 14, no. 3 (2005): 404. https://www.jstor.org/stable/20081271; Judt, *Postwar*, 24.

12. Josef Fraenkel, "Noah Barou: The Man from Poltava," in Henrik F. Infield, ed., *Essays in Jewish Sociology, Labour and Co-operation in Memory of Dr. Noah Barou 1889–1955* (London and New York: Thomas Yoseloff, 1962), 7.

13. Hagit Lavsky, *New Beginnings: Holocaust Survivors in Bergen-Belsen and the British Zone in Germany, 1945–1950* (Detroit: Wayne State University Press, 2002), 99.

14. Schwartz accompanied Earl G. Harrison, envoy of President Truman, who visited the camps for displaced persons in July 1945. He subsequently directed relief programs in the camps. See Yehuda Bauer, *Out of the Ashes: The Impact of American Jews on Post-Holocaust European Jewry* (Oxford: Pergamon Press, 1989), chap. 3.

15. Zweig, *German Reparations*, 33.

16. Sagi, *German Reparations*, 70. See also Neima Barzel, "Dignity, Hatred and Memory," *Yad Vashem Studies* 24 (1994): 252.

17. Sagi, *German Reparations*, 69.

18. Benjamin Ferencz in a testimony given to the Hebrew University Oral History Division ("HUJI") in April 1971, 3.

19. Nahum Goldmann in a testimony given to HUJI, on November 14, 1961, 2.

20. An example of the contention that Israel initiated the reparations process and the formation of the Claims Conference appears in a statement made by Foreign Minister Sharett in a cabinet meeting on October 25, 1951. See "Minutes of Government Meeting 5/312, Section 7, Israel Enlists Jewish Organizations," *Sharett .org.il*, n.d., accessed on October 20, 2019, http://www.sharett.org.il/cgi-webax y/sal/sal.pl?lang=he&ID=880900_sharett_new&act=show&dbid=bookfiles&dataid =2212.

21. Cited in Ganin, *An Uneasy Relationship*, 27.

22. Ganin, *An Uneasy Relationship*, 27.

23. Ganin, *An Uneasy Relationship*, 36.

24. *Jewish Telegraphic Agency*, September 1, 1949.

25. Cited in Ganin, *An Uneasy Relationship*, 37.

26. Ganin, *An Uneasy Relationship*, 93.

27. Sagi, *German Reparations*, 191–192; Angelika Timm, *Jewish Claims against East Germany: Moral Obligations and Pragmatic Policy* (Budapest: Central European University Press, 1997), 67.

28. Timm, *Jewish Claims against East Germany*, 86.

29. Günter Bischof, "Victims? Perpetrators? 'Punching Bags' of European Historical Memory? The Austrians and their World War II Legacies," *German Studies Review* 27, no. 1 (2004): 18. https://www.jstor.org/stable/1433546; Robert Knight, "National Construction Work and Hierarchies of Empathy in Postwar Austria," *Journal of Contemporary History* 49, no. 3 (2014): 492. https://www.jstor .org/stable/43697322. On the extremely limited Austrian compensation for victims, see chap. 7 below.

30. See, for example, Manfred Kittel, *Die Legende von der "Zweiten Schuld": Vergangenheitsbewältigung in der Ära Adenauer* (*The Legend of the "Second Guilt": Dealing with the Past in the Adenauer Era*) (Berlin: Ullstein, 1993), 41.

31. Constantin Goschler, "German Compensation to Jewish Nazi Victims," in Jeffry M. Diefendorf, ed., *Lessons and Legacies: New Currents in Holocaust Research*, vol. VI (Evanston, IL: Northwestern University Press, 2004), 373.

32. Goschler, *Schuld und Schulden*, 31.

33. Axel Frohn, "Introduction: The Origins of Shilumim," in Axel Frohn, ed., *Holocaust and Shilumim: The Policy of Wiedergutmachung in the Early 1950s* (Washington, D.C.: German Historical Institute, 1991), 1–2.

34. Frohn, *Holocaust and Shilumim*, 2. For a different view on the use of the term *Wiedergutmachung* see Hockerts, "Wiedergutmachung in Deutschland," 167–170.

35. On the Union (*die Vereinigung der Verfolgten des Naziregimes*) see Goschler, *Schuld und Schulden*, 125–126. Goschler adds that at the time, other victims such as homosexuals, and Germans who had undergone forced sterilization did not participate in the discussions on compensation.

36. Goschler, "German Compensation to Jewish Nazi Victims," 403.

37. Sagi, *German Reparations*, 69.

38. On the importance of Barou's visit to Blankenhorn, see Nahum Goldmann, "A Noble Son of Jewry," in *Essays in Jewish Sociology*, 10–11.

39. Gerhart Riegner, *Never Despair: Sixty Years in the Service of the Cause of Human Rights* (Chicago: Ivan R. Dee, 2006), 378. See also Michael Brecher, "Images, Process and Feedback in Foreign Policy: Israel's Decisions on German Reparations," *The American Political Science Review* 67, no. 1 (1973): 86.

40. Goldmann, *Memories*, 256.

41. Jelinek, "Political Acumen," 87–88.

42. Vogel, *The German Path to Israel*, 33.

43. Jelinek, "Political Acumen," 80.

44. Gardner Feldman, *The Special Relationship between West Germany and Israel*, 55.

45. Ronald W. Zweig, "'Reparations Made Me,' Nahum Goldmann, German Reparations, and the Jewish World," in *Nahum Goldmann: Statesman without a State*, 242.

46. The letter appears in *Documents Relating to the Agreement between the Government of Israel and the Government of the Federal Republic of Germany* (Jerusalem: Ministry of Foreign Affairs, 1953), 12.

47. *Documents Relating to the Agreement*, 12.

48. Brecher, "Images, Process and Feedback," 77.

49. Brecher, "Images, Process and Feedback," 75; and Günther Gillessen, *Konrad Adenauer and Israel*, The Konrad Adenauer Memorial Lecture 1986 (Oxford: St. Anthony's College, 1986), 5.

50. Jelinek, "Political Acumen," 88.

51. See Weitz, "HaDerech LeWassenaar," 19; and "Speech by Menahem Begin in the *Knesset* on January 7, 1952," *Knesset.gov.il*, n.d., accessed on October 20, 2019, http://main.knesset.gov.il/About/Occasion/Pages/BeginSpeech4.aspx.

52. This claim appeared in the *Herut* newspaper on January 4, 1952. See Tom Segev, *The Seventh Million: The Israelis and the Holocaust*, trans. Haim Watzman (New York: Hill and Wang, 1993), 214.

53. *Documents Relating to the Agreement*, 23–24.

54. Jemima Rosenthal, ed., *Foreign Policy Documents of the State of Israel*, vol. 5 (Jerusalem: Government Printer, 1991), Document 276, p. 386.

55. *Foreign Policy Documents of the State of Israel*, Document 328, pp. 452–455.
56. *Foreign Policy Documents of the State of Israel*, Document 366, pp. 514–516.
57. Sagi, *German Reparations*, 75.
58. Felix Shinnar, *Be-Ol Korach U-regashot, Bishelichut Hamedina, Yahasei Israel-Germanyah, 1951–1966* (*The Burden of Necessity and Feelings, On Behalf of the State: Israel-German Relations, 1951–1966*) (Jerusalem: Schocken, 1967), 19.
59. Sagi, *German Reparations*, 75.
60. See Minutes of the Conference on Jewish Material Claims held on October 25–26, 1951, p. 10.
61. Minutes of the Conference on Jewish Material Claims held on October 25–26, 1951, p. 63. Nevertheless, *Aguda* remained a member of the Claims Conference and played a central role in the deliberations on how to allocate German funds. See chaps. 4 and 6.
62. Minutes of the Conference on Jewish Material Claims held on October 25–26, 1951, p. 45.
63. Minutes of the Conference on Jewish Material Claims held on October 25–26, 1951, p. 46.
64. Minutes of the Conference on Jewish Material Claims held on October 25–26, 1951, p. 68.
65. Minutes of the Conference on Jewish Material Claims held on October 25–26, 1951, p. 84.
66. Minutes of the Conference on Jewish Material Claims held on October 25–26, 1951, p. 86. For details of the Israeli claim, see Israeli Notes of March 12, 1951 to the four Occupying Powers concerning reparations cited in *Documents Relating to the Agreement*, Document 5, pp. 20–24.
67. Minutes of the Conference on Jewish Material Claims held on October 25–26, 1951, p. 87.
68. Resolution of the Conference on Jewish Material Claims against Germany, on the subject of material claims from Germany, New York, 26 October 1951. See *Documents Relating to the Agreement*, Document 15, p. 46.
69. "Minutes of Israeli government meeting held on October 25, 1951," *Sharett.org.il*, n.d., accessed on October 20, 2019, http://www.sharett.org.il/cgi-webaxy/sal/sal.pl?lang=he&ID=366979_sharett&act=show&dbid=bookfiles&dataid=2201.
70. Nahum Goldmann in a testimony given to HUJI, on November 14, 1961, pp. 8–9. and Zweig, *German Reparations*, 32–33.
71. Brecher, "Images, Process and Feedback," 92.
72. The prime minister's statement in the *Knesset* on January 7, 1952 concerning reparations. See *Documents Relating to the Agreement*, Document 20, 57.
73. Weitz, "HaDerech LeWassenaar," 250.
74. Letter from Alex Easterman to Maurice Perlzweig dated April 25, 1951, Central Zionist Archives (CZA), WJC Files, C2\1782-90.
75. See the letter of Eli Rock, director of JDC office in Berlin to Moses Leavitt, vice president of the JDC of October 5, 1951. JDC Archives, Item # 608158. See also Zweig, *German Reparations*, 28. The status of the JDC in the founding meeting of the Claims Conference was "observer" and not "participant."

76. Goldmann, *Memories,* 141.
77. Telephone interview of the author with Benjamin Ferencz on August 12, 2015.
78. Vogel, *The German Path to Israel,* 36.
79. Letter from Jerome Jacobson to Leavitt of October 8, 1951. See JDC Archives, Item # 608151.
80. Cited in Nahum Goldmann, *Community of Fate: Jews in the Modern World, Essays, Speeches and Articles* (Jerusalem: Israel Universities Press, 1977), 79.
81. Shinnar, *Be-Ol Korach U-Regashot, Bi-Shelichut Ha-Medina,* 19.
82. Goldmann, *Memories,* 251.

Chapter 3

From Temporary Committees to a Permanent Institution

Change of Mandate to Ensure Immortality

Organizations seek eternal life. In the middle of the twentieth century, states and individuals set up institutions to perform tasks resulting from the catastrophe caused by the Second World War: millions uprooted, famine, and the crimes perpetrated by the Third Reich. Although within a decade, they had completed their mission, some seventy years later, many continue to function. Political scientists describe international organizations in terms of living organisms that change over time.[1] Private and intergovernmental agencies adopted survival strategies, including changes to their original mandates, replacement of staff, and the search for new sources of funding.

The Claims Conference exemplifies the quest for self-preservation. Originally set up for the limited purpose of presenting Jewish claims against Germany, the temporary committees completed their task with the signing of the Luxembourg Agreement. How did the negotiating team metamorphose into a permanent organization? Historians of the organization take this evolution for granted.[2] According to one account, "by presenting their own global claim the Jewish organizations were ensuring a life for the Claims Conference after the negotiations were completed."[3] This interpretation may benefit from hindsight.

At the founding meeting, Goldmann declared that he would call another conference within six months to "review the situation, maybe then we will see there is nothing in the whole business, or maybe we will have to change policies."[4] This indicates his uncertainty regarding German willingness to agree to the demands of the Claims Conference or the continued existence of the alliance after the termination of the negotiations. In June 1952, Goldmann wrote: "I think generally that we must try to have the Conference dissolved as soon as possible after we have distributed the money and not make out of it a new permanent Jewish organization."[5] He later stated, in connection with the Luxembourg Agreement, that "the favorable outcome was far from a foregone conclusion, for at one point in the negotiations an unfavorable outcome had loomed as the likelier prospect."[6] Furthermore, for a period of over a year, the Claims Conference was not incorporated as a legal entity. This fact strengthens the view that until they reached a settlement with West Germany, Goldmann and his partners did not know if the negotiating party would continue to exist.

The Claims Conference worked out a settlement in the tripartite negotiations on reparations. After the initial breakdown of talks, Goldmann persuaded Chancellor Adenauer to overcome internal German opposition and honor the undertaking he had begun. Achieving a settlement on the payment of reparations was not in itself sufficient justification for the continued existence of the diaspora coalition. The transformation of the temporary negotiating party required an additional agreement between member organizations on their continued cooperation and a change of mandate. The evolution of the temporary negotiating delegation into a permanent and powerful organization is the subject of this chapter.

TEMPORARY NEGOTIATOR AND DEALMAKER

Direct talks on compensation for crimes perpetrated by Germany against the Jews commenced on March 21, 1952, in Wassenaar, a suburb of The Hague. Three delegations from Israel, West Germany, and the Claims Conference conducted two separate sets of negotiations. In the morning, Israeli representatives presented their claims to German officials, and in the afternoon, the Claims Conference submitted its demands. The German negotiators, Professor Franz Böhm and Dr. Otto Küster, were lawyers, untainted by Nazi Party membership. Foreign Minister Sharett headed the Israeli delegation. The other members were a diplomat (Shinnar) and the treasurer of the Jewish Agency (Dr. Giora Josephthal). Both Shinnar and Josephthal were born in Germany but received instructions to refrain from using their mother tongue in the negotiations.[7] Moses Leavitt of the JDC headed the Claims Conference delegation. He was well acquainted with postwar Germany since his organization administered welfare programs for Jewish displaced persons in the country. Ferencz, the director general of the JRSO, and Robinson of the WJC also participated in the delegation. Goldmann, the godfather of the Claims Conference and negotiations on reparations, remained in the wings. In a later interview he said that he decided to wait until an impasse was reached and then intervene on "the highest level."[8]

Israel and the diaspora delegation drafted their demands for reparations in different terms. The state submitted one claim to West Germany for the payment of the sum of $1 billion to be discharged in cash (1/3) within five years and commodities (2/3) in annual installments. Since Israel had not existed at the time of the Second World War, it could not base this claim on the Grotius concept of repairing the illegal act. Instead, it demanded the defrayment of the cost of absorbing five hundred thousand Holocaust survivors.[9] The Claims Conference demanded relief for crimes perpetrated by the Third Reich against Jewish victims under two separate headings: compensation for individuals, survivors and heirs, and a claim for a lump sum. The relief for individuals sought by the delegation involved amendments to German legislation on a broad range of issues. These included restitution of movable property, the extension of the indemnification laws enacted in the US occupation zone to the entire territory of West Germany, and compensation for victims from East Germany, Austria, and former employees of Jewish communal institutions. The second claim was for compensation in the sum of $500 million, a figure based on the value of property stolen from Jews that had not been restored and for which there were no heirs (the global claim).

The negotiations were protracted and, as Goldmann had predicted, took place mainly outside the negotiating rooms in Wassenaar. West Germany sought to link the payment of compensation for crimes against Jews to the outcome of the Conference on German External Debts. This conference was conducted simultaneously in London and its subject was German defaults on loans taken out by the Weimar Republic to pay reparations prescribed by the Treaty of Versailles after the First World War. Dr. Hermann Abs, the chief German negotiator on repayment of debts, advocated the suspension of negotiations on compensation for Holocaust victims until a settlement had been reached with the country's creditors. In the words of one Claims Conference delegate, "The Germans were claiming poverty and they thought that if they would combine the two things, it would cost them less."[10] After two weeks of talks, the delegations at Wassenaar dispersed without any fixed date for the resumption of negotiations.

The next stage of the negotiations consisted of requests to third parties to exert pressure on the German government. Ferencz approached the US High Commissioner in Germany, John J. McCloy, and asked for his assistance. Similarly, the WJC requested the intervention of the British government. Both attempts failed and West Germany refused to return to the negotiation table. Two meetings between Chancellor Adenauer and Goldmann saved the day (and the negotiations). At the first meeting, which took place at the chancellor's home in Rhöndorf on April 20, 1952, Goldmann talked of the moral significance of German compensation for Jewish victims of National Socialism. He urged Adenauer to prevent the negotiations from declining into horse trading. Following the meeting, the chancellor overruled his financial advisor, Abs, and instructed Böhm (Küster had resigned in protest against his government's intransigence) to continue negotiations. This time, Goldmann participated in the talks, acting both in the name of the state and the diaspora. At a second meeting on June 10, 1952, the chancellor, Goldmann, and Shinnar reached an agreement on the amounts to be paid by West Germany and the terms and method of payment. Over the next two months, the lawyers of the German and Claims Conference delegations worked out the details of amendments to legislation for the benefit of individual claimants.

The dynamics of the negotiations indicate the importance of personal relations in international diplomacy. Goldmann, the statesman without a state, was instrumental in the conclusion of a settlement. His relationship with the chancellor led to a breakthrough and the achievement of a favorable settlement for both Israel and the diaspora delegation. The US State Department predicted, according to Goldmann, that the Germans would pay US $400 million in compensation, less than half the final total sum.[11] Goldmann impressed Adenauer. Kagan, the chief implementer of the agreements between the Claims Conference and West Germany, later said that "Nahum was a real cosmopolitan in the best sense of the word . . . he was a man of culture . . . he and Adenauer had a common language."[12] Goldmann's tools were his sophistication and diplomatic skills and not the formal standing of a state emissary, which he lacked. He continued to foster a close relationship with the chancellor in the following decades. This direct channel to the head of the Federal Republic helped to overcome obstacles raised by the German bureaucracy in the discharge of its contractual duties.

THE LUXEMBOURG AGREEMENT AND ITS IMPACT ON THE CLAIMS CONFERENCE

On September 10, 1952, West Germany signed three agreements: one with Israel (the Luxembourg Agreement) and two with the Claims Conference (see figure 3.1 below). The Luxembourg Agreement provided for the payment of DM 3 billion (equivalent to approximately $715 million) to Israel. The German negotiators drafted understandings reached with the Claims Conference in the form of protocols because of their objection to the signing of a treaty with a "private body."[13] The provisions of the protocols stipulated who would (and would not) receive compensation from West Germany in the first decade after the war. They also constituted the basis for an extension of the mandate of the diaspora alliance and its modus operandi.

Protocol 1—Compensation for Individuals

Protocol 1 to the Luxembourg Agreement laid down the ground rules on compensation for Hitler's victims. One German historian described this

Figure 3.1 Moshe Sharett Signing the Luxembourg Agreement with Nahum Goldmann on his left and Giora Josephthal on his right. *Source*: Courtesy of the United States Holocaust Memorial Museum photo archives and Benjamin Ferencz, photograph 41623.

agreement as "the Magna Carta of compensation history."[14] The protocol stipulated a list of amendments to federal laws to be enacted by West Germany. These amendments benefited victims of the Third Reich, Jews, and non-Jews chiefly of German origin. It is important to note that the diaspora delegation (and not Israel) advocated compensation for individual victims. Moreover, in the course of the negotiations and in order to secure its own claim, Israel renounced the right of its citizens to compensation for personal injuries under German legislation.[15] Accordingly, victims who entered Israel before 1953 were entitled only to a one-time small payment for loss of freedom under German legislation provided that they belonged to the sphere of German language and culture.

The first provision of Protocol 1 stated that West Germany would adopt legislation "so as to ensure that the legal position of persecutees throughout the Federal territory be no less favorable than under the General Claims Law now in force in the US Zone."[16] Pursuant to this provision, the *Bundestag* enacted the Federal Law on Compensation of Victims of National Socialist Persecution (in German, the *Bundesentschädigungsgesetz*, known as the "BEG") in September 1953. This legislation adopted the compensation laws enacted by German states (*"Länder"*) in the US zone during the period of occupation that were characterized by a "lack of uniformity."[17]

The Federal Law awarded compensation to victims of Nazi persecution. It defined victims as individuals oppressed because of political opposition to National Socialism, race, religion, or ideology who suffered as a consequence the loss of life, damage to limbs or health, loss of liberty, property or possessions, or harm to vocational or economic pursuits.[18] At the request of the Claims Conference, the *Bundestag* extended the definition in the Federal Law to include two groups formerly not entitled to compensation, namely, expelled persecuted victims and stateless persons.[19] Previous legislation of the German states had tied compensation to residence in West Germany at the time of filing a claim. By 1952, many Jewish survivors had left Europe to build a new life elsewhere. The Claims Conference negotiated a revision enacted as paragraphs 150 and 160 of the BEG. According to these provisions, an expellee who was not a resident of West Germany and a victim who was stateless or a refugee under the 1951 Geneva Convention Relating to the Status of Refugees had a claim for damages if they belonged to the "German sphere of language and culture."[20] To meet the latter requirement, survivors had to prove proficiency in the German language. They also had to file a claim before the deadline of December 31, 1969.

The Claims Conference failed to obtain West German consent to compensate all Jewish victims of the Third Reich. The Federal Law denied compensation to two main categories: victims from Austria and East European Jews who did not speak German.[21] In addition, Jews who spoke German but lived in countries without diplomatic relations with West Germany, including Soviet Bloc countries, were not entitled to compensation under the federal legislation adopted in 1953.[22] The Claims Conference demanded the inclusion of survivors from Austria in the projected legislation but not Jews from Eastern Europe, in view of Cold War politics. The German Cabinet rejected the demand on the grounds that Austrian survivors should seek redress from their former government.[23] For five decades, the Austrian government limited compensation to small one-time payments to former citizens persecuted on grounds of race and religion and to Jews for loss of assets and discriminatory taxes paid by them after the *Anschluss*.[24] In this context, a Claims Conference negotiator aptly stated that "the Austrians got away with murder."[25] The end result of the Claims Conference negotiations was eligibility for survivors who met the following combined terms: (a) residence in Germany before the war or after the enactment of the BEG; (b) proficiency in German; (c) filing a claim before the BEG deadline; (d) non-residence in Eastern Europe or immigration to Israel after 1953.

Other provisions of Protocol 1 defined terms of entitlement, methods of computation of compensation, and benefits for survivors. One example was the recognition of a presumption of death of Holocaust victims before West German probate courts. The purpose of this clause was to overcome bureaucratic demands for a death certificate for Jews murdered in concentration camps and before firing squads. Another provision was for renewed payment of pensions to Jewish veterans of the First World War residing outside West Germany after their suspension by the "National-Socialist regime of terror." In addition, the protocol contained a provision on the compensation of former German victims for household goods seized in European ports.[26]

Victims who became Israeli citizens before 1953 were not entitled to compensation for personal injuries under German legislation. In response to public pressure, the *Knesset* enacted two laws in 1954 and 1957 granting financial benefits to Israeli citizens. Initially, the *Knesset* limited compensation to persons disabled due to participation in Allied or partisan forces during the Second World War.[27] Other Holocaust survivors, the vast majority, did not receive any compensation during a period of nine years after the founding of the state. Eventually, in response to lobbying by Holocaust survivors, including a demonstration outside the *Knesset* and complaints that Israel was the only country that did not compensate victims, a second law was enacted.[28] This law granted financial aid to non-combatants who immigrated to Israel before 1953 and suffered disability due to Nazi persecution.[29] Israeli legislation was limited to people disabled due to the war. The state did not pay compensation to individuals interned in ghettoes or camps who did not meet the definition of disabled, unlike the German legislation. In addition, the sums paid by Israel to survivors were much lower than German reparations.

The Claims Conference was the only INGO that lobbied successfully on behalf of individual victims less than a decade after the war. Over the course of six decades, one million victims received compensation under the BEG totaling approximately DM 80 billion. Eighty percent of the compensation went to claimants abroad, half of them in Israel.[30] In 1965, Norman Bentwich of URO said that "no similar case is recorded of the voluntary payment of indemnities by a state to its own subjects and foreign subjects on account of crimes and outrages committed by a former government."[31]

This achievement contrasted with the refusal of West Germany to pay compensation to other groups of Nazi victims in the war aftermath. These groups included German citizens compelled to undergo sterilization, homosexuals interned in concentration camps, and forced laborers. They did not receive redress for many decades. To this day, Germany refuses to compensate victims of the Nazi *Lebensborn* program. To promote the growth of Germany's healthy "Aryan" population, the SS kidnapped thousands of foreign children with blond hair and blue eyes and placed them with German families. In 2018, a court in Cologne rejected a claim by a victim of the *Lebensborn* program to compensation.[32] Furthermore, other countries such as Holland and France refused to compensate their own citizens and residents for state-inflicted suffering in the Second World War. Another example of a state violation of human rights is the incarceration of Japanese Americans by the US government without due process during the Second World War. Japanese Americans had to wait forty-three years until the Civil Liberties Act of 1988 provided a presidential letter of apology and $1.65 billion in reparations.[33] A third example is that of refugees from Germany and Austria and Italian residents interned in the United Kingdom as enemy aliens during the Second World War. They have yet to receive compensation from the British government.

Protocol 2 — Global Payment to the Claims Conference

In addition to compensation for individual survivors, the Claims Conference demanded the payment of a lump sum. The basis of this global claim was the benefit derived by Germany from property seized by its government and the National Socialist Party that had not been restored to the original owners or their heirs. Protocol 2 stated that West Germany would pay the sum of DM 450 million (equivalent at the time to approximately $107 million) for the benefit of the Claims Conference.[34] The protocol specified that the sum was to be used "for the relief, rehabilitation and resettlement of Jewish victims of National Socialist persecution, according to the urgency of their needs."[35] Furthermore, use of the funds was limited to victims living outside Israel at the time of the execution of the agreement.

The delegation initially presented a global claim of $500 million. In the course of the negotiations, West Germany proposed a single payment to Israel and none to the Claims Conference on the grounds that the latter was not a representative body. Goldmann rejected the proposal and insisted on the payment of reparations to the alliance of diaspora organizations. At the same time, he agreed to a substantial reduction, without consulting members of the delegation.[36] An explanation for this partial waiver appears in a letter written by Goldmann before the commencement of negotiations. According to Goldmann, since the individual claims may amount to $500 million: "I do not expect for a moment that [the Germans] should make out another bill in addition to what Israel will get, and therefore we may have to make substantial concessions in our claims."[37] In other words, Goldmann recognized the priority of Israel's claims over those of the organizations. Therefore the Claims Conference delegation agreed to receive a sum from West Germany that represented less than one quarter of its original claim. The subsequent authorization of Goldmann's consent to a reduction of the global claim by members of the diaspora delegation reflected their consent to the preference of claims of the fledgling state and individual survivors, mainly from Germany, over their own.

Payment of reparations by a state to an organization was, at the time, a novel concept. Goldmann described the German consent set forth in Protocol

2 as "truly revolutionary."[38] In a report to the Claims Conference shortly after signing the Luxembourg Agreement, he explained:

> The concept of a global payment to be made to a nongovernmental ad hoc committee, possessing no juridical status in international law is admittedly unprecedented; however, although difficult, we did succeed in persuading the Germans on this issue. It was important to obtain at least partial settlement of the Conference claims not only because the amount involved ($107 million) will enable us to extend additional help to Jewish victims of Nazism, but also because it establishes a precedent of major significance for the future.[39]

West Germany undertook to pay the global claim in fourteen annual installments, in cash and commodities, to the state of Israel.[40] These payments covered both commitments to Israel under the Luxembourg Agreement and to the Claims Conference under Protocol 2.[41] Israel and the Claims Conference signed a separate agreement stating that one-third of all German payments received by the state would be held in trust for the organization. Of this sum, 18.333 percent was to be used in Israel and assigned by the Claims Conference in agreement with the state of Israel to organizations operating there. The remaining 15 percent was intended for relief, rehabilitation, and resettlement of Jewish victims of Nazi persecution in the diaspora.[42] The outcome of Protocol 2 and the agreement with Israel was that the Claims Conference received annual installments of approximately $10 million each (equivalent to approximately $90 million in present value) for use outside Israel.[43] In addition, Israel and the Claims Conference agreed to decide jointly on the allocation of annual sums amounting to approximately $11 million to organizations operating in the state during the same term. In practice, Israel decided unilaterally on the use of this sum.[44]

TRANSFORMATION OF THE STATUS AND MANDATE OF THE CLAIMS CONFERENCE

The founding members limited the mandate of the Claims Conference to the presentation of claims to West Germany for reparations. The temporary negotiating party completed its task with the signing of the protocols and the agreement with Israel. The members now had two options: to assign the distribution of funds provided under Protocol 2 to another entity and disband the alliance or to turn into an institution that would exist, at least until the end of the payment of reparations under the Luxembourg Agreement, with an adapted mandate.

A majority of the members supported continued cooperation between the diaspora organizations. Contrary to his undertaking, Goldmann did not convene a second conference to examine if there was still a need for the entity and to redefine the nature of future activities. Instead, shortly after the execution of the protocols with West Germany, a meeting of the presidium of the Claims Conference took place. Dr. Israel Goldstein, American rabbi and representative of the WJC, maintained that the diaspora alliance had accomplished its main job. He suggested turning over future work to other organizations and proposed that "the responsibilities of the Conference should be reduced to the absolute minimum."[45] In response, Blaustein stated that he was "amazed by the opinion of Dr. Goldstein that the primary responsibility of the Conference ended with the obtaining of the funds." He added that disbursement was also a primary function of the organization. No other participant expressed support for Goldstein's minimalist view. At a later meeting, Blaustein repeated that the allocation of funds from Germany was the main function of the Claims Conference.[46] An examination of the minutes of the different committees did not disclose a formal discussion on the change and extension of the organization's aims.

The existence of a source of funds, German reparation payments, prolonged the existence of the new entity. Once in place and in accordance with Parkinson's Law, no member wished to end the novel non-ideological alliance.[47] The funds constituted both a divisive element and a powerful incentive for the alliance to continue to function. It took eighteen months for executives and representatives of the members with different ideologies and interests to formulate a disbursement policy. This process of grappling and negotiating aims and structures following internal or external developments characterizes many associations and communities. Developments compel organizations to "struggle to redefine themselves to survive and prosper in a changing environment."[48] The achievement of consent on an allocation policy (discussed in the following chapter) indicated the desire of all parties involved to extend their cooperation and enabled the Claims Conference to continue to function.

The adaptation of a mandate by INGOs for self-preservation has been a common phenomenon. Other faith-based organizations created in response to the horrors of the Second World War adopted similar strategies. The nongovernmental agency Cooperative for American Remittances to Europe (CARE) offers one example. In 1945, twenty-two members, including labor unions and religious groups, set up a temporary agency to raise funds from American individuals for the purchase, packaging, and delivery of person-to-person packages to needy Europeans in the immediate postwar crisis. The packages were in fact surplus rations purchased from UNRRA and the US Army. By 1949, when food scarcity in most European countries had almost disappeared and consequently, fundraising sharply declined, CARE reinvented itself. Members and executives transformed an organization originally focused on European recovery into an international relief agency.[49] American government funds supplanted private donations and government donated food commodities replaced military surpluses. Another example is the LWR (Lutherans World Relief). The original mission of the organization was to raise funds for fellow Lutherans in war-torn Europe. After completing this task, the LWR transformed itself into a cooperative dedicated to collecting clothing for needy individuals in Korea.

CONCLUSION

The efforts of the Claims Conference negotiators resulted in German consent to pay reparations to a small number of victims of National Socialism. This achievement benefited two clearly defined groups: Jews who had lived in Germany in 1933 and Jews living in Germany from 1953 onward. In 1933, there were 500,000 Jews in Germany, approximately 3 percent of world Jewry. Those who survived the war and direct descendants of murdered German Jews were entitled to compensation from West Germany. In addition, between 10,000 to 20,000 Jews living in Germany in 1953, the year of the enactment of the BEG, were entitled to direct compensation.[50] The combined number of both groups attests to the fact that most Holocaust victims did not receive any compensation under the BEG. Moreover, the BEG awarded much higher sums for material losses, such as the loss of earnings or potential earnings than bodily damage or incarceration.[51] Nevertheless, the settlement negotiated by the Claims Conference for the compensation of individuals, including those living outside Germany, established an important precedent. Over the following decades, the number of survivors entitled to direct reparations greatly increased, especially after German reunification.

Like other organizations, the Claims Conference was not the product of a well thought through strategy but instead, reacted to events and adapted to changing circumstances. It proved the finding of a study of NGOs that "it is hard to escape the charge that networks are formed largely by default rather than design."[52] Furthermore, the metamorphosis illustrated that there is nothing more permanent than a temporary solution. Members and their representatives wished to continue their cooperation and consequently devised a strategy to meet the institutional needs of both their own organizations and the alliance between them.

Political scientists and sociologists of organizations have proposed conflicting theories to explain the causes of change in organizations. The earliest and still dominant approach attributes altered agendas and functions to external forces. Realist and constructivist theorists claim that change occurs due to external (exogenous) forces involving developments in the biophysical and social setting of the institutions.[53] They implicitly view staff and members as passive players, incapable or unwilling to determine the course of action adopted by the organization in which they serve. Contemporary accounts of change apply this approach to describe how post–Cold War factors and globalization "forced" organizations set up by states and communities to make changes. For example, according to Brian Smith, the mission of the LWR changed "at the urging of the departments of State and Defense and representatives of the UN."[54] This statement overlooks the desire of members of the organization to continue their cooperation, despite the termination of the original mission.

A second theory connects change in international organizations to internal forces. Proponents of this approach contend that international bureaucrats working within international organizations transform their own institutions over time. They view change as the outcome of struggles between members or staff over power and resources. Two studies of faith-based organizations emphasize their autonomy and the impact of agency leadership. In both cases, insiders altered aims or modes of conduct.[55] It should be noted that some scholars have harshly attacked the search for causes of change in the identity of leaders and the internal workings of international organizations.[56]

An examination of the early history of the Claims Conference supports the theory that both external and internal factors resulted in its transformation from temporary negotiator to permanent distributor of funds. German consent to provide reparations to the diaspora alliance constituted the external cause. This agreement was supplemented by the broad implicit consent of members and representatives to the redefined aim of distribution of funds. The achievement of agreements on both the external and internal fronts ensured an afterlife for the new diaspora alliance.

NOTES

1. Julia Gray, "Life, Death, or Zombie? The Vitality of International Organizations," *International Studies Quarterly* 62 (2018): 2.

2. See, for example, Zweig, *German Reparations*, chap. 4 and Sagi, *German Reparations*, chap. 14.

3. Zweig, *German Reparations*, 34.

4. Minutes of the Conference on Jewish Claims against Germany held on October 25–26, 1951, p. 223.

5. Letter from Nahum Goldmann to Israel Goldstein dated June 26, 1952, CZA - Nahum Goldmann's Offices in New York and Geneva (NG Archive), Z6\1621–135.

6. Goldmann statement to Claims Conference Board of Directors Meeting held on January 30, 1960, AJC Archives (AJCA), CJH, RG 347, Gen. 10, Box 286, Folder 2.

7. Shinnar had gone to school with the German negotiator, Dr. Otto Küster, in Stuttgart. See Shinnar, *Be-Ol Korach U-regashot*, 28.

8. Nahum Goldmann in a testimony given to HUJI, on November 14, 1961, 23.

9. The refusal of East Germany to participate in the negotiations led to a reduction of the original claim by $500 million.

10. Maurice Boukstein in a testimony given to HUJI on June 28, 1971, 12.

11. Nahum Goldmann in a testimony given to HUJI, on November 14, 1961, 28.

12. Saul Kagan in an oral testimony given in 2003–2004 to Larry Zuckerman, JDC Archives.

13. Sagi, *German Reparations*, 163.

14. Hockerts, "Wiedergutmachung in Deutschland," 181.

15. See the letter of Sharett to Adenauer dated September 10, 1952, accompanying the Luxembourg Agreement and cited in *Documents Relating to the Agreement*, 143. For criticism of Israel's waiver of compensation from West Germany for personal injuries of Nazi victims see Yossi Katz, *The Forsaken: Israel, the Reparations Agreement and the Question of Compensation and Restitution for Nazi Survivors* (Israel: Ministry of Defense, 2009) (in Hebrew).

16. Article 1 of Protocol 1. See *Documents Relating to the Agreement*, 152.

17. Kurt Schwerin, "German Compensation for Victims of Nazi Persecution," *Northwestern University Law Review* 67, no. 4 (1972): 492.

18. See chap. one of the BEG. For the full text of the BEG see "Bundesgesetz zur Entschädigung für Opfer der nationalsozialistischen Verfolgung (Bundesentschädigungsgesetz - BEG)," *Bundesministeriums der Justiz und für Verbraucherschutz*, accessed on October 20, 2019, https://www.gesetze-im-internet.de/beg/BEG.pdf.

19. Nehemiah Robinson, *Ten Years of German Indemnification* (New York: Claims Conference, 1964), 23.

20. See Schwerin, "German Compensation," 509–511; Goschler, "German Compensation to Jewish Nazi Victims," 391.

21. In the case of Western Europe, West Germany concluded "global agreements" with countries occupied during the Second World War for the payment of funds to be used for compensation of individual victims. See chap. 7.

22. Goschler, "German Compensation to Jewish Nazi Victims," 391.

23. On negotiations between the Claims Conference and the Austrian government, see chap. 7.

24. Sagi, *German Reparations*, 160. See also Eric Rosand, "Confronting the Nazi Past at the End of the 20th Century: The Austrian Model," *Berkeley Journal of International Law* 20, no. 1 (2002): 202.

25. Maurice Boukstein in a testimony given to HUJI on June 28, 1971, 14.

26. Protocol 1 to the Luxembourg Agreement, section I, clauses 11 and 20 and section II, clause 2.

27. The Law for Persons Wounded in the War Against the Nazis, 1954.

28. See *Divrei Haknesset* 286 (April 10, 1957): 1773–1775.
29. The Law for Disabled Victims of Nazi Persecution, 1957.
30. Hockerts, "Wiedergutmachung in Deutschland," 184.
31. Norman Bentwich, "Nazi Spoliation and German Restitution: The Work of the United Restitution Office," *Leo Baeck Institute Yearbook* 10 (1965): 223–224.
32. See "No Compensation for Lebensborn Children Abducted by SS," *Deutsche Welle,* July 6, 2018, accessed on February 26, 2020, https://www.dw.com/en/no-compensation-for-lebensborn-children-abducted-by-nazi-ss/a-44556995.
33. Alice Yang Murray, "'Military Necessity,' World War II Internment, and Japanese American History," [Review] *American History* 25, no. 2 (1997): 319.
34. Article 1 of Protocol 2 to the Luxembourg Agreement.
35. Article 2 of Protocol 2 to the Luxembourg Agreement.
36. Sagi, *German Reparations*, 140; Zweig, *German Reparations*, 37. See also Vogel, *The German Path to Israel*, 50. Goldmann is quoted as making a proposal on a reduced claim "without having consulted and without authorization."
37. Letter from Nahum Goldmann to Israel Goldstein dated February 14, 1952, CZA - NG Archive, Z6\1621–140.
38. Goldmann, *Memories*, 251.
39. See report by Nahum Goldmann to the Policy Committee of the Claims Conference of September 25, 1952 in the JDC Archives, Item # 608164.
40. Articles 1–3 of the Luxembourg Agreement.
41. On the complicated manner of payment of the global reparations to the state and organization, see Yeshayahu A. Jelinek, "Implementing the Luxembourg Agreement: The Purchasing Mission and the Israeli Economy," *Journal of Israeli History* 18 (1997): 191–209.
42. Agreement between the government of the State of Israel and the Conference on Jewish Material Claims against Germany signed in New York on September 10, 1952. See CAHJP, Claims Conference file no. 15001.
43. West Germany paid the full sums owed under the Luxembourg Agreement and Protocol 2 in eleven annual installments commencing in 1954 and terminating in 1964.
44. Claims Conference Executive Committee held on March 19, 1954, CAHJP, Claims Conference File no. 16601b, p. 9.
45. Minutes of Presidium Meeting of the Claims Conference held on October 2, 1952, CAHJP, Claims Conference File no. 16601, p. 6.
46. Minutes of Presidium Meeting of the Claims Conference held on of December 11, 1952, CAHJP, Claims Conference File no. 16601, pages unnumbered.
47. See, for example, implementation of Parkinson's Law in the case of the International Monetary Fund, Herbert G. Grubel, ed. *World Monetary Reform: Plans and Issues* (Stanford: Stanford University Press, 1963), 163.
48. Dennis R. Young, "Organizational Identity and the Structure of Nonprofit Umbrella Associations," *Nonprofit Management and Leadership* 11, no. 3 (2001): 292.
49. Heike Wieters, "Reinventing the Firm: From Post-War Relief to International Humanitarian Agency," *European Review of History* 23, no. 1–2 (2016): 116–135. https://doi.org/10.1080/13507486.2015.1117424.

50. According to a 1950 census, the number of Jews in West Germany was 21,000 but in 1952, the AJC estimated that 10,000 Jews still lived in the country. See "Jewish Population in Germany Greatly Reduced Since 1950," *Jewish Telegraphic Agency*, May 16, 1952, accessed on October 20, 2019, https://www.jta.org/1952/05/16/archive/jewish-population-in-germany-greatly-reduced-since-1950.

51. Goschler, "German Compensation to Jewish Nazi Victims," 393.

52. Anna Ohanyan, "Policy Wars for Peace: Network Model of NGO Behavior," *International Studies Review* 11, no. 3 (2009): 478. https://www.jstor.org/stable/40389139.

53. O. R. Young, *Governance in World Affairs* (Ithaca and London: Cornell University Press, 1999), 151.

54. B. H. Smith, *More than Altruism: The Politics of Private Foreign Aid* (Princeton, NJ: Princeton University Press, 2014), 51.

55. Loramy Conradi Gerstbauer, "The Whole Story of NGO Mandate Change: The Peacebuilding Work of World Vision, Catholic Relief Services and Mennonite Central Committee," *Nonprofit & Voluntary Sector Quarterly* 39 (2010): 849; Kauffman, "Politics, Programs and Protests," 250. https://doi.org/10.1177%2F0899764009339864.

56. Andrew Moravcsik, "Theory and Method in the Study of International Negotiation: A Rejoinder to Oran Young," *International Organization* 53, no. 4 (1999): 811–814. https://doi.org/10.1162/002081899551084.

Chapter 4

Reparations for Victims?

Formulation of a Policy to Strengthen the Alliance

The payment of reparations to an organization for distribution to members of a community was unprecedented in the 1950s. Transatlantic distributions of funds by non-state actors were generally limited to organizations motivated by philanthropy and altruism. Individuals and states donated funds to organizations such as Caritas, UNRRA, and the JDC on a voluntary basis for the alleviation of poverty.[1] German compensation received by the Claims Conference under an international treaty differed from humanitarian aid. Consequently, the officers and directors had no direct models to guide them on how to disburse the funds.

In retrospect, it is clear that the Protocol 2 reparations paled in comparison to payments made by the West German government to individual survivors.[2] According to one estimate, in the same period, 300,000 victims received compensation totaling $547 million.[3] In other words, individual victims received five times the entire sum awarded to the Claims Conference pursuant to Protocol 2. Nevertheless, the Claims Conference received a significant sum from West Germany intended to assist survivors. Moreover, the future of the organization depended on the success or failure of its members to agree on an allocation policy and its implementation.

Assessments of how the Claims Conference dispensed German funds provided under Protocol 2 differ greatly. The journalist Marilyn Henry described these activities as "sacred spending."[4] According to Ronald Zweig, who was commissioned by the Claims Conference to research the reparations process, the allocations contributed to the reconstruction of West European Jewry, and the organization instituted "a remarkably effective deliberation process."[5] Others rejected this rosy-eyed view of the allocation process and termed the activities of the Claims Conference a flagrant breach of the letter and spirit of the Luxembourg Agreement.[6] This chapter explains the system devised by the Claims Conference for the allocation of funds received from West Germany from 1954 to 1964.

FORMULATION OF AN ALLOCATIONS POLICY

West Germany and the Claims Conference had quite different views on the purpose of the reparation payments provided under Protocol 2. For various reasons, states frequently delegate tasks to international organizations that they cannot or do not wish to perform. According to international relations scholars Michael Barnett and Martha Finnemore: "delegation rarely results in unproblematic service of state interests. Mandates need to be interpreted, and even with oversight the agenda, interests, experience, values and expertise of IO [international organization] staff heavily color any organization's response to delegated tasks."[7] The allocation of reparations by the Claims Conference illustrates the problem of charging an international organization with performing a task that the delegating state preferred to avoid.

Who Defines the Purpose of the Reparation Funds?

West Germany paid the sum of DM 450 million to the Claims Conference as compensation for the crimes of the Nazi regime. The intention was to wipe the slate clean. From the German point of view, reparations were intended to meet the claims of victims who were not entitled to compensation under domestic legislation. The successor state wished to curtail its liability. In his book on the politics of reparations, Goschler described the German expectation that the payments, at least from a material perspective, would end their atonement.[8]

At the negotiating table, the German delegation proposed the distribution of the reparations to needy survivors who were not entitled to compensation under the proposed federal legislation. They wanted to ensure that the funds would go "to the people the Nazis had damaged and not in a broader sense."[9] To accomplish this, they suggested stipulating in Protocol 2 that the funds would be paid to "needy surviving victims." The negotiating team at Wassenaar rejected this proposal. When asked why he objected to the word "needy," Goldmann replied that the deletion would give the Claims Conference more room to act and would prevent future arguments with the Germans on the manner of distribution of the funds.[10] Leavitt, another member of the negotiating team, wrote in the course of the negotiations that "the Germans tried to maneuver in such a way that the global sum of the Conference was to be used for unsuccessful claimants for indemnification and restitution . . . I had to fight this concept strenuously over and over again."[11]

Eventually, the Claims Conference and West Germany agreed on a definition of the organization's mandate for the disbursement of reparations. Protocol 2 specified three distinct criteria intended to fulfill German expectations. These included (a) definition of the beneficiaries—Jewish victims of National Socialist persecution living outside Israel; (b) use of funds—for relief, rehabilitation, and resettlement; and (c) determination of priorities—on the basis of urgency of the victims' needs.[12] Accordingly, the Claims Conference was authorized to use the funds to solve the immediate problem of individual victims still suffering hardships due to persecution and displacement.

The allocation policy prescribed by the Claims Conference did not comply with German intentions. West Germany provided the funds and prescribed the terms of payment, but the Claims Conference acted autonomously. It allocated reparations based on its understanding of the needs of communities and member organizations.

Decision-Making by American Organizations and Executives, Not Victim Associations

American organizations and executives played a decisive role in determining how to use German funds. Goldmann established the Claims Conference headquarters in New York, where he lived at the time. As president of the WJC, he was well acquainted with American Jewish organizations.[13] Always an astute diplomat, the decision to locate the Claims Conference headquarters in New York and not in neutral Switzerland, his other home base after the war, reflected Goldmann's appreciation of the shifting center of the Jewish diaspora. The first office of the Claims Conference was on the premises of the JDC at 270 Madison Avenue. Kagan, secretary of the organization later stated, "my office was next to Eddie Warburg's."[14] This physical proximity between the two organizations contributed to the development of a symbiotic relationship, which is illustrated below.[15]

A majority of the Claims Conference members accepted the principle established by the successor organizations that "world Jewry" should benefit from the reparations.[16] The result was the formulation of an allocation policy by the American-dominated alliance intended to benefit an entire community. The vast majority of Holocaust victims and their heirs lacked representation in the body that based its existence on their suffering. Therefore they were unable to participate in the decision-making process. Survivors from Germany and in Germany vociferously protested, to no avail. British members also objected to the distribution of funds in their part of the world by American organizations, arguing that they were better acquainted with survivors' needs. The British members were overruled.

The Council of Jews from Germany and the *Zentralrat* proposed that a part of the reparations should be set aside for distribution to victims. After the conclusion of the Luxembourg Agreement, Rabbi Dr. Leo Baeck (a survivor of *Theresienstadt*) questioned the administration of reparation funds by the Claims Conference. He contended that the Council had a right to a share of the reparation funds, in view of the stipulation in the preamble to Protocol 2 that the National Socialist regime had confiscated property from Jews in Germany.[17] Van Dam of the *Zentralrat* complained about the preference of wealthy Jewish groups over the impoverished community in Germany.[18] The Claims Conference dismissed both objections.

During the following decade, tension characterized relations between German and American member organizations. After the rejection of applications submitted by the Council of Jews from Germany to the Claims Conference, Baeck contacted Blankenhorn of the German Foreign Office and discussed the possibility of filing an appeal against the allocations to the arbitration court prescribed by the Luxembourg Agreement.[19] On learning of this discussion, Goldmann sent a letter to Kagan describing Baeck "as a pseudo-saint, one who should be removed from Jewish life if at all possible."[20] Several months later, the Claims Conference again rejected an application filed by the Council for allocations intended to fund relief payments to refugees. In a letter of complaint sent to the Claims Conference, the Council wrote:

> When the first funds were distributed in 1954 the Conference rejected completely the social and cultural projects submitted by us. The allocation for 1955 was equally disappointing. In the social field, the needs of the 150,000 Jewish refugees from Germany and Austria residing in the United States were ignored, although we had submitted detailed evidence showing that the assistance rendered by communal and Jewish organizations was of a kind which made additional relief an urgent necessity.[21]

The Claims Conference refused to change its decision and explained the rejection on the grounds that existing welfare organizations provided sufficient care to Nazi victims. In addition, the Claims Conference rejected applications for the funding of cultural projects to perpetuate the achievements of German Jewry.

The Board of Deputies of British Jews also objected to the central role of American organizations in the allocation process. Immediately after the signing of the protocols with West Germany, Sir Barnett Janner, a British politician and the head of the Board of Deputies between 1955 and 1964, proposed the establishment of a body that would operate in Europe.[22] In a subsequent meeting on the incorporation of the Claims Conference, Janner said that "there was a feeling among the European groups that they were excluded from the executive work."[23] He proposed that the Board of Directors create a committee of European representatives to deal specifically with allocations in Europe. Shad Polier of the American Jewish Congress opposed the "division of interest along geographical or any other lines." Janner's proposal was put to the vote and defeated by a large majority. Janner then suggested holding a meeting of the Board of Directors in Europe once a year and that one-third of the members of the Executive Committee represent European organizations. The presidium committee rejected both proposals.[24]

The issue arose once more in an Executive Committee meeting held in January 1953. Janner repeated his proposal for the establishment of a European committee to deal with applications for funds originating in Europe, since "such a committee would be in the best position to command all the necessary facts to make recommendations."[25] Barou of the British section of the WJC supported the idea of a European committee. Lewin, the *Aguda* representative, also advocated the creation of a screening and recommendation committee in Europe including members of the relevant Jewish communities. American representatives on the committee, especially Leavitt of the JDC, strongly opposed the proposal. The latter intended his own organization to take a leading role in the allocation process. The creation of a European committee would have frustrated his intention and challenged his plans on the future relationship between the reparation funds and the JDC.[26] Janner deferred his proposals for later consideration.

The British representatives never gave up their request to create a European committee. They raised the issue again and again. By June 1953, the request was made "for the record."[27] Americans outnumbered Europeans on all committees and rejected any attempts at power-sharing. The structure of the organization created by Goldmann and identity of the majority of its members ensured American control of operations.

The decisive role of American organizations and executives reflected the transition of power in diaspora politics after the Second World War. The destruction of European Jewry led to a "transatlantic shift."[28] American executives and the American way of doing things directed all types of international organizations, inside and outside the Jewish world, including the successor organizations in postwar Germany. The Claims Conference was part of this trend, despite protests and opposition from European members and representatives.

Reparations for Organizations, Not Individuals

The existence of an umbrella organization representing a broad range of members with a regular flow of income from an external source was a novelty. Members discussed and disputed how to disburse German reparation payments. They finally reached an arrangement that reshaped the identity of the Claims Conference and strengthened ties between its members.

The first principle of the distribution policy was to give preference to organizations over individuals. In the eyes of the directors and executives of the Claims Conference, the purpose of the German reparation funds was not to provide aid to needy survivors but instead to rebuild Jewish life in Europe. Goldmann explained this position a few years later in a speech to the organization's Board of Directors:

> The German funds were not given exclusively for individual victims of Nazi persecution. More than that, the funds are to rebuild Jewish life, particularly on the destroyed continent of Europe . . . it was more important for the Conference to make a lasting contribution to Jewish life which was destroyed by Nazis than to give large portions of its funds for temporary relief.[29]

Blaustein, chairman of the non-Zionist AJC, had participated in negotiations with the Germans on reparations and viewed himself as the most important executive in the Claims Conference after Goldmann. He too supported the idea of preferring groups over individuals and proposed replacing the term "survivors" in Protocol 2 with "reconstruction of Jewish life."[30] The proposal was not adopted but the idea of using reparation funds for "reconstruction" persisted.

Blaustein's preoccupation with relations between Israel and the diaspora may explain his support for use of funds for the reconstruction of Jewish life. A year after the establishment of the new state, Blaustein at the head of an AJC delegation conducted a four-week tour of the country. Subsequently, he delivered an address on NBC radio fittingly entitled "Israel Through American Eyes." In the talk, he said that the AJC "warmly welcomes Israel as a home for Jews who want to go there or need to go there."[31] In other words, Israel was one of the many options for Jews looking for a home. Throughout the talk, he distinguished between American non-Zionists with whom he identified, and Israel, which he portrayed as an undeveloped entity with the potential of following the American path to success. In his words: "We feel certain that with our aid, Israel like our own United States, can become a positive force for democracy and for international peace and order."[32]

The understanding reached with Israeli prime minister Ben-Gurion in August 1950 did not end friction between the sides. A speech made by Ben-Gurion at the opening of the Twenty-Third World Zionist Congress in 1951 included frequent references to the "Jewish nation" [quotation marks in the AJC minutes citing the speech]. The meeting took place in Jerusalem and the subject on the agenda was the future role of Zionism. The Congress adopted a resolution granting the WZO the status of representative of the

Jewish people. Ben-Gurion's speech and the WZO resolution prompted the following impassioned response of Blaustein in a meeting of the AJC Administrative Committee:

> We oppose as completely false and unrealistic any view that American Jews can be convinced that Israel is the only place where Jews can live in security and dignity. We reject the notion, from whatever source it emanates, that American Jews are in any sense "exiles" . . . Confidence in the security of American Jewry's future here and in the possibility of continuing to build a rich and meaningful life that embodies the best in the American and Jewish traditions has never been greater or more justified than it is at present.[33]

One month later, in discussions on AJC participation in the Claims Conference, Blaustein again repeated his view that Israel and its diaspora mouthpiece, the Jewish Agency, should not head or dominate the new alliance.[34]

Blaustein did not explain to fellow members of the Claims Conference why he advocated using German funds for reconstruction instead of for needy survivors. His wish to strengthen the diaspora and create a counterbalance to Israel's claim to lead world Jewry offers one explanation. Another explanation is his background as a wealthy businessman and president of the elitist AJC. Whatever the reason, his preference of the community over the individual contributed to forging a policy that served other member organizations of the Claims Conference.

Kagan, secretary of the Claims Conference, explained the organization's attitude to individual claims. In a speech delivered at the 1954 JDC country directors' conference, he said:

> The Conference would basically like, I am sure, to concentrate on the type of projects that are of a lasting nature . . . the vanity of the Conference [is] to be able to demonstrate that its funds have been used in such a manner that there is evidence, as long as Jewish life will continue, that the Conference has done something . . . I was rather unhappy when [Moses W. Beckelman, director-general of JDC overseas operations] told me . . . "we have 27,000 people who are in need of daily, regular assistance" . . . the hard-core which the Conference cannot ignore, with which the Conference has to deal. But it is also with an eye to the future that the Conference must direct a good part, and I hope a major part, of its efforts in the years to come.[35]

Kagan was involved in the different allocation programs at the level of both general principles and details.

Reparations for Long-Term Projects, Not Immediate Needs of Victims

In its first annual report, the organization spelled out its understanding of how reparation funds should be allocated. The report stated: "The Conference . . . had to single out projects of lasting value from those of transient benefit."[36] Three years later, at a meeting of the Claims Conference, Blaustein discussed the conflict between the desire to make a lasting impression and the immediate needs of victims. In his words:

> The most enduring contribution we can hope to make for the relief and rehabilitation of Nazi victims lies in the creation of communal institutions and facilities which will be strong enough to provide for these needs after the final curtain has fallen on Conference activities. But as a limiting factor in our planning for the future years, we are constantly faced with demands for urgently needed relief programs, demands which may not yield to very substantial reductions during the lifetime of the Conference.[37]

Preference for long-term projects over immediate relief reflected Jewish philanthropic practices that had been prevalent since the early twentieth century. The logic behind this approach was the ideology developed by the *Haskalah*, the Jewish Enlightenment. This outlook advocated that a change in the economic structure of the beneficiaries, namely their occupation and/or location, would prevent a need for assistance from their coreligionists in the future. The idea was to "reconstruct" Jews or Jewish life wherever it was located, instead of funding emigration and charity.[38] Reconstruction required the transfer of funds to institutions and training facilities, not individuals. An earlier example of reconstruction was the Agro-Joint project aimed at teaching Russian Jews skills in order to turn them into productive Soviet citizens and enable their integration into the local society.[39]

In the aftermath of the First World War, leaders of communities and aid organizations debated the most effective use of funds raised by philanthropies. One view advocated the use of funds to meet the immediate needs of victims of the war. The opposing view supported investment in long-term solutions. In 1920, the director general of JDC operations in Europe called for "the suspension of all palliative relief activities and the reorganization of the work along specialized functional-reconstructive lines."[40] The JDC continued this policy in Eastern Europe after the Second World War with the result that in at least one case, Hungary, it "inadvertently condemned these survivors and their offspring to a type of imprisonment behind the Iron Curtain."[41]

Leaders of the Claims Conference asserted that reconstruction programs (and not palliative relief) would make the most difference to the lives of beneficiaries. This did not coincide with West Germany's intention. In addition, emphasizing reconstruction contrasted with American and

British officials who led UNRRA and viewed the question of postwar relief "primarily as a matter of procurement: matching raw material supplies to the populations in greatest need."[42]

Reconstruction of Jewish life was an ongoing process. It required member organizations to convene and elect long-term projects that fit in with the object of rebuilding Jewish life. Officers and directors allocated funds for institutions and culture. In the first five years of allocations, the Claims Conference granted funds to the JDC for the construction, expansion, or repair of 313 institutions primarily in Western Europe, including fifty-five community and youth centers, forty-eight homes for the aged, thirty-eight day schools, thirty-one religious institutions, twenty-eight children's and youth homes, twenty-three summer camps, nineteen supplementary schools, nineteen kindergartens, fourteen *yeshivot*, and eight hospitals and clinics.[43]

The JDC was another member of the Claims Conference with clear ideas on the utilization of reparation funds. Leavitt, vice president of the JDC, which operated both in Israel and Europe was a key figure in the Claims Conference (see figure 4.1). In a speech to the presidium in October 1952, he outlined his proposal and explained the logic behind it. According to the proposal, the reparation funds should be channeled through the JDC as much as possible for distribution in Europe.[44] Leavitt put forward several justifications for the assignment of a greater part of the German payments to his organization. First, the proposal would save Israel the "excessive foreign currency obligation" of granting dollars to the Claims Conference.[45] According to this argument, Israel would provide Israeli pounds for JDC operations in the country. A corresponding dollar amount would be used by the organization for its European programs on behalf of the Claims Conference. In addition, the JDC had experience operating in Europe and had already established a system of controls over beneficiary organizations. Granting a majority of the funds to the JDC would also prevent the duplication of programs. Leavitt concluded his speech by stating that the JDC refused to receive instructions from the Claims Conference on the manner of expenditure of said funds.

Discussions on how to spend the reparation funds came at a critical time for the JDC. By the late 1952, the key missions facing the organization in the postwar era—welfare and relief to displaced persons in Central Europe and the first wave of mass immigration to Israel—were almost over. The vast majority of Jewish refugees had found new homes and no longer required day-to-day assistance from the JDC.[46] Similarly, the initial influx of immigrants from Europe, Asia, and Africa to the newly established state ended in 1951. The scaling down of JDC operations was accompanied by a drastic reduction of income, mainly generated by the United Jewish Appeal (UJA). The organization's annual budget dropped from $72 million in 1948 to $21 million in 1952.[47] The future of the organization, in particular in Europe

Figure 4.1 Moses Leavitt. *Source*: Courtesy of the JDC Archives, item #2740.

where former major sites of its activities were now located behind the descending Iron Curtain, was unclear.

The reparation funds offered a solution for the JDC. Executives of the organization were quick to appreciate the opportunity afforded by the Claims Conference. The JDC General Counsel summarized the position in a letter to Leavitt:

> The JDC's internal thinking was never to seek an augmentation to spend for needy Nazi persecutees outside of Israel over the JDC program by an amount equivalent to the gain of the Conference. In fact, the corollary in JDC's mind was to a large extent to seek a replacement of JDC-UJA expenditures for these expenditures by Conference assets while permitting the amount thus released to be diverted for use in Israel. In this process JDC serves as the machinery which enables the entire shift and balancing to be effectuated.[48]

The JDC had a history of adapting to changed circumstances in order to continue its ad hoc existence. For instance, at the beginning of the 1930s, when Stalin decided on the forced collectivization of farms, including those previously purchased by the JDC as part of the Agro-Joint project, the organization did not cut its losses and terminate involvement in Soviet Russia or encourage emigration. Instead, it concluded that it would be doing the greatest service to Soviet Jewry by remaining engaged in the project. To this end, the organization funded by American capitalists, such as Julius Rosenwald, "lauded the *positive* effects of collectivization on the colonies."[49]

Leavitt explained to his colleagues why his organization should act as the chief operator and receive all or most of the German payments. At a meeting in October 1952, after proposing that the funds should be allocated to his organization, Leavitt opposed a British suggestion to set up a European committee for the distribution of German funds. His view was that the Claims Conference was in no position to determine allocations to individual organizations. Chaos would ensue and the "JDC would have to step out of the picture."[50] In a subsequent meeting of the Executive Committee, Leavitt rejected a proposal raised by Barou, the British WJC representative and initiator of talks on reparations, to give victims of Nazi persecution a voice in the allocation of funds for their needs. According to Leavitt, "The needs of individuals, as compared to the need of others, can only be assessed by functioning organizations." He added that "practically everywhere the JDC operates through local institutions."[51]

Kagan strengthened the JDC's claim by announcing that no money would be allocated in the United States or Canada in the first year. He gave two contradictory reasons for this decision: first, the United States could take care of its community requirements and second, the entire annual payment would not meet existing needs.[52] In the discussion that followed, Leavitt said that the JDC was not a "beneficiary" and would be happy to step aside if the Conference could do the job themselves.[53] Leavitt, as well as the other committee members, were fully aware that the Claims Conference did not have the personnel or the expertise to screen applications and therefore no one took his threat at face value.

Surprisingly, the idea that a major share of the reparations would go to only one of the twenty-two members of the Claims Conference did not encounter great opposition. The JDC had at that time almost forty years' experience operating in Europe. Its status as a leading transnational player was reinforced by the function it performed as the operating agent on behalf of the JRSO together with the Jewish Agency. Goldmann later said that disregard of the JDC by the Claims Conference "would have been more than silly, it would have been fantastic" and would have created chaos and overlapping.[54] Before the 1950s, the JDC operated chiefly in Central and Eastern Europe whereas the Claims Conference sought to reconstruct Jewish life in Western Europe but no one commented on this shift.

Blaustein initially protested Leavitt's proposal for the distribution of reparation funds by the JDC. He rejected the idea that the Conference would become the adjunct of the JDC and argued that no organization should be compelled to channel its applications through any other organization.[55] He added that the problem of supervision was not as complicated or difficult as what Leavitt presented. Over time, he withdrew his opposition to the allocation of the majority of the funds to the JDC but insisted on supervision by the Claims Conference.[56]

European organizations, including the Council of Jews from Germany, the *Alliance*, and British members of the WJC objected to the distribution of funds in their part of the world by an American organization, but they were in the minority. Goldmann argued that allocating funds to the JDC would save the Claims Conference the need to create a new transnational network. This logic of reduced administrative costs clearly influenced American member organizations. Janner, like Blaustein, opposed Leavitt's attempt to avoid accountability to the Claims Conference on the use of the funds.[57] Goldmann concurred and said that the JDC would report regularly on what it did with the money. He added that he did not foresee terrible conflicts between the two organizations.

The discussions resulted in the adoption of the JDC proposal with minor modifications. Kagan drafted a decision approved by the Executive Committee to allocate to the JDC the bulk of the money for relief, namely $6,744,250 of the first annual installment of approximately $9 million. The decision continued that "certain projects or increased operations on which they may agree with the communities be taken care of by this money and that JDC is obligated to use that part of the money for the increased operations."[58]

The decision to grant three quarters of the Claims Conference funds to the JDC for allocation in Europe served both organizations. The former benefited from an existing transnational network with expertise on disbursements acquired over the years. Awarding funds for use in Europe also prevented disputes between American members. The majority of these members operated on a national basis only or collected funds for Israel. The desire for American control of the funds fit in with the proposal submitted by Leavitt. At the same time, the decision provided a much needed new source of funding for the JDC and ensured its continued functioning on the European continent.

Special Categories of Beneficiaries

Aguda was another member organization determined to participate in the allocation of funds. This organization promoted the interests of Orthodox Jews and aimed to reestablish the authority of prominent rabbis as the supreme institution of Jewish life. At the Claims Conference, Lewin, the *Aguda* representative, lobbied on behalf of refugee rabbis. In a meeting of the Executive Committee, he talked of "one group in America in a desperate situation who require help," namely refugee rabbis.[59] In response, Goldmann proposed setting up a fund of $40,000 for refugee rabbis. Lewin rejected this as a "drop in the sea" and said that the fund should be extended to at least half a million dollars. Goldmann then suggested a pension fund for "rabbis, old people and other non-rabbinical people." Nothing came of the proposal for a fund for "old people," but a month later, the Executive Committee set up two funds of $100,000 each, one for needy rabbis in the United States, Canada, and England and one for "deserving communal leaders."[60] A committee including Lewin was appointed to implement the program for needy rabbis in the United States, and the British Chief Rabbi was asked to control the distribution of funds in England. Similarly, Barou, Leavitt, Janner, and a representative of the Council of Jews from Germany were appointed to the committee for allocation of funds to former communal leaders.

The Claims Conference had decided not to allocate funds to individuals. Nevertheless, apart from Goldmann, none of the committee members, communal leaders, or rabbis themselves questioned why rabbis and communal leaders, all men like the organization's executives, should receive preferential treatment. As noted above, the first decision taken by the presidium was to distribute funds to organizations, not individuals. Why did rabbis and communal leaders merit a pension unlike other survivors who were simply "old people?" No explanation of this discrimination appears in the Claims Conference documents. The granting of funds to needy rabbis promoted the aims of the *Aguda* and contributed to its support of the Claims Conference. In addition, the appointment of Lewin, Janner, Barou, and Dr. Rudolph Callman of the Council of Jews from Germany to the committees overseeing allocation of these funds helped reduce tensions between them and other executives and assisted in securing continued cooperation in the framework of the Claims Conference.

Finally, Goldmann requested approval for use of part of the German funds for cultural purposes. This was a field close to his heart. In the 1920s, he was involved in several Jewish and Zionist cultural enterprises including co-editing the *Encyclopedia Judaica* with Dr. Jacob Klatzkin in German and in Hebrew.[61] Further evidence of Goldmann's interest in culture was the decision of the WJC, which he headed, at the end of the 1950s, to establish the museum *Beth Hatefutsoth* in Israel. The purpose of the museum was to depict Jewish life, culture, and spiritual values.[62] More importantly, the creation of a cultural fund gave the Claims Conference a purpose, apart from channeling funds to others for distribution.

In a meeting of the presidium, Goldmann called for the Claims Conference to spend funds on cultural activities. The basis for the proposal was that Germany had destroyed not only Jewish life and property in Europe but also all cultural life. Goldmann contended that the resurrection of such activities was a legitimate Jewish need.[63] No one opposed the proposal and the Board of Directors subsequently decided to allocate funds for cultural activities.[64] Goldmann recommended allocating the sum of $700,000 (approximately 10% of the total allocations projected for 1954) for cultural and educational programs.[65] He recruited Salo Baron to determine procedures for the allocation of funds. Baron recommended the creation of two advisory committees, one for Europe and another for the United States, which he would head. Goldmann and Baron nominated academics and rabbis (all men) to the committees, and the groundwork was now in place for allocations.

RESULTS OF THE ALLOCATION PROCESS

Claims Conference members and executives believed that they were better qualified to determine how to disburse German funds than survivors and victims' associations. Decisions by elites on how to aid members of a community echoed the approach of "great" men to philanthropic enterprises in the previous century.[66] Blaustein of the AJC, Warburg of the JDC, and other oligarchic leaders of member organizations drew on their experience from the world of philanthropy.

Fears of uncontrolled migration of persecuted kin in Eastern Europe and North Africa had prompted the activism of affluent West Europeans in the first half of the twentieth century. They donated funds and intervened with governments in an attempt to improve the lives of communities of their less fortunate brethren in situ. The undeclared purpose was to reduce mass emigration, which they believed would increase antisemitism at home.[67]

Undue influence of elite groups or superrich individuals continues to prevail in the philanthropic world. According to a recent study, "Compared with ordinary donors, elite philanthropists hold greater sway over recipient organizations and enjoy more sustained control over how money is spent."[68] The application of philanthropic principles to reparations indicates the problem of allocation of compensation by an undemocratic entity. The result was that tycoons decided how to allocate funds granted under Protocol 2 and intended to compensate Holocaust victims. The latter had little or no say in the matter.

The allocation process achieved the objectives defined by the Claims Conference. Directors and executives distributed funds among their own parent organizations. Of the total sum paid under Protocol 2 amounting to $107 million, the Claims Conference granted the JDC close to $76.5 million (approximately 70%).[69] The balance went almost entirely to projects sponsored by members such as funds for rabbis and communal leaders and Holocaust memorials or grants to other members and affiliated entities.

NOTES

1. See for instance, Eric Werker and Faisal Z. Ahmed, "What do Nongovernmental Organizations Do?" *The Journal of Economic Perspectives* 22, no. 2 (2008): 77. DOI: 10.1257/jep.22.2.73

2. On the contribution of the Claims Conference to extending German legislation to cover a broader range of Jewish victims and the processing of claims, see chap. 7.

3. Schwerin. "German Compensation," 515.

4. Henry, *Confronting the Perpetrators*, 185.

5. Zweig, "Review of *Confronting the Perpetrators*," 346.

6. See, for example, Finkelstein, *The Holocaust Industry*, 86; Teitelbaum, *Hapitaron Habiologi*, 293–299.

7. Michael Barnett and Martha Finnemore, *Rules for the World: International Organizations in Global Politics* (Ithaca and London: Cornell University Press, 2004), 22.

8. Goschler, *Schuld und Schulden*, 12.

9. Minutes of Presidium Meeting of the Claims Conference held on July 30, 1952, CAHJP, Claims Conference File no. 16601, p. 4.

10. Minutes of Presidium Meeting of the Claims Conference held on July 30, 1952, CAHJP, Claims Conference File no. 16601, p. 4.

11. Letter from Leavitt to Seymour Rubin dated August 16, 1952, CAHJP, Claims Conference File no. 7022.

12. Article 2 of Protocol 2 to the Luxembourg Agreement.

13. See Reinharz and Friesel, "Nahum Goldmann, Jewish and Zionist Statesman – An Overview," 10.

14. Saul Kagan oral testimony given in 2003–2004 to Larry Zuckerman, JDC Archives. Edward Warburg served as president of the JDC from 1939 to 1964.

15. The term "symbiotic relations" appears in Zweig, *German Reparations*, 85.

16. See chap. 1, p. 35.

17. Letter from Dr. Walter Breslauer to the Claims Conference dated May 10, 1955, AJC Archives, CJH, RG 347, Gen. 10, Box 292, Folder 4.

18. Jay Howard Geller, *Jews in Post-Holocaust Germany, 1945–1953* (Cambridge, UK: Cambridge University Press, 2005), 240.

19. Yeshayahu A. Jelinek, "Leo Baeck, Nahum Goldmann and the Money from Germany (A Document)," *Studies in Contemporary Jewry: An Annual*, vol. V (1989): 237.

20. Letter from Goldmann to Kagan dated May 28, 1954, CZA, Nahum Goldmann Collection, File Z6/1811.

21. Letter from Dr. Walter Breslauer to the Claims Conference dated May 10, 1955, AJC Archives, CJH, RG 347, Gen. 10, Box 292, Folder 4.

22. Minutes of Presidium Meeting of the Claims Conference held on September 23, 1952, CAHJP, Claims Conference File no. 16601, p. 5.

23. Minutes of Membership Meeting of the Claims Conference held on December 29, 1952, CAHJP, Claims Conference File no. 16601, p. 9.

24. Subsequently, the Claims Conference agreed to hold annual board meetings in Europe every other year. See chap. 6 p. 133 below.

25. Minutes of Executive Committee Meeting of the Claims Conference held on January 7, 1953, CAHJP, Claims Conference File no. 16601, p. 9.

26. The JDC had a history of fearing competition over resources and prestige from other philanthropies. See for example the case of the Agro-Joint project Jonathan Dekel-Chen, *Farming the Red Land: Jewish Agricultural Colonization and Local Soviet Power, 1924–1941* (New Haven and London: Yale University Press, 2005), 86.

27. Minutes of Executive Committee Meeting of the Claims Conference held on June 23, 1953, CAHJP, Claims Conference File no. 16601a, p. 6.

28. Dekel-Chen, "Philanthropy, Diplomacy, and Jewish Internationalism," 511.

29. Meeting of the Board of Directors of the Claims Conference, January 1956, cited in Zweig, "'Reparations Made Me,'" 248–249.

30. Minutes of Presidium Meeting held on July 30, 1952, CAHJP, Claims Conference File no. 16601. On the use of funds for reconstruction purposes, see chap. 6 below.

31. Jacob Blaustein, *Israel Through American Eyes* (New York: The American Jewish Committee, 1949), 4.

32. Blaustein, *Israel Through American Eyes*, 11.

33. "AJC Administrative Committee held on Monday, November 19, 1951," p. 6, *AJC Archives*, accessed on October 20, 2019, http://ajcarchives.org/ajcarchive/DigitalArchive.aspx.

34. "AJC Administrative Committee held on Wednesday, December 12, 1951," p. 4, *AJC Archives*, accessed on October 20, 2019, http://ajcarchives.org/ajcarchive/DigitalArchive.aspx.

35. JDC 1954 Country Directors Conference, JDC Archive, Collection Geneva, 1945–1954 ("JDC Archive, Geneva"), File Admin. 30, Film 006, slide 509, p. 296.

36. *Conference on Jewish Material Claims against Germany – Report 1954* (New York: The Organization, 1955), (hereinafter *the First Annual Report*) and *Conference on Jewish Material Claims against Germany – Annual Report 1964* (New York: The Organization, 1965), 8.

37. Claims Conference Board of Directors Meeting held on January 19, 1957, AJC Archives, CJH, RG 347, Gen. 10, Box 286, Folder 1.

38. Jonathan Dekel-Chen, "One Big Agrarianizing Family," *Jewish History* 21 (2007): 265. https://www.jstor.org/stable/20728550.

39. Jonathan Dekel-Chen, "An Unlikely Triangle: Philanthropists, Commissars and American Statesmanship meet in Soviet Crimea, 1922–37," *Diplomatic History* 27, no. 3 (2003): 353. https://www.jstor.org/stable/24914417.

40. Zosa Szajkowski, "'Reconstruction' vs. 'Palliative Relief' in American Jewish Overseas Work (1919-1939)," *Jewish Social Studies* 32, no. 1 (1970): 16–17.

41. Dekel-Chen, "Philanthropy, Diplomacy and Jewish Internationalism," 526; Kinga Frojimovics, "Different Interpretations of Reconstruction: The AJDC and the WJC in Hungary after the Holocaust," in David Bankier, ed., *The Jews are Coming*

Back: *The Return of the Jews to their Countries of Origin after WWII* (Jerusalem: Yad Vashem, 2005), 286–292.

42. Clavin, "International Organizations," 155.

43. These figures are taken from the Study Committee Report of September 1958, AJHS, CJH, Conference on Jewish Material Claims against Germany Collection 1955–1972, Call 1–319, Folder 4.

44. Minutes of Presidium Meeting held on October 2, 1952, CAHJP, Claims Conference File no. 16601, p. 4.

45. Minutes of Presidium Meeting held on October 2, 1952, CAHJP, Claims Conference File no. 16601, p. 3.

46. The number of Jews in Germany, Austria and Italy (where DP camps were situated) declined from 250,000 in 1947 to 39,000 at the end of 1950. See Malcolm J. Proudfoot, *European Refugees: A Study in Forced Population Movement* (London: Faber and Faber, 1957), 362.

47. Zweig, *German Reparations*, 74.

48. Letter from Jerome J. Jacobson to M. W. Beckelman of September 3, 1953, JDC Archives, Microfilm Reel 148.

49. Dekel-Chen, *Farming the Red Land*, 140.

50. Minutes of Presidium Meeting held on October 2, 1952, CAHJP, Claims Conference File no. 16601, p. 8.

51. Minutes of Executive Committee Meeting held on January 7, 1953, CAHJP, Claims Conference File no. 15001, pp. 11–12.

52. Minutes of Executive Committee Meeting held on March 19, 1954, CAHJP, Claims Conference File no. 16601b, p. 22.

53. Minutes of Executive Committee Meeting held on March 19, 1954, CAHJP, Claims Conference File no. 16601b, p. 29.

54. 1954 JDC Country Directors Conference, JDC Archives, Geneva Collection 1945–1954, File Adm. 30, slide 473, p. 260.

55. Minutes of Presidium Meeting held on October 2, 1952, CAHJP, Claims Conference File no. 16601, p. 6.

56. See Minutes of Executive Committee Meeting held on March 19, 1954, CAHJP, Claims Conference File no. 16601b, p. 22, where Blaustein suggested that the money be deposited in a special fund.

57. Janner proposed that the JDC: "act as an agent for distribution under guidance and supervision" of the Claims Conference in Minutes of Executive Committee Meeting held on March 19, 1954, CAHJP, Claims Conference File no. 16601b, p. 22.

58. Minutes of Executive Committee Meeting held on March 19, 1954, CAHJP, Claims Conference File no. 16601b, p. 26.

59. Minutes of Executive Committee Meeting held on March 19, 1954, CAHJP, Claims Conference File no. 16601b, p. 24.

60. Minutes of Executive Committee Meeting held on April 23, 1954, CAHJP, Claims Conference File no. 16601b.

61. Reinharz and Friesel, "Nahum Goldmann, Jewish and Zionist Statesman – An Overview," 7.

62. See Nahum Goldmann, *Beth Hatefutsot Museum of the Jewish Diaspora* (Tel Aviv: Museum of the Jewish Diaspora, 1980), pages unnumbered. In 2021, *Beth Hatefutsot* was renamed Anu Museum of the Jewish People.

63. Minutes of Presidium Meeting held on October 2, 1952, CAHJP, Claims Conference File no. 16601, p. 5.

64. Minutes of Executive Committee held on May 11, 1953, CAHJP, Claims Conference File no. 16601a.

65. Minutes of Executive Committee held on October 5, 1953, CAHJP, Claims Conference File no. 16601a.

66. Dekel-Chen, "Philanthropy, Diplomacy and Jewish Internationalisms," 511.

67. Carole Fink, *Defending the Rights of Others,* 17. On the tension between donors and recipients see also Bernard D. Weinryb, "East European Immigration to the United States," *The Jewish Quarterly Review* 45, no. 4 (1955): 511 and 520–524.

68. Emma Saunders-Hastings, "Plutocratic Philanthropy," *The Journal of Politics* 80, no. 1 (2018): 151. https://doi.org/10.1177%2F002083451806800201.

69. Report of the executive vice chairman to the JDC Executive Committee Meeting, Wednesday, May 27, 1964, JDC Digitized Archives, Item #ID 811904.

Chapter 5

Power Begets Power

Inclusion and Exclusion

The Claims Conference emerged in response to the call of Chancellor Adenauer to negotiate with representatives of "world Jewry" (*Judentum*) on compensation for victims of the Third Reich. The term "world Jewry" defies a generally accepted definition. Individuals who identified as Jews and those who entered the category of Jews according to traditional Jewish law (*Halacha*) were two examples of "world Jewry." Both communities are characterized by a high degree of diversity. Clearly, not all members of either community could participate in negotiations on reparations. Goldmann created an entity to speak in their name. This leadership body contended that it was the sole spokesman for diaspora Jews worldwide, both in negotiations with West Germany and in the subsequent allocation of funds. It adopted policies with wide-reaching implications, influencing the lives of millions of individuals.

The Claims Conference based its legitimacy on the high number of member organizations and their different countries of origin and ideologies. The founders and executives of the Claims Conference repeatedly emphasized the broad nature of the alliance. At the opening session of negotiations with West Germany, Leavitt, on behalf of the Claims Conference delegation, declared that he spoke "in the name of the most important Jewish organizations in the world."[1] Similarly, in a board meeting on the organization's first budget, Goldmann explained that the members constituted "the representative variety of Jewish organizations all over the world more than any other super organization or organization of organizations in this respect can do it or is doing it from the point of view of the variety and the difference of opinion" [Lack of punctuation in the original stenographic text].[2] In a 2004 interview, Kagan compared the participation of orthodox *Aguda* alongside the World Union of

Progressive Judaism in the Claims Conference to "putting together the Pope and Pat Robertson."[3]

Scholars have unquestioningly accepted this self-portrait. According to one account, the organizations invited by Goldmann to participate in the founding conference "included every shade of opinion in world Jewry (except Communists)."[4] Another history of the organization repeated this conclusion, adding that the invitees were selected "to include as representative a list of Jewish groups as possible, both geographically and ideologically."[5] Other studies of the Claims Conference did not examine the accuracy of the description of the organization as an agent with a broad, almost all-encompassing membership.[6]

The Claims Conference presents a case study of the exclusion and inclusion of different sectors in an entity that purported to represent a community. Who decided on the identity of members of a transnational nongovernmental organization and to what extent did they represent their entire constituency? Examining the selection of members of the Claims Conference challenges the accuracy of its self-portrayal as the speaker on behalf of an entire community. It also raises the question whether the choice of members was motivated by the desire to represent a broad cross section of Jews and Nazi victims or, alternatively, the need to create a functional coalition.

SELECTION OF MEMBER ORGANIZATIONS OF THE CLAIMS CONFERENCE

One person alone decided on the constituency of the body created to represent "world Jewry" in negotiations for reparations. Goldmann, in the name of the Jewish Agency, invited twenty-two organizations to attend a meeting at the Waldorf-Astoria hotel in October 1951. He did not consult with leading American organizations, the JDC or the AJC on the choice of constituents.[7] The participants at this meeting were the founding members of the entity that emerged from the discussions, the Claims Conference.[8] Subsequently and before the conclusion of negotiations with the Germans, two additional organizations joined the Claims Conference, the CBF and the *Zentralrat*.[9]

At first sight, it is not clear what connected the founding members of the Claims Conference or why Goldmann selected them from among hundreds of Jewish organizations worldwide. In a 1961 interview, Goldmann explained the logic behind his choice. He sent out invitations to organizations: "From the United States, England, Canada, Australia, South Africa and Argentina. I selected these countries primarily for the reason that we needed Allied support to have any chance of getting anywhere with the Germans."[10] This explanation does not stand up to examination. Argentina and Canada, for example, did not occupy Germany at the end of the war and therefore had no influence over the country. In addition, the statement does not clarify why, out of the multitude of organizations in a given country as well as the many Jewish communities worldwide, Goldmann chose one and not another to constitute the new body representing world Jewry on the issue of reparations.

Members of the Claims Conference included many groups and individuals who had cooperated with Goldmann in the past. Goldmann was a serial creator of umbrella organizations. In his autobiography, he wrote:

> The most natural instrument for strengthening it [survival of the Jewish people] is an organization comprising the innumerable Jewish associations all over the world and designed to provide the Jewish people with an address, enabling it to collaborate systematically on the solution of its problem.[11]

Without the diaspora, Goldmann argued, Israel would become a "civilization of a small people with parochial, provincial interests, influenced by the civilizations surrounding it."[12] In this context, it is interesting to note that according to US official documents, Goldmann told the State Department in 1950 that he would use his influence to prevent American Jews from exerting pressure on their government with regard to its policy toward Israel.[13]

In addition to the WJC and the Claims Conference, Goldmann played a key role in the establishment of the Conference of Presidents of Major American Jewish Organizations in 1955 (the Conference of Presidents). He was also instrumental in the creation of the Conference of Jewish Organizations (COJO) in 1958.[14] In the first decade after the establishment of the Jewish state and in just six and a half years, Goldmann had created three new alliances of organizations and leaders.

In his many autobiographies and articles, Goldmann did not explain why he engaged in alliance-building. A possible motivation was his wish to reinforce Jewish existence outside the state of Israel. Although president of the WZO, Goldmann was preoccupied with strengthening diaspora communities and rebutting Israel's claim to act as the sole spokesman on Jewish matters.[15] Goldmann emphasized the importance of diaspora Jewry in a speech made in London in 1965:

> Israel's link with the diaspora means a two-way passage for just as Israel will culturally influence the Jews in diaspora, so it must remain open to the cultural impact of diaspora Jewry. Otherwise it may become just a small, very able, gifted and dynamic people in the Middle East.[16]

Figure 5.1 that shows the plaque outside Goldmann's Jerusalem residence reflects the uneasy relations between the state and diaspora leader. The text

Figure 5.1 **Plaque outside Nahum Goldmann's Jerusalem Apartment.** *Source*: photograph by the author.

ignores the pivotal role played by Goldmann in negotiations on reparations and makes no mention of the Claims Conference.

The Claims Conference differed significantly from the WJC and the other organizations created by Goldmann. The latter functioned as advocacy groups, three of many lobbies promoting different agendas, with restricted resources at their disposal. These entities exercised limited influence on the lives of others. The Claims Conference had both power and a steady flow of income.

Goldmann tended to invite the same people and organizations to participate in his different projects. Ten member organizations of the WJC participated in the Claims Conference and six delegates to the opening session of the WJC subsequently attended the founding meeting of the Claims Conference fifteen years later.[17] Similarly, seven of the eight American founding members of the Claims Conference were members of the Conference of Presidents.[18]

In conclusion, the selection process for members of the Claims Conference bore a striking resemblance to earlier practices. In the Middle Ages, large taxpayers, selected or nominated from among the wealthiest Jews in the community, appointed themselves leaders of local associations. Local rulers charged Jewish communities protection fees for the right of residence in their territory. The response of the Jews was to "band together" and form local associations (*Landjudenschaften* and in Hebrew, *Kehal Medinah* or *Bnei ha-Medinah*) for the distribution of the tax between all members of the community.[19] Lay leaders of the associations had virtually unlimited power over their members. The most far-reaching prerogative of the leaders was the right to grant permission to a Jew from outside the territory to settle there or to permit the son of a resident to succeed the place of his father. The earliest known example of a secular local association is documented in Alsace in the memoirs of *Josel* of Rosheim. In 1510, Josel wrote that he had been elected "leader and head" of a *gemeiner judischheit*, a Jewish association located in Lower Alsace. As leader of the association, it was his duty "to watch carefully over the community and administer its affairs."[20]

Over five centuries later, one person created an institution with the power to determine policies influencing the lives of people who had no say in his election. In the case of Josel, wealth had granted him the status of head of a body allocating the payment of taxes between members of the community and granting or denying Jews from outside the territory the right to settle there. In the second half of the twentieth century, a combination of diplomatic skills and connections inside and outside the Jewish world (a *macher*, in Yiddish) enabled Goldmann to establish the Claims Conference and select its members. This organization then assumed the function of leader of world Jewry on reparations.

HOMOGENEITY OF MEMBERS

A high degree of similarity characterized the original members of the new coalition. Scholars have emphasized that "every shade of opinion" was represented in cooperation between organizations with rival ideologies. By way of example, the Jewish Agency and the American Zionist Council joined forces in the framework of the alliance with the non-Zionist *Alliance* and the Anglo-Jewish Association. Capitalists, such as the oil tycoon Blaustein of the AJC, worked together with the proletarian Jewish Labor Committee. Orthodox *Aguda* sat alongside non-orthodox organizations. This finding of a pluralistic membership relied solely on one aspect of the members of the Claims Conference, namely their stated ideologies, and ignored other characteristics.

A different approach to the question of pluralism or homogeneity is to conduct a broader examination of the Claims Conference members. Did they share common institutional features and values? Furthermore, did they represent all sectors and individuals who identified as Jews or were persecuted by Germany as Jews? This examination does not support the pronouncement of a representative all-inclusive association.

All twenty-two members of the alliance were male-only or male-dominated organizations. Founded after the commencement of the Cold War, all members of the Claims Conference came from countries belonging to the Western bloc. Eight founding members were American organizations, and seven were based in Europe—three from the United Kingdom, two from France, and two represented Jews in and from Germany. One member, the Jewish Agency, acted on behalf of the state of Israel. Two invitees, the WJC and *Aguda* claimed to act on a worldwide basis. In addition, Goldmann invited organizations representing four relatively small Jewish communities in Australia, Canada, South Africa, and Argentina to join the alliance. Figure 5.2 shows a breakdown, by country of origin, of the member organizations of the Claims Conference at the time of signing the protocols to the Luxembourg Agreement.

All but four of the original members of the Claims Conference were engaged in advocacy, not relief work. Seven members were umbrella organizations or institutions representing Jewish communities in Britain, France, Germany, Canada, South Africa, Australia, and Argentina. Three members were orthodox synagogue councils. Only two members, the Council of Jews from Germany and the *Zentralrat*, represented Holocaust survivors and none represented individuals who did not identify as Jews but entered the definition of Jews (non-Aryans) prescribed by the Nuremberg Race Laws.

Almost all the founding members were undemocratic and many, such as the AJC, the Anglo-Jewish Association, and the Canadian Jewish Congress, were controlled by members of the patrician strata of their communities. A striking exception was the American Jewish Congress, which was created in response to Jewish suffering in Europe in the First World War. On June 10, 1917, 325,000 voters, including women, went to the polls to elect representatives to the Congress.[21] Following the elections, Rabbi Wise, future honorary president of the organization, as well as co-founder of the WJC (together with Goldmann), said:

> Are we forever to suffer men to think and act for us . . . because they have decreed that we are not fit to be trusted with the power of shaping our own destiny?

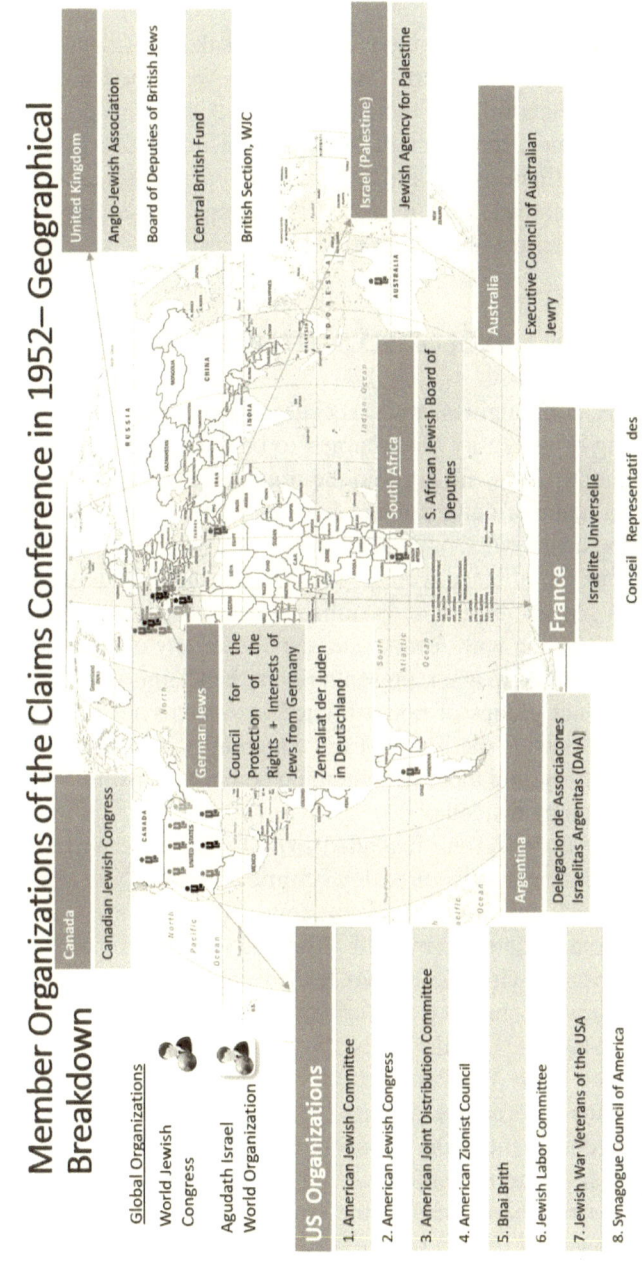

Figure 5.2 Geographical Breakdown of Member Organizations of the Claims Conference in 1952. *Source:* by the author.

Among the first of earth's peoples to advocate and to insist upon popular autonomy, shall we be the last to welcome the renewal of the spirit of democracy?[22]

More than three decades later, other Jewish organizations, including most members of the Claims Conference, still had not welcomed the "spirit of democracy," and a handful, not thousands, elected their leaders. Even the WJC, arguably the most representative Jewish transnational organization in the 1950s, was an alliance of mainly self-appointed representatives of different Jewish communities. Few, if any, of the delegates were elected by all members of the public they purported to represent.

EXCLUDED SECTORS

Many individuals, communities, and associations were not represented in the founding meeting of the entity that claimed to be the spokesman for "world Jewry." Subsequently, they did not join the organization that evolved. These included a broad range of non-affiliated Jews as well as organizations representing women and survivors.

All members of the alliance were organizations. Individuals without any connection to an organization or an established community, whether due to a lack of self-identification with Jews or Judaism or for any other reason, were excluded from membership and representation in the Claims Conference.[23] In addition, two distinct groups of non-affiliated Jews were not invited to join the alliance: those outside the limits of the community, according to Claims Conference executives, and those for whom no communal institutions existed in the lands where they resided.

The first non-affiliated group excluded from the alliance was composed of individuals with fewer than three Jewish grandparents. Nazi persecution policies targeted not only self-professing Jews but also these individuals, many of them Roman Catholic by faith. The supplement to the Nuremberg Laws defined a person with one or two Jewish grandparents as *Mischlinge*. According to a census conducted in Germany in 1939, the number of mixed Jews was over 110,000.[24] In the early 1940s, five thousand Christians of Jewish origin lived in the Warsaw ghetto.[25]

Both the Claims Conference and its members refused to include these victims in their constituency. During negotiations on reparations, a German negotiator asked his Claims Conference counterpart whether he represented this group. Professor Böhm, head of the German delegation, stated, "Hitler had not discriminated in persecution between Jews and Christians of Jewish extraction, and the problem therefore arose in connection with the latter category."[26] Chief Claims Conference negotiator Leavitt replied:

The Chancellor had spoken of meeting representatives of the Jews of the world, not of victims of Nazi action. The Conference did not, and could not represent all such victims, regardless of religion, and could therefore only speak in terms of Jewish victims, and their heirless property.[27]

Consensus existed between the leaders of the Claims Conference that individuals with fewer than three Jewish grandparents or those practicing a different religion were not part of the community and the organization did not speak on their behalf. Goldmann subsequently agreed with German negotiators that these individuals, "Christian Jews," would receive compensation directly from the German government from a fund of DM 50 million initially intended for the Claims Conference and deducted from the payment made under Protocol 2 (originally set at DM 500 million).

A second category of non-affiliated individuals not invited to join the Claims Conference were those living in countries where no Jewish communal institutions existed. In 1951, large numbers of Holocaust survivors lived in lands with no representative organizations including those behind the Iron Curtain and in North Africa. The number of Jews in postwar Eastern Europe was 2.85 million, over a quarter of the total number of world Jewry and three times as many Jews as in Western Europe.[28] Jews in North Africa numbered 580,000 in 1951.[29]

Reasons for the absence of local Jewish organizations differed in each context. In Eastern Europe, state policy prevented the formation of communal organs. In North Africa, lack of internal solidarity between different elements of the local Jewish population impeded the formation of "homegrown" centralized organizations.

The timing of the creation of the Claims Conference prevented the invitation of Jews from Eastern Europe to join the new alliance. Stalin's postwar antisemitic crusade and the descending Iron Curtain marked the end of significant Jewish institutional life in Russia and neighboring countries, as well as the danger of cooperation with Jews in the West. The last Jewish organization created in Russia before the establishment of the Claims Conference was the Jewish Antifascist Committee. This committee, founded in 1942 "to influence American Jewry, and through them public opinion in the US, in favor of Soviet policy," came to a tragic end.[30] In addition, religious life as a whole was under attack. Restoration of public religious activity following Soviet efforts to mobilize support for its war effort reached a peak from 1945 to 1948.[31] In 1948, a bout of closures of Jewish communities commenced as part of a national anti-religious campaign. In the same year, the authorities also banned the distribution of the *Black Book of Soviet Jewry* in which authors Ilya Ehrenburg and Vasily Grossmann detailed Nazi persecution of Soviet Jewry. This account did not comply with the official narrative that viewed the murder of Jews as part of the general history of the Second World War. Soviet authorities began a campaign depicting Jews as dangerous cosmopolitans with international links (especially with American capitalism and imperialism) and dubious national loyalties.[32] By the time Goldmann sent out invitations to the inaugural meeting of the Claims Conference, cooperation between Soviet Jewry and a Western organization promoting the payment of reparations to individual victims was inconceivable.

None of the member organizations of the Claims Conference originated from Jewish communities in North Africa or other Arab lands, such as Iraq. Many of these communities did not have their own centralized institutions for administering communal affairs. Maghreb communities were made up of different groups of émigrés whose city of origin determined their identity. In Casablanca, for example, Spanish-speaking Jews who traced their roots to the Inquisition had little in common with Arabic-speakers originating from the city of Rabat. When the *Alliance* set up a school in the city in 1897, it called for the establishment of a committee composed of representatives of the different synagogues to administer communal affairs. The committee, known as the *junta*, soon disbanded. According to the historian Yaron Tsur, the lack of Jewish solidarity in the region prevented the establishment of central organs representing the entire community of a city or country.[33]

Members of the Claims Conference operated in lands where no local communal institutions existed but did not claim to act as spokesmen for indigenous Jewish populations. The JDC and *Alliance* conducted activities in Eastern Europe and North Africa at different times throughout the 1950s and 1960s, promoting education and providing relief.[34] They were well acquainted with conditions in these regions, however, their interests and those of the local communities did not always coincide. The *Alliance*, for instance, set out to educate Jews in the tradition of French secular society.[35] They were outsiders with their own agenda. In his book on the impact of nationalism on the Jews of Morocco, Tsur describes how the *Alliance* did not adopt the Western reformist model of integration into the culture of the local Muslim population, viewed by the organization as "backwards, despotic and oppressive."[36] Instead, the organization imposed French culture and values on the Jews of Morocco. Consequently, it is questionable whether the Western transnational organizations filled the role of authentic spokesmen for these non-affiliated Jews excluded from the coalition.

In addition to the non-affiliated Jews, large sectors of organized Jewish life did not participate in the Claims Conference. Jewish women's organizations are a prime example. Goldmann did not invite a single women's association to join the new alliance engaged in lobbying for reparations and allocating them. Both the global community and National Socialist victims included men and women. None of the members, many of them men-only institutions at the time, such as the Board of Deputies of British Jews and *Aguda,* saw anything irregular in the absence of women from an entity claiming to speak "in the name of the most important Jewish organizations in the world."

A form of blindness to the gender composition of different Jewish international activities preserved their traditional structure. All seventeen founders of the *Alliance* were men.[37] Women worked as teachers but did not participate in the organization's management or committees. The Zionist movement, which viewed itself as modern and emancipatory, also took a very traditional approach to the question of gender. In the first ten Zionist congresses between 1897 and 1911, only 2 to 5 percent of attendees were women.[38] In this period, there were no female representatives on the Action Committees. When they spoke at congresses, female participants limited themselves to topics pertaining to women and their duties within the Zionist movement. Emma Gottheil, one of the few female participants in the fourth congress, stated "we know that it is not up to us women to solve the great problems, we leave this to our husbands and brothers."[39]

Attempts to join and participate in existing Jewish organizations around the turn of the twentieth century taught women that "a certain amount of separatism from men afforded them more independence and autonomy over their actions."[40] Accordingly, they set up their own organizations. In 1893, Mrs. Hannah Solomon of Chicago invited women from the United States of America to represent their respective communities in the National Council of Jewish Women (NCJW).[41] In 1912, the famous Bertha Pappenheim (Anna O) and Sadie American founded the International Council of Jewish Women. At its World Congress of Jewish Women held in Vienna in 1923, organizations from over twenty countries discussed the problems of refugees and orphans, aid for emigration, and support for Palestine. Similarly, Henrietta Szold, together with other Jewish women in America, created their own Zionist organization, Hadassah, in 1912. Five years later, Hadassah had established thirty-three chapters across the United States with 2,710 members, and it played a central role in laying the foundations for medical treatment in Palestine.[42] Across the Atlantic, Vera Weizmann, wife of the future first president of the state of Israel, together with Rebecca Sieff and Romana Goodman, founded the Federation of Women Zionists in Britain in 1919. This was to become the British and leading branch of the Women's International Zionist Organization (WIZO).

At least one of the women's organizations, Hadassah, was larger than many members of the Claims Conference, such as those from Australia and South Africa. In 1931, the male-led Zionist Organization of America (ZOA) had 13,500 members compared to Hadassah's 44,000.[43] By 1948, the number of Hadassah members had risen to 250,000.[44] Rose Luria Halprin, the national president of Hadassah, served on the Board of Directors of the Claims

Conference in the years 1954 and 1955, in her capacity as representative of the Zionist General Council.[45] Hadassah conducted campaigns to ensure its autonomy within the Zionist movement but there is no record of an application from Hadassah to join the Claims Conference.

In addition to the traditional nature of all-male community leadership, the postwar backlash against feminist activism explains the non-inclusion of women's organizations in the Claims Conference. In the United States, where the Claims Conference was incorporated and operated, the 1950s signaled a conservative turn in women's lives and a return to domesticity. This was the age of the suburban housewife, the dream image of the young American woman, allegedly content to play the role of wife and mother. In the words of Betty Friedan, "In the fifteen years after World War II, this mystique of feminine fulfillment became the cherished and self-perpetuating core of contemporary American Culture."[46] A significant drop occurred in the number of nongovernmental organizations created by women in the two decades after the war, and they played a smaller role in advocacy networks and campaigns.[47] Against this backdrop, the exclusion of women's organizations from the Claims Conference did not encounter opposition.

In retrospect, the absence of women's organizations deprived them of a say in this leadership body. It also prevented their participation in the deliberations on how to allocate German reparations intended for the diaspora. The decision not to benefit from the knowledge and experience acquired by women's organizations in the field of relief work over a period of thirty years appears all the more striking.

Victims and survivors were also underrepresented in the reparations agency. Only two members represented victims of the Holocaust and they both acted on behalf of Jews from or in Germany. Associations of survivors originating from outside Germany did not participate in the organization. Over the years, victim organizations criticized their exclusion from the alliance. Their protests eventually succeeded, and in 1989, the Claims Conference admitted American and Israeli survivor organizations. At present, survivor organizations constitute four of its twenty-seven members. A lack of awareness of the gender imbalance of the Claims Conference prevented any correction. To this day, not one of the members of the Claims Conference is a women's organization.[48]

In conclusion, examining the institutional identity of the members of the Claims Conference reveals that it was not a pluralistic coalition. Instead, it represented a small, elite group selected by Goldmann to fit into his view of the "most important Jewish organizations in the world" and conducive to his leadership. In this sense, the Claims Conference followed in the footsteps of the WJC. A patriarchic partnership excluding one-half of the people did not represent world Jewry.[49] The selection of members of the Claims Conference illustrates the force of tradition in Jewish self-governance. Inclusion and exclusion are evidence of both the strength of those selected as members and the weakness of those outside this circle of policymakers. The exclusion of a high number of individuals from participation in the policy-making entity reflected their situation. This included residence in many countries, political conditions where they lived, and fragmentation between different groups focusing on specific fields. Moreover, groups representing specific sectors were unwilling to cooperate with one another on matters pertaining to the entire community and avoided confrontations with the establishment. The result was the perpetuation of medieval forms of self-governance.

ENTRY BARRIERS: THE REJECTION OF APPLICATIONS TO JOIN THE CLAIMS CONFERENCE

After the establishment of the Claims Conference, many organizations submitted requests to join the coalition. The corporation's by-laws provided for the admission of new members, subject to obtaining the consent of a two-thirds majority.[50] In practice, the issue was almost never put to the vote.

Member organizations of the alliance held very different views on the question of applications to join the Claims Conference. The issue arose at a meeting of the executive committee that took place four months after its formation. Adolph Held of the Jewish Labor Committee (JLC) stated:

> It is in the interest of the Conference to include in its membership as many legitimate Jewish organizations as possible . . . to have the largest possible representation so as to give it greater influence in the Jewish community . . . we should look with favor upon the idea of having other organizations join in order to lend their voice in the Jewish community.[51]

Colonel Bernard Bernstein of B'nai B'rith shared this view and proposed that "we should welcome the membership of Jewish organizations who are sympathetic to our purposes." Dr. Maurice Perlzweig of the Council of Australian Jewry opposed all admissions on the grounds that once an applicant had been admitted, "there would be no logical basis on which to turn down any future applications by any other organizations." Goldstein, a representative of the WJC, added:

> The Conference has already achieved a certain history of working together, at meetings and discussions, of arriving at decisions. That history is important. It is therefore important to continue as far as possible the present *modus operandi*. Changes would only create disturbances and would not strengthen the work.[52]

According to Goldstein, cooperation over a period of four months constituted "history" and was sufficient grounds for rejecting new members. He added that the question to be considered was whether the organization now represented a fair cross section of the Jewish people and answered in the affirmative. The proposal by Held to admit organizations identifying with the aims of the Claims Conference was put to the vote and rejected.

The issue arose again three years later after eight organizations filed applications to join the alliance. This time, Goldstein was more open to the idea and suggested designating a sub-committee to screen the applicants. The representative of the Synagogue Council of America added that in the judgment of many, the alliance was not sufficiently representative, there are "some conspicuous omissions" and new members should be admitted. In his response, Goldmann talked of the "fine representative character of this gathering."[53] The meeting's attendees refrained from voting on Goldstein's proposal to set up a screening committee.

As in other matters, the Claims Conference developed a method for avoiding confrontation with applicants. The organization did not turn down applications but instead deferred them to the next meeting. In his explanation of the practice, Goldmann stated: "Out of politeness we didn't say 'no' because this may be interpreted as a judgment on the merits of these organizations, but we said we want to keep this 'club as a closed shop.'"[54] The members adopted this line of action in the case of applications submitted by eight organizations. A majority of eleven for and five against resolved to defer the decision to the next meeting.

Only three organizations were admitted to the Claims Conference in the course of over three decades after its founding. Two members, the CBF and the *Zentralrat*, joined the entity before the commencement of negotiations with West Germany. The motivation for their admittance was the strengthening of the new alliance and not the will to create a more pluralistic entity.

The Claims Conference accepted the application of the CBF to prevent friction between organizations operating in Germany. Created in 1933 by Otto Schiff, nephew of the American banker and philanthropist Jacob Schiff, this organization financed and coordinated the emigration of thousands of refugees from Germany and Austria, mainly young persons (sent on the *Kindertransport*) and their resettlement.[55] The CBF was subsequently involved in seeking the restitution of Jewish property in the British zone of postwar Germany in the framework of the Jewish Trust Corporation. According to Leavitt, "If the Central British Fund is thus antagonized, there will be difficulties in the whole British Zone."[56] This fear led the Claims Conference to approve the CBF application. Another applicant was the *Zentralrat*, an entity created in Munich on July 19, 1950, to represent the Jews living in Germany.[57] Clearly, it was politically astute to have a local member when negotiating with West Germany on reparations. In 1957, the Claims Conference admitted a third organization, the World Union for Progressive Judaism (WUPJ). The WUPJ was created in 1926 to unite progressive Jewish movements around the world.[58] Blaustein proposed the admittance of the WUPJ because they "represent a branch in Jewry which is at present not represented."[59] A majority vote adopted the proposal.

The Claims Conference rejected all other applications for membership. The British Relief Committee of Jews from Czechoslovakia is an example of an organization that tried, unsuccessfully, to join the Claims Conference. This organization represented not only victims of the Holocaust but also a community from Eastern Europe, both underrepresented groups in the Claims Conference. In a letter dated December 18, 1952, the committee wrote:

> We feel that representatives of Jews from countries in Central and East Europe which were occupied by Germany should be admitted to the Conference because Jews from those countries were among the foremost victims whose indemnification is now at stake. Our organization can, of course, only speak for the Jews of Czechoslovakian origin but we admit that similar organizations of Jews originating from other occupied countries have an equal title to representation in the Conference.[60]

The members turned down this application, as well as the Committee's subsequent request for allocation of funds from German reparations received by the Claims Conference, without explanation. [61]

CONCLUSION

The track record of the Claims Conference on the admission of new members reinforces the image of the organization as a "closed shop." Not only Goldmann but also a majority of the members rejected applications to join the coalition. This finding, together with the homogeneity of its members, undermines the description of the organization as a representative body incorporating every shade of opinion.

Management theorists define organizational culture as the degree to which members have similar beliefs about the best way of doing things. The closer the shared values of members, the stronger the organizational culture. Theorists contend that culture as homogeneity is a pervasive force because shared beliefs reduce or eliminate differences in objectives and promote efficiency. This benefit comes at the cost of more delegation and less monitoring, experimentation, and reduced information collection.[62] The common values of the member organizations contributed to the stability of the Claims Conference and the decision-making process, especially in the potentially explosive field of allocation of reparations. These objectives were achieved at the expense of those groups excluded from the organization. Inclusion of a broader cross section of world Jewry and a wider range of victims of National Socialist persecution may have challenged the mode of operation of the Claims Conference and altered the manner of allocating reparations.[63] The cohesion of the alliance took precedence over a truly representative organization embracing all sectors of world Jewry or victims persecuted by the Third Reich as Jews.

NOTES

1. See the document headed "Erklärung der 'Conference on Jewish Material Claims Against Germany' zur Eröffnung der Verhandlungen mit den Vertretern der Deutschen Bundesrepublik," CAHJP, Claims Conference File no. 8132.

2. Minutes of Meeting of Board of Directors held on February 5–6, 1955 CAHJP, Claims Conference File no. 16602, p. 2.

3. Saul Kagan in a testimony given to the JDC Archives on April 2, 2003. Pat Robertson served as a Southern Baptist minister before becoming a media mogul (a televangelist).

4. Sagi, *German Reparations*, 76.

5. Zweig, *German Reparations*, 27.

6. Marilyn Henry mentions in a footnote that Holocaust survivors were not directly represented. See Henry, *Confronting the Perpetrators*, 23, footnote 27.

7. Letter from Jerome Jacobson to Leavitt of October 8, 1951, JDC Archives, Item #608151. See also Zweig, *German Reparations*, 28.

8. One of the two entities that attended the founding meeting of the Claims Conference as observers, not full participants, the Council of Jewish Federations and Welfare Funds, did not subsequently become a member. In addition, the Jewish War Veterans of the United States of America that attended the founding meeting subsequently terminated its membership after the signing of the Luxembourg Agreement.

9. See p. 112 below.

10. Nahum Goldmann in a testimony given to HUJI, on November 14, 1961, 7–8.

11. Goldmann, *Memories*, 125.

12. Goldmann, *Community of Fate*, 36.

13. *Encyclopedia Judaica*, 2nd ed., vol. 7 (Detroit: Thomson Gale, 2007), 716.

14. *Encyclopedia Judaica*, 2nd ed., vol. 7, 716.

15. An example of this claim is Israel's statement in the notes to the four Allies in March 1951 that it is "the only state which can speak on behalf of the Jewish people." See chap. 2, p. 52.

16. Goldmann, *Community of Fate*, 36.

17. A list of the delegates to the first session of the WJC appears in *Protocole du Premier Congrès Juif Mondial: Genève, 8–15 Août 1936* (*Minutes of First World Jewish Congress: Geneva, August 8–15, 1936*). (Geneva: WJC, 1936), vii.

18. See "Member Organizations," *Conference of Presidents of Major American Jewish Organizations*, n. d., accessed on October 20, 2019, https://www.conferen ceofpresidents.org/about/members.

19. Michael A. Meyer, ed. *German-Jewish History in Modern Times*, vol. I, *Tradition and Enlightenment 1600–1780* (New York: Columbia University Press, 1996), 196; Bernard D. Weinryb, *The Jews of Poland: A Social and Economic History of the Jewish Community in Poland from 1100 to 1800* (Philadelphia: Jewish Publication Society, 1973), 73. See also Israel Bartal, *The Jews of Eastern Europe, 1772–1881*, trans. Chaya Naor (Philadelphia: University of Pennsylvania Press, 2005), 20.

20. Weinryb, *The Jews of Poland*, 198. A full version of *Josel's* diaries appears in Isidor Kracauer, "Rabbi Joselmann de Rosheim," *Revue des Études Juives* 16 (1888).

21. On the elections to the American Jewish Congress, see Jonathan Frankel, "The Jewish Socialists and the American Jewish Congress Movement," *YIVO Annual of Jewish Social Science* 16 (1976): 288–302.

22. Cited in Eli Lederhendler, *Jewish Responses to Modernity: New Voices in America and Eastern Europe* (New York and London: NYU Press, 1994), 126.

23. According to a 2013 Pew research of American Jewry, 14 percent of Jews born in the years 1928–1945 and 19 percent of those born in the years 1946–1964 did not identify as Jews on the basis of religion. Figures for other countries are not available. See "A Portrait of Jewish Americans," *Pew Research Center*, October 1, 2013, accessed on October 20, 2019, https://www.pewforum.org/2013/10/01/jewish-american-beliefs-attitudes-culture-survey/#fn-17239-1.

24. "Mischlinge," *Holocaust Education & Archive Research Team*, n. d., accessed on October 20, 2019, http://www.holocaustresearchproject.org/holoprelude/mischlin ge.html.

25. On the Jewish-Christian communities of the Warsaw ghetto see Peter F. Dembowski, *Christians in the Warsaw Ghetto: An Epitaph for the Unremembered* (Notre Dame, IN: University of Notre Dame Press, 2005).

26. Meeting of 13th Plenary Session of Negotiations on Reparations held on June 27, 1952, CAHJP, Claims Conference File no. 8092, p. 1.

27. Meeting of 13th Plenary Session of Negotiations on Reparations held on June 27, 1952, CAHJP, Claims Conference File no. 8092, p. 2.

28. The figures are taken from DellaPergola, "Reflections on the Multinational Geography of Jews After World War II," Table 1 on p.16.

29. Leon Shapiro, "World Jewish Population," *American Jewish Yearbook* 52 (1951): 231–233.

30. Shimon Redlich, "The Jewish Antifascist Committee in the Soviet Union," *Jewish Social Studies* 31, no. 1 (1969): 29.

31. Yaacov Ro'i, "The Reconstruction of Jewish Communities in the USSR, 1944–1947," in *The Jews are Coming Back*, 187.

32. Olga Baranova, "Early Historiography of the Holocaust: The Example of the Soviet Union," in Regina Fritz, Éva Kovács, and Béla Rásky, eds., *Als der Holocaust noch keinen Namen hatte: zur frühen Aufarbeitung des NS-Massenmordes an den*

Juden (Before the Holocaust Had a Name: On the Early Coming to Terms with NS Mass Murder of Jews) (Vienna: New Academic Press, 2016), 188.

33. Yaron Tsur, "Reshito shel Ha-irgun Ha-kehilati Be'Casablanca," (The Beginning of the Communal Organization in Casablanca) in Israel Bartal, ed., *Kehal Yisra'el: Ha-shilton Ha-'atsmi Ha-Yehudi Le-dorotav* (Jerusalem: Merkaz Zalman Shazar, 2001), vol. 3, 175–179 and Yaron Tsur, *Kehilah Keru'ah: Yehude Maroko veha-le'umiyut, 1943–1954 (A Torn Community: Moroccan Jews and Nationalism, 1943–1954)*. (Tel Aviv: Am Oved, 2001), 46–47.

34. On the intermittent operations of the JDC in Poland after the war see Anna Sommer Schneider, "Behind the Iron Curtain: The Communist Government in Poland and its Attitude towards the Joint's Activities, 1944–1989," in Avinoam Patt, Atina Grossmann, Linda G. Levi, and Maud S. Mandel, eds., *The JDC at 100: A Century of Humanitarianism* (Detroit: Wayne State University Press, 2019), 316–360.

35. Michael M. Laskier, "Aspects of the Activities of the Alliance Israélite Universelle in the Jewish Communities of the Middle East and North Africa: 1860-1918," *Modern Judaism* 3, no. 2 (1983): 147.

36. Tsur, *Kehilah Keru'ah,* 49.

37. André Chouraqui, *L'Alliance Israélite Universelle et la Renaissance Juive Contemporaine: Cent Ans d'Histoire (Alliance Israélite Universelle and the Contemporary Jewish Renaissance: A Century of History)* (Paris : Presses Universitaires de France, 1965), 29.

38. Priska Gmür, "'It Is Not Up To Us Women to Solve Great Problems': The Duty of the Zionist Woman in the Context of the First Ten Zionist Congresses," in Wayne van Dalsum and Vivian Kramer, eds., *The First Zionist Congress in 1897: Causes, Significance and Topicality,* trans. Heiko Haumann (Basel: Karger, 1997), 293.

39. This citation is taken from the minutes of the Fourth Zionist Congress held in London in 1900. See Gmür, "'It Is Not Up To Us Women,'" 295.

40. Mary McCune, *The Whole Wide World without Limits: International Relief, Gender Politics and American Jewish Women, 1893–1930* (Detroit: Wayne State University Press, 2005), 26.

41. Rebekah Kohut, "Jewish Women's Organizations in the United States," *The American Jewish Year Book* (September 12, 1931–September 31, 1932/5692): 174.

42. McCune, *The Whole Wide World without Limits,* 26.

43. Mary McCune, "Formulating the 'Women's Interpretation of Zionism': Hadassah Recruitment of Non-Zionist American Women, 1914–1930," in Shulamit Reinharz and Mark A. Raider, eds., *American Jewish Women and the Zionist Enterprise* (Waltham, MA: Brandeis University Press, 2005), 90–91.

44. Shirli Brautbar, *From Fashion to Politics: Hadassah and Jewish American Women in the Post World War II Era* (Boston: Academic Studies Press, 2012), 22.

45. The names of the directors, including "Mrs. Samuel W. Halprin," appear in the annual reports of the organization. See *Conference on Jewish Material Claims against Germany – Annual Report 1954* (New York: The Organization, 1954), page unnumbered and *Conference on Jewish Material Claims against Germany – Annual Report 1955* (New York: The Organization, 1955), pages unnumbered. Halprin served as president of Hadassah in the years 1947–1952.

46. Betty Friedan, *The Feminine Mystique* (New York: W. W. Norton & Co., 1963), 18. For a different view on the idealization of this period see Joanne Meyerowitz, *Not June Cleaver: Women and Gender in Postwar America, 1945–1961* (Philadelphia: Temple University Press, 1994); Stephanie Coontz, *The Way We Never Were: American Families and the Nostalgia Gap* (New York: Basic Books, 1993); Deborah L. Nelson, "Introduction," *Women's Studies Quarterly* 33, no. 3/4 (2005): 10–23.

47. Berkovitch, "The Emergence and Transformation of the International Women's Movement," 117.

48. On the inclusion of victim organizations among members of the Claims Conference, see Henry, *Confronting the Perpetrators*, 222.

49. On the exclusion of women from Jewish history see Pamela Nadell, "Rereading Charles S. Liebman: Questions from the Perspective of Women's History," *American Jewish History* 80, no. 4 (1991): 510.

50. Membership Meeting of Claims Conference, Inc. held on December 29, 1952, CAHJP, Claims Conference File no. 15001, pages unnumbered.

51. Minutes of Executive Committee Meeting of the Claims Conference held on February 29, 1952, CAHJP, Claims Conference File no. 15000, p. 6.

52. Minutes of Executive Committee Meeting of the Claims Conference held on February 29, 1952, CAHJP, Claims Conference File no. 15000, pp. 7–8.

53. Transcript of Claims Conference Meeting (no details of which committee) held on January 14, 1956 at YIVO premises, CAHJP, Claims Conference File no. 16604, pp. 34–35.

54. Transcript of Claims Conference Meeting held on January 14, 1956, at YIVO premises, CAHJP, Claims Conference File no. 16604, p. 36.

55. See Joan Stiebel, "The Central British Fund for World Jewish Relief: Transactions & Miscellanies," *Jewish Historical Society of England* 27 (1978): 51–60.

56. Minutes of Executive Committee Meeting of the Claims Conference held on February 29, 1952, CAHJP, Claims Conference File no. 15000, p. 9.

57. *Zentralrat der Juden in Deutschland-Geschichte, n.d.*, accessed on October 20, 2019, https://www.zentralratderjuden.de/der-zentralrat/geschichte/.

58. See "About the World Union for Progressive Judaism," *World Union for Progressive Judaism,* n. d., accessed on October 20, 2019, https://wupj.org/about-us/history/.

59. Summary of Discussion of Claims Conference Board of Directors Meeting held on January 19–20, 1957, CAHJP, Claims Conference File no. 16605, p. 25.

60. See Letter of British Relief Committee of Jews from Czechoslovakia to the Claims Conference dated December 18, 1952, in CAHJP, Claims Conference File no. 15001.

61. See Claims Conference Membership Meeting of January 14, 1956, JDC Archives, Item #812684 and CAHJP, Claims Conference File no. 15001.

62. Eric Van der Steen, "Culture Clash: The Costs and Benefits of Homogeneity," *Management Science* 56, no. 10 (2010): 1718. https://www.jstor.org/stable/40864736.

63. According to a JDC official in a discussion with the author on November 16, 2015, since the admission of survivor organizations to the Claims Conference in 1989, decision-making has become much harder and there is "lots of bickering" at board meetings.

Chapter 6

Internal Operations
Organizational Logic and Experts

The disbursement of German reparations was a major activity of the Claims Conference after the signing of the Luxembourg protocols. In 1954, the organization received the first payment under Protocol 2, by a circuitous route, and the last installment in 1964. Like other postwar coalitions, the Claims Conference projected the image of a rational, professional entity seeking to promote the interests of an entire community. In its many publications, it described the allocations system in terms of objective norms implemented by professional personnel without any ulterior motives.

The legitimacy of modern global organizations is invested in legalities, procedures, and rules. Organizational theorists describe how institutional rules (to which they refer as "myths") provide more than tools for day-to-day operations. Instead, they promote legitimacy and enhance survival prospects.[1] In addition, the postwar generation of international organizations emphasized the professionalism of their staff. In this context, the historian Patricia Clavin wrote: "The stress on expertise represented the continued power of the idea that the world could be directed by using figures, numbers and statistical categories."[2]

A fuller understanding of the allocation process explains who did and did not receive reparations from the organization. The Claims Conference distributed funds behind closed doors. Internal documents disclose both the ground rules for the distribution of German funds and the manner of their implementation. The nature of the rules combined with the powers of the administrators prevented outside influence or even an understanding of how the allocations system worked.

ACQUISITION OF AUTHORITY

The founders of the Claims Conference created an entity that resembled international organizations outside the Jewish world. The object was to incorporate the most advanced ideas on the structure and operations of institutions operating across borders. Members and executives of the Claims Conference employed a number of elements to enhance the status of a communal leader: organizational structure, rationality of actions, and professionalism of executives.

Three organs of the Claims Conference administered the allocation process: the Secretariat, Executive Committee, and Board of Directors. This tripartite structure resembled that of the League of Nations, the model for twentieth-century intergovernmental and nongovernmental organizations.[3] The purpose of the separate organs was to distinguish between the formulation of policy by representatives of the member organizations and its execution by the staff. The latter was supposed to have a single loyalty, to the Claims Conference, and not to its members. Goldmann first gained knowledge of the functioning of international organizations from the League of Nations. As head of the WJC, he reported to the League on frequent breaches of the Minorities Treaties and discriminatory practices directed against Jews in the interwar period and was well-acquainted with its mode of operations. The tripartite structure of the Claims Conference was part of the effort to present to states and individuals a modern entity governing "world Jewry" in the field of reparations.

The emphasis on the application of neutral, objective rules to the allocation of reparations was also intended to increase the authority of the Claims Conference. The initial allocations policy contained only rudimentary guidelines. Directors and executives of the organization had the task of translating vague rules into operative decisions. In its annual reports, the organization described the allocation process in technical terms devoid of political interests. It published lists of figures and tables. The first annual report stated that the organization was "impelled to weigh the urgent needs of each community in relation to those of every other one, and to evaluate every individual project submitted."[4] The report contained guidelines on how to apply for German funds. The second annual report described a survey, "the first of its kind," of 11,000 individuals living in eleven countries who received allocations in cash from the Claims Conference.[5] To ensure compliance with the allocations system, the organization appointed a study committee that published its findings.[6] The object was to demonstrate the neutrality of the allocation process for the distribution of German reparations.

The role of the administrator or bureaucrat was a fundamental aspect of the Claims Conference. A small number of individuals determined who would benefit from the funds provided under Protocol 2 to the Luxembourg Agreement. In an attempt to prevent public criticism, the Claims Conference and the JDC, which played a key role in the allocation process, emphasized the professionalism and experience of their administrators, who were guided solely by objective considerations. In a 1954 conference of JDC country directors and Claims Conference officials, Beckelman, director general of JDC overseas operations, said: "You are to assume that there is nobody in this room who is not a professional colleague."[7] His colleague, Charles Jordan, head of the Paris office, added, "Men and women of the JDC were in fact at times substitute community leaders. But they were also professional people who had benefited from the rapid advancement in the field of social service particularly in the United States."[8] To this day, the Claims Conference cites its reliance on (nameless) experts in the allocation process. According to its website, committees composed of experts from around the world help guide the staff in developing recommendations to the Allocation Committee.[9]

ALLOCATION SYSTEM STRUCTURED TO SERVE MEMBERS

Minutes of meetings on allocations and correspondence between member organizations reveal a different picture. The Claims Conference devised a system for the disbursement of reparations that almost exclusively served its members, first and foremost, the JDC. Organizational theorists define umbrella bodies as "primarily member-serving versus public beneficiary organizations."[10] They provide services to members, not individuals or unrelated groups of clients. The Claims Conference meets this definition.

Multiple Roles of Executives

In practice, there was no rigid division between the different organs of the Claims Conference. Many executives played more than one role. The more positions they filled as officers, directors, and members of the executive committee, the greater their influence on the allocations. Applications for funds filed by member organizations had an advantage over requests by unconnected entities. The Claims Conference, together with the JDC, appointed a person to review the request and make recommendations (the "rapporteur"). Jordan of the JDC described the requirements of a rapporteur as follows: "The job of rapporteuring demands understanding and objectivity in dealing with communities and their requirements. . . . Many experts participated in the rapporteuring."[11] The rapporteur was elected on the basis of his acquaintance with the country in which the applicant operated. Frequently, he was associated with the organization that filed the application.[12] Findings of the rapporteurs were submitted to the executive committee and subsequently to the Board of Directors for their final decision.

Directors of the Claims Conference voted on the allocation of funds to the member organizations they represented. The decision to award funds to the director's own organization involved a conflict of interests between duties owed to the Claims Conference and to the entity or community that appointed them. The representative of the South African Jewish Board of Deputies argued that directors should not vote on issues relating to the member organizations represented by them. In his words:

> Mr. Chairman, it seems to me that there is something seriously wrong, and I say this with all humility, in the procedure . . . of the meeting of the Board of Directors. . . . In the first place, as I conceive the functions of the Board of Directors, it is to examine impartially, as far as they are able to, all claims . . . I think it is not proper for the directors to vote when there is controversy on a particular issue affecting them personally or affecting the organization they represent.[13]

No action was taken on this proposal, and directors continued to vote on allocations for uses and organizations in which they had a personal interest. The *Aguda* representative demanded funds to serve the needs of orthodox communities such as *yeshivot*, ritual baths, and schools. Similarly, Leavitt of the JDC, the main beneficiary of the funds, participated and voted in meetings of the Board of Directors and executive committee on allocations, including to his own organization. The decision to allow directors to vote, despite possible conflicts of interest, benefited member organizations at the expense of other groups, primarily individual victims of Nazi persecution.

Absence of Formal Appeals Procedure

There was no formal appeals procedure for unsuccessful applicants. At an early stage, representatives of the WJC and B'nai B'rith complained about the lack of an appeals tribunal. Goldmann described the demand for an objective board of appeals as "absurd" and added that it was "impossible and destructive to envisage a system where they [the directors] would directly hear all applicants and directly screen applications."[14] The only course available to applicants was to ask a director to lobby on their behalf at the next meeting of the Board. In the words of Polier, American Jewish Congress director:

> The Board was in fact merely functioning as an "appeals court" between various applications, satisfying groups of pressure claims, without an overall, organized

approach to the whole budget. He felt that rather than concern itself with how to spend ten million dollars a year, the organization should take the long-range view of how the most permanent good could be achieved.[15]

Other directors did not share Polier's criticism and they did not alter the procedures. Applicants connected to member organizations could ask a representative to present their appeal against the rejection of their application at a Claims Conference board meeting. Individuals and entities who were not associated with member organizations were denied the opportunity to try and overcome a rejection of their request.

At least two applicants whose applications were rejected sought relief from the Supreme Court of New York County. In one case, the Jewish Secondary Schools Movement requested an order to hold a meeting of the Claims Conference Board of Directors in England.[16] In another case, a Holocaust survivor asked the court to order the Claims Conference to award him $20,000 to cover his resettlement costs.[17] The court rejected both cases on the grounds of the petitioners' lack of standing. The rulings attest to the finality of Claims Conference decisions on how to disburse German reparation funds and the lack of recourse for applicants without connections to members of the alliance.

Accountability

The approach of the Claims Conference to disclosure of information on the allocation process again illustrates how its procedures were geared to member organizations and not the general public. The organization, like other NGOs at the time, conducted the allocation process with a complete lack of transparency. Details of filed applications and recommendations made by rapporteurs were distributed only to officers and directors of the organization. The public did not receive information on denied applications. Even applicants were not informed of the reason for rejection of their requests. Annual reports issued by the Claims Conference specified allocations made but contained no information on requests turned down. In a 1958 board meeting, Harry Goodman, representative of *Aguda*, called for the admission of representatives of the Jewish press to the discussions. He added:

> Now the Jewish world is without the slightest shadow of doubt very interested in the manner in which the Claims Conference conducts its proceedings. It is interested to know the views which various people express. These views till now have been in the utmost secrecy . . . I think the Jewish public should know what is happening.[18]

The motion was seconded but when put to a vote, a large (silent) majority rejected it. Directors did not feel any obligation to share information on the operation of the allocation process with the public. An article published in 1965 by the London *Jewish Chronicle* attacked this policy:

> No adequate defence of this procedure has ever been put forward. . . . The secrecy which surrounds the claims procedure only encouraged unjustified requests and fueled the disquiet of those who questioned the morality of an institution which gave the Board of Directors the right to decide on allocations, when a number of them had a direct organizational interest in them.[19]

The refusal to open proceedings to the press reflected the view of directors and officers that they were not accountable to the public they claimed to represent. This approach undermined the image projected by the organization of a modern entity directed on the basis of professional, not political, considerations.

As part of the effort to counter external and internal criticism of improper conduct, the Claims Conference commissioned a review by a study committee in 1958. The mandate of this committee was to examine the "principles, priorities and procedures which govern the allocation of Conference funds."[20] Member organizations criticized the manner of reparations disbursements. The findings were directed to this group only and not to other stakeholders. The study committee was made up of the same people who had determined the original allocation policy, and included Goldmann, Blaustein, Leavitt of the JDC, Jules Brunschvig of the *Alliance*, who was also vice president of the Claims Conference, and Polier. The committee did not consult unrelated organizations or groups of victims who did not receive allocations. Unsurprisingly, the study committee upheld the organization's allocations policy. The members concluded that:

> we believe that the existing principles governing the allocation of Conference funds for the relief and rehabilitation and cultural and educational reconstruction for Jewish victims of Nazi persecution are sound, and should be retained without change for the next three years.[21]

The findings enabled the organization to continue to distribute funds, first and foremost to member organizations, without clear criteria or full disclosure.

Definition of Eligibility: Procedures not Objective Criteria

The allocations system provides further evidence of the organizational culture developed by the Claims Conference. Allocating funds required defining the terms of eligibility. This need arose due to the large number of applications filed with the Claims Conference. In the first year of operations, the organization received requests for funds totaling more than $54,000,000, five times the sum available for distribution.[22] Beckelman, the JDC official who formulated guidelines for applications to the Claims Conference, talked about the need for a "necessary system of priorities."[23] He proposed a system for the screening of applications by the JDC that was subsequently adopted by the Board of Directors. At the outset, member organizations had demanded the right to supervise the use of reparations by the JDC. Accordingly, all requests for allocations, together with the recommendation of the rapporteur, were submitted to the Board of Directors for approval.

Disbursement of reparations by an organization differed from direct German compensation to victims of National Socialism. West Germany granted annuities or single payments on the basis of detailed criteria specified by legislation. The BEG defined the types of victims and losses that qualified for compensation. The advantage of this model was identical treatment for similar cases. The drawback was that it required a sophisticated bureaucratic system to oversee it. Another possibility was to divide the available sum by the number of victims and to distribute the compensation equally to all people who met the definition prescribed by the organization. The West German Foreign Office proposed this model to the Claims Conference, but Goldmann immediately rejected this suggestion on the grounds that the money should go to groups, not individuals. In a speech to the Board of Directors, he described his conversation with the German President on the subject:

> I said "President Hallstein, what you want us to do could make our life very easy. We will figure out so and so many refugees. We have $10 million a year and everybody could get $20 or $25, so we would hand it over and it would be a very easy life. . . . It's an eternal conflict—who is first? The community or the individual? . . . we say we'd give something for the survival of the Jewish people, to Judaism, synagogues, children, schools etc. and we give to needy people but not to individuals, to groups."[24]

This approach contrasted with the policy adopted by the United States government when it decided to compensate Japanese Americans for their incarceration during the Second World War. Under the 1988 Civil Liberties Act, each living individual who had been interned received $20,000.[25] In the first decade of its operations, the Claims Conference chose a different method tailored to the needs of its members.

Procedures, not criteria, determined the fate of applications to the Claims Conference for the allocation of reparations. The Claims Conference, together with the JDC, published a list of principles on the disbursement of funds.[26] The first rule stated that all allocations must be governed by the organization's contractual obligations. Other rules stipulated who did and did not qualify for allocations. Recognized and functioning relief organizations were eligible for grants. New institutions and individuals did not qualify, except in special cases. The rules also prescribed uses that did not qualify for grants including compensation for past losses or expenditures. These principles emphasized procedural aspects of filing applications and criteria for disqualifying requests for funds. They provided almost no information on the types of use that did merit grants. In an early meeting of the executive committee, Goldmann criticized the committee on cultural and religious applications for attempting to prescribe principles of eligibility: "There has been a slight misunderstanding among the members of the committee regarding their task—instead of limiting themselves to a discussion of procedures, they attempted to define criteria for actual allocations."[27] A lack of clear and objective guidelines on the intended use of the funds enabled the Claims Conference to distribute funds at its discretion and released it from the need to ensure compliance with predetermined criteria.

Criticism of the absence of criteria for the allocation of reparation funds came from outside and inside the organization. In 1953, Zachariah Shuster, AJC European Director, wrote to a colleague: "My major difficulty in developing a clear policy on the entire matter of allocations from the Conference, is that thus far I have been unable to discern from all the material we have received here the guiding principles adopted by the Conference on this subject."[28] Nevertheless, there is no evidence that Blaustein, the AJC president, or other officers demanded the establishment of a set of criteria for the allocation of funds.

The cultural committee of the Claims Conference also complained of the lack of guidance on the exercise of its duties. In a letter sent to members of the Executive Committee in 1954, Dr. Judah Shapiro, director of the cultural and educational department, wrote:

> No mandate was given to the Cultural Advisory Committee clearly instructing the group as to its role. The committee therefore defined its own responsibilities. It was never clear whether such a committee should formulate the general scope of the program to be undertaken and indicate broad lines for the program, or whether it should, as it did, concern itself with the specific requests and recommend precise allocations on each of the applications.[29]

At the 1954 conference of JDC country directors, Kagan explained the Claims Conference decision not to prescribe criteria for allocations. In his words:

> Some reference has been made to the absence of principles and I will confess to you that we have had discussions about formulating a rather full and clear

statement of principles in advance, and it was my personal view and continues to be, that it would be doctrinaire. It is true that it would be convenient and easy, because every piece of paper would be tested against this cubby-hole of principle . . . I think we have to struggle through this empirical approach, step by step, benefit and profit from our mistakes, and not be ashamed to stand up and say, "We have made a mistake."[30]

The subject arose again in a meeting of the Claims Conference executive committee held in 1955. Polier emphasized the need for rules to determine how to disburse the German funds. According to the minutes: "Mr. Polier stated that there were two issues here involved, which were not being separated. One is the question of the procedures, and the other is basic principles of allocation. He felt that the latter was of primary importance."[31] In response, the members appointed a subcommittee to present a working paper the next meeting. The paper duly reiterated the procedural rules in place and refrained from defining criteria for the allocation of funds.[32] In conclusion, the Claims Conference made allocations on a "non-doctrinaire" basis. Most directors and officers valued their freedom of action over the risk of making mistakes. The result was inconsistencies in the allocation of reparation funds.

Selective Application of Rules

Implementation of allocation rules often differed from case to case. Officers and directors did not explain how they applied the rules or the discrepancies between similar claims. This conduct contradicted the image of a rational and impersonal system devised by a modern organization.

Figures published by the organization show the uneven distribution of reparations between different countries. The total sum allocated to the United Kingdom (where between 45,000 to 55,000 victims settled) during the first twenty years of the organization's existence amounted to $1,885,293.[33] Sweden, with only 6,500 survivors, received a larger sum of $1,961,780. Australia, a new home to 28,000 survivors, received 40 percent more than the United Kingdom, although it had half as many survivors. Figure 6.1 shows the total allocations per survivor in each country from 1952 to 1972.

The statistics also show inconsistencies in the distribution of reparations. A guiding principle of the allocators was that the funds should go to countries occupied by Germany or disproportionately burdened by heavy influxes of Nazi victims.[34] Nevertheless, three European countries (Switzerland, Spain, and Portugal) received reparation funds although they were not occupied during the war nor did they offer shelter to considerable numbers of Holocaust

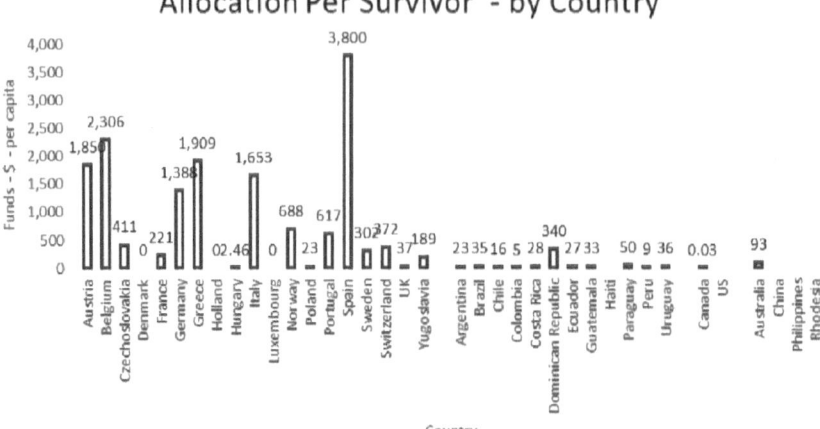

Figure 6.1   Allocation per Survivor by Country in 1952–1972. *Source*: By the author.

survivors. No explanation for this deviation appears in the organization's annual reports.

The discrimination between South America and North America illustrates the Claims Conference mode of operations. Twelve countries in Latin America received funds totaling $2,838,543, mainly for the relief and rehabilitation of approximately 100,000 refugees from Germany and Austria. The Claims Conference did not allocate any funds for the relief and rehabilitation of the 100,000 victims who settled in the United States. Instead, it allocated $2,880,4660 to North America, earmarked entirely for research, publication, and salvaging Jewish cultural treasures.[35] Canada, with between 45,000 to 55,000 survivors, received a total of $15,000. At the same time, the organization granted $1,454,000 to twenty-two *yeshivot* in the United States and Canada. This allocation also violated the predetermined rules of distribution to Nazi victims since, according to the organization, only one half of the students met this definition.

Decision-Making Procedures as Tools for Promoting Cooperation

The Claims Conference had a much wider range of members than the JDC or the successor organizations. Moreover, officers and directors were accustomed to different organizational cultures. This situation constituted a challenge. Minutes of meetings disclose three different practices employed to reach a consensus on the distribution of reparations. One method was the recognition (especially by Goldmann) of situations when an issue should or should not be put to a vote. The second method was to refer recommendations on disputed allocations to smaller committees where opponents to the official line constituted a minority, thereby ensuring the adoption of the original proposal. A third method was to allocate funds to pet projects of member organizations and their representatives. Below are illustrations of the different methods.

No vote was taken on the decision to direct reparation funds primarily to Western Europe, excluding the United Kingdom. In a March 1954 meeting of the Executive Committee, Goldmann announced that "it has been decided that no money for relief will be allocated in the United States nor in Canada. . . . This same principle is being applied for England."[36] Two European members of the committee, the Council of Jews from Germany and the British Board of Deputies, objected but Goldmann did not clarify how it was decided and did not put the issue to a vote. The policy of directing funds to Western Europe appears to be a logical outcome of the decision to allocate a major share of the funds to the JDC. Protocol 2 stipulated that the funds were to be used outside Israel for victims of National Socialist persecution. In 1954, the JDC was unable to operate in Eastern Europe. At the time, Western Europe's largest Jewish community was in the United Kingdom, where many victims of National Socialism had resettled. However, the JDC had never operated in England or Scotland. Consequently, leaders of the Claims Conference decided to focus on Western Europe, excluding the United Kingdom because this was the only location that matched all the requirements of the agreements with West Germany and between the member organizations.

Another example of the art of refraining from putting an issue to the vote was the shifting of reparation funds from the reconstruction of West European Jewry to the Relief-in-Transit program. Initiated by the JDC in the early 1920s, this program financed food and clothing parcels sent to starving Jews in Soviet Russia through the International Red Cross and other organizations.[37] The JDC operated the program once again after the Second World War for the benefit of Jews in Eastern Europe.[38] Little evidence on how Relief-in-Transit worked is available, and JDC officials refuse to discuss how they elected individuals who received parcels.[39]

The Claims Conference allocated a large share of German payments designated for Nazi victims to the JDC Relief-in-Transit program. In 1955, the Claims Conference granted $1,823,143 to the program.[40] Over the years, the sums spent on food and clothing parcels increased. The decision to redirect a major share of reparations from Western to Eastern Europe was not put to a vote. Officers and directors of the Claims Conference did not question this change of policy. They received extremely limited information on the use of funds from JDC officials, but nevertheless, by 1963, the Relief-in-Transit program accounted for more than 80 percent of reparation funds designated for general relief.[41]

The German government took issue with the allocation of reparation funds to the Relief-in-Transit program. In a letter to the Claims Conference in 1964, the German Foreign Office wrote:

> It is our belief that payments effected in countries behind the Iron Curtain neither show their nature as reparations nor their provenance from German sources stemming from Protocol 2 of the Hague Agreement. Secondly, the persecutees and the Claims Conference itself . . . point again and again to the difficult situation of the so-called post 1953 cases. It is exactly this group of persons who should be benefitted by payments out of the DM 450 million fund in accordance with the provisions of Protocol 2 of the Hague Agreement; we learn, however, from your Annual Report that this can obviously not sufficiently be accomplished because part of the means at your disposal is being spent for relief-in-transit.[42]

The German protest had no effect. Directors of the Claims Conference did not reconsider the policy or even demand explanations on how the program worked. Instead, the organization continued to award larger and larger sums to the Relief-in-Transit program of its member organization, the JDC. On the other hand, many survivors who settled in the United States, Canada and the United Kingdom, as well as those who left Eastern Europe after 1953 ("the so-called post-1953 cases") and did not qualify for direct German compensation, received nothing.

A different general organizational practice for the resolution of disputes adopted by Goldmann was to refer controversial issues to a smaller committee. Members of the Claims Conference requested the allocation of funds to North African Jews. Lewin submitted the proposal, stating that "North African Jewry has been part and parcel of this terrible Holocaust which European Jewry went through."[43] Goldmann replied that since the countries had not been occupied by Germany, only a very small number of refugees in Morocco and Algiers qualified for reparations. Leavitt then stated that Jews in North Africa already received more help from the JDC compared to the past. In view of the differences of opinion, the board instructed the Executive Committee to consider whether German funds should be applied to "not victims (*sic*) of Nazi persecution residing in any part of North Africa."[44] Subsequently, the Claims Conference did not allocate funds for use in North Africa.

The directors again used the practice of referral to a committee to resolve the question of allocations to the United Kingdom. In a discussion held by the Board in 1958, Janner questioned the rejection of British applications for the support of Jewish schools attended by the children of refugees. He argued that it was of "utmost importance" to give them the opportunity to receive the kind of training they would have obtained if their parents had not been uprooted.⁴⁵ Goldmann proposed that the study committee examine the issue. Goldmann's proposal prevented an escalation of the dispute between the JDC that opposed allocation of funds for use in England and the British directors. The study committee had the power to advise a future change of policy and the award of funds to Jewish day schools. Instead of supporting a rejection of the British application, Goldmann provided a solution that pleased a majority of the parties. He then put the issue to a vote. Eleven directors voted in favor of referring the matter to the study committee, while eight voted against.

The third method was to grant funds to projects advocated by member organizations and of special importance to their representatives. The Claims Conference granted $12,000 (equivalent to $106,000 today) for a community center in Spain. The center was intended to serve a Jewish community that numbered officially seventy members, half of whom were Moroccan students.⁴⁶ Blaustein lobbied strongly for the allocation. He advocated that for the first time since 1492, there was an opportunity to again build up a Jewish community in Spain. Several directors objected to the allocation on different grounds, but Blaustein prevailed. None of the directors commented on the fact that the proposal did not comply with the rule limiting allocations to projects in countries occupied by Germany during the war. In another case, directors approved an application for the grant of $75,000 for Jewish poultry farmers from New Jersey. B'nai B'rith, a member organization of the Claims Conference, filed the application for funds to provide loans to members hard hit by the general economic situation and hurricane Hazel.⁴⁷ The allocation again contravened the rule prescribed by the Claims Conference of not granting funds in the United States. When the subject of the grant arose before the applications meeting, no one asked why poultry farmers, not all of whom were Nazi victims, unlike other refugees and survivors residing in the United States, would receive reparations. Grants approved by directors and officers to projects of special importance to member organizations contributed to the strength of the alliance and a lack of friction.

The ability to overcome disputes and reach amicable solutions on the distribution of reparations attested to directors and officers who appreciated the importance of the alliance. To further their cooperation, executives waived ideological differences. They also refrained from asking questions. In most cases, member organizations allowed Claims Conference officers and the JDC to distribute communal funds with little or no intervention.

POLICYMAKERS AND EXPERTS

Very few Claims Conference executives and officers had formal qualifications in the field of administration or experience in welfare work. Many directors, such as Goldmann, Janner, Maurice Boukstein of the Jewish Agency, Shad Polier of the American Jewish Congress, and Rudolph Callman of the Council of Jews from Germany, were lawyers. Their legal experience contributed to the success of negotiations with West Germany on amendments to federal and state legislation for the benefit of victims. However, legal training did not provide tools for relief work or the screening of applications for aid. Other officers were industrialists (Blaustein trained as an engineer and Bronfman was president of the alcoholic beverage company Seagram) or religious leaders (such as Goldstein and Dr. Hugo Gryn). Shapiro was a professor of contemporary Jewish thought at the Hebrew Union College and held leading positions at the Hillel Foundation, the YIVO Center for Advanced Jewish Studies, and the Labor Zionist Alliance. The only officer with experience in relief work was Leavitt, the treasurer of the Claims Conference. He trained as a chemical engineer but directed social welfare operations in his role as vice president of the JDC. Kagan, who managed the affairs of the Claims Conference for more than forty-seven years (with one brief and unhappy interruption) had no formal higher education.[48] Furthermore, most of the officers or directors had not been inmates of Nazi concentration camps or ghettos and therefore did not have first-hand knowledge of the victims' needs.[49]

A majority of the officers and directors who determined the allocation policy and oversaw its implementation lacked formal training in finance or budget planning. Many received their training in the distribution of public funds from their service in the JRSO.[50] Unlike the Claims Conference, the JRSO was not bound by contractual restrictions. It allocated the bulk of the proceeds from its sale of private and communal heirless assets to the Jewish Agency and the JDC. These recipients used the funds to finance ongoing programs and did not earmark JRSO proceeds for assistance to Nazi victims. Arguably, it was the JRSO experience and not the professionalism or expertise of directors and officers that determined the Claims Conference policy on allocations.

For all officers and directors, the Claims Conference was a part-time occupation of secondary importance and frequently one of many organizations in which they were involved. It was not only Goldmann who served in numerous entities and "straddled the organizational divide."[51] Blaustein headed Amoco and led the AJC, his primary interest outside the business world. Leavitt served as treasurer in the Claims Conference and acted simultaneously as vice president of the JDC. Janner was an MP throughout the period of allocation of reparations and headed the Board of Deputies of British Jews from 1955 to 1964. Kagan acted as the JRSO secretary following his discharge from the US Army and continued in this position after Goldmann recruited him to the Claims Conference. For most of the period of the allocations under Protocol 2, Kagan was secretary of both the JRSO and the Claims Conference.[52] As a result, the time available to officers and directors of the Claims Conference to closely read thousands of applications for allocations and oversee the functioning of the organization's different committees as well as the JDC, the main recipient of reparation funds, was strictly limited.

Involvement in the Claims Conference provided an opportunity to travel the world and attend meetings but no other remuneration. The sole monetary benefit to directors and nonexecutive officers was reimbursement of travel expenses for attending meetings. Meetings were held in New York and Europe, on an alternating basis. The terms of office restricted service as a policymaker in the Claims Conference to a small group of wealthy men with limited time on their hands. These men had the authority to overrule recommendations submitted by social workers acquainted with the different communities and their needs. Lawyers and industrialists, not experts, decided whether to accept or reject requests for the allocation of reparation funds.

END BENEFICIARIES OF THE ALLOCATIONS

Communal leaders prioritized the reconstruction of West European Jewry, at the expense of compensation for past wrongs. Qualification for reparations depended on circumstances extraneous to the persecution suffered or physical and mental damages sustained by the victim. The determining factors included the applicant's geographic location and communal affiliation. The result was that only a minority of Holocaust survivors benefited directly from reparations paid to the Claims Conference pursuant to Protocol 2.

The system devised by the diaspora alliance favored those sectors with prior experience of applying for public funds. In the first five years of allocations, $992,283 went to *yeshivot* and rabbinical schools, compared to allocations of $222,246 to teachers' seminaries and $303,519 to adult education.[53] In addition, one group that posed a threat to the image of the Claims Conference and its members received a disproportionate share of the reparation funds. Members of the group were residents of the last displaced persons camp in Germany, located at *Föhrenwald*, who received $540,000 from the Claims Conference.[54] Recipients included individuals who had settled in Israel after the Second World War and returned to Germany in search of a better life. In the eyes of the JDC, the continued existence of the camp more than a decade after the end of the war amounted to a "complete failure in our efforts to solve the problem of the camp."[55] The allocation of reparation funds resolved the issue, both for the displaced persons and the JDC.[56] Other groups of victims, whether due to lack of familiarity with the system or because they concentrated all their efforts on rebuilding their lives and had no desire to look back, did not receive any compensation.

The policies devised by the organization resulted in the award of small sums to a large number of projects. So, for instance, in 1956, a representative of the French welfare organization, *Fonds Social Juif Unifié*, commenting on the allocation of Claims Conference funds to 140 projects, complained that

> sixty percent of the money had been spread over a series of very small projects. When these were examined more closely it would seem that they involved minor repairs or small material investments or equipment whereas the major projects . . . were only the small minority of these cases.[57]

Another example is the allocation of $65,000 for constructing, renovating, and equipping six centers in Italy.[58] Annual reports of the organizations contain long lists of institutions that received grants from the Claims Conference but no details on the size of the grants. This enabled the organization to state that the reparations benefited a large number of individuals.

CONCLUSION

Politics played a major role in the distribution of reparations by the Claims Conference in the years 1954 to 1964. Allocations were geared to meet the needs of member organizations and strengthen the alliance between them. To achieve this end, the organization prescribed loose rules and applied them arbitrarily. Moreover, policymakers and implementers lacked training and skills in the fields of administration, finance, and welfare work.

In 2009, top executives of the Claims Conference admitted the difficulty inherent in the allocation of funds by an organization. In their words, "Fighting and struggling for the money, however difficult, is far easier and more morally clear than when it comes to distribution, which becomes messier, harder, and uglier."[59] The statement contrasts with the picture presented in earlier annual reports and press releases. Nevertheless, the organization continued to distribute funds behind closed doors, with limited disclosure of its internal workings.

Questionable uses of reparations were not limited to the Claims Conference. In 1964, West Germany agreed to provide one million pounds to British victims of National Socialism. The British Foreign Office adopted a narrow definition of what constituted National Socialist persecution. On the basis of this definition, it rejected claims from former British prisoners of war including survivors of an escape attempt from the Sachsenhausen concentration camp. Politicians and journalists denounced the Foreign Office, and the Ombudsman subsequently published a damning report on "defects in the administrative procedure."[60] The lack of generally accepted criteria for the payment of reparations to individuals, together with damages far exceeding available resources, denied victims compensation both in the case of the Claims Conference and under the Anglo-German Agreement for Compensation to Victims of Nazism.

The actual workings of the allocation system, like those of other international agencies engaged in relief work in the aftermath of the Second World War, undermine the idea that rational norms and professional, impersonal considerations dictated governance. The operations of UNRRA exemplify the gap between theory and practice. At the outset, American policymakers intended to provide basic resources to war-torn countries. Subsequently, US Secretary of State Dean Acheson criticized UNRRA because the bulk of its supplies "went to the wrong places and were used for wrong purposes." Instead, he formulated a new system of priorities to "do the most good from the standpoint of promoting US security and national interest."[61] Both UNRRA and the Claims Conference illustrate the balance of power between the provider of funds and potential recipients. States and organizations determined who received public funds to further their own interests. Needy victims or individuals lacked influence or political power and therefore had no say in the matter.

NOTES

1. John W. Meyer and Brian Rowan, "Institutional Organizations: Formal Structures as Myth and Ceremony," *American Journal of Sociology* 83 (1977): 340; Gili S. Drori, John W. Meyer, and Hokyu Hwang, eds. *Globalization and Organization: World Society and Organizational Change* (Oxford: Oxford University Press, 2006), 15–16. For an example of how an organization acted to safeguard its autonomy see Michael Barnett and Liv Coleman, "Designing Police: Interpol and the Study of Change in International Organizations," *International Studies Quarterly* 49, no. 4 (2005): 593–619. https://www.jstor.org/stable/3693502.

2. Clavin, "International Organizations," 160.

3. Patricia Clavin, "The Role of International Organizations in Europeanization: The Case of the League of Nations and the European Economic Community," in Martin Conway and Kiran Patel, eds., *Europeanization in the Twentieth Century: Historical Approaches* (Basingstoke, Hampshire: Palgrave Macmillan, 2010), 110–131.

4. *Conference on Jewish Material Claims against Germany – Report 1954* (New York: The Organization, 1955), 8 and 92–93.

5. *Conference on Jewish Material Claims against Germany—Report 1955* (New York: The Organization, 1956), 16.

6. *Five Years Later: Activities of the Conference of Jewish Material Claims against Germany, 1954–1958* (New York: The Claims Conference, 1959), 70–75.

7. JDC 1954 Country Directors Conference, JDC Archive, Geneva, 1945–54, File Admin. 30, Film 006, slide 213, p. 2.

8. JDC 1954 Country Directors Conference, JDC Archive, Geneva, File Admin. 30, Film 006, slide 291, p. 80.

9. See "Grants Process," *Claims Conference*, n. d., accessed on March 10, 2020, http://www.claimscon.org/for-agencies/applications/process/.

10. Rose Melville, "Nonprofit Umbrella Organisations in a Contracting Regime: A Comparative Review of Australian, British and American Literature and Experiences," *The International Journal of Not-for-Profit Law* 1, no. 4 (1999): unnumbered pages.

11. Summary of Discussion of Claims Conference Board of Directors Meeting held on January 31, to February 1, 1960, in Amsterdam, AJCA, RG 347, Gen. 10, Box 286, Folder 2, p. 2.

12. The allocation procedures stated that rapporteurs for review of requests for financial assistance for relief, rehabilitation and resettlement would be appointed by the Claims Conference together with the JDC. The latter was the main beneficiary of these funds. See Claims Conference Executive Committee Minutes of June 2, 1953, CAHJP, Claims Conference File no. 16601a.

13. Claims Conference Board of Directors Meeting held on January 14, 1956, CAJHP, Claims Conference File no. 16604, transcript of tape 20, unnumbered pages.

14. Minutes of Claims Conference Executive Committee Meeting held on February 4, 1955, CAHJP, Claims Conference File no. 16601b, p. 14.

15. Minutes of Claims Conference Executive Committee Meeting held on February 4, 1955, CAHJP, Claims Conference File no. 16601b, p. 14.

16. Matter of Jewish Secondary Schools v. Conference of Jewish Material Claims 11 Misc. 2d. 358 (N.Y. Sup. Ct. 1958).

17. Revici v. Jewish Material Claims 11 Misc. 2d. 354 (N.Y. Sup. Ct. 1958).

18. Claims Conference Board of Directors Meeting held on October 11–12, 1958, CAHJP, Claims Conference File no. 16611, transcript of reel 1, p. 20 to reel 2, p. 1.

19. *Jewish Chronicle*, March 12, 1965, p. 24.

20. See Report of the Study Committee, September 1958, American Jewish Historical Society ("AJHS"), CJH, Conference on Jewish Material Claims Against Germany Collection 1955–1972, Call 1–319, Folder 4, p. 1.

21. Report of the Study Committee, September 1958, AJHS, CJH, Conference on Jewish Material Claims Against Germany Collection 1955–1972, Call 1–319, Folder 4, p. 2.

22. See *Conference on Jewish Material Claims against Germany; Annual Report 1954* (New York: The Claims Conference, 1954), 95.

23. Letter of Moses Beckelman to *Internationale Komitee für Jüdische KZ-ler und Flüchtlinge in Österreich*, dated November 19, 1953, in JDC Digitized Archives, Item #ID 2504697.

24. Claims Conference Board of Directors Meeting held on January 14, 1956, CAJHP, Claims Conference File no. 16604, transcript of tape 13, p. 127.

25. Rhoda E. Howard-Hassmann, "Getting to Reparations: Japanese Americans and African Americans," *Social Forces* 83, no. 2 (2004): 827. https://www.jstor.org/stable/3598349?seq=1.

26. These principles are set out in *the First Annual Report*, 92–93.

27. Minutes of Executive Committee Meeting of the Claims Conference held on June 23, 1953, CAHJP, Claims Conference File no. 16601a, 3–4.

28. Letter from Zachariah Shuster, AJC European Director to Dr. Eugene Hevesi – AJC, Paris Office dated November 20, 1953, AJCA, CJH, RG 347, Gen. 10, Box 287, Folder 5.

29. Report of Cultural Advisory Committee attached to a memorandum from Shapiro to the Executive Committee dated March 17, 1954, AJCA, CJH, RG 347, Gen. 10, Box 287, Folder 3.

30. JDC 1954 Country Directors Conference, JDC Archives, Collection Geneva 1945–54, File Admin. 30, Film 006, slide 508, p. 295.

31. Claims Conference Executive Meeting held on May 15, 1955, AJCA, CJH, RG 347, Gen. 10, Box 288, Folder 2.

32. Claims Conference Executive Meeting held on September 28, 1955, AJCA, CJH, RG 347, Gen. 10, Box 288, Folder 2.

33. All the figures in this paragraph and figure 6.1 are taken from *Twenty Years Later: Activities of the Conference of Jewish Material Claims against Germany, 1952-1972* (New York: The Claims Conference, 1973).

34. *Five Years Later*, 70.

35. *Twenty Years Later*, 119.

36. Claims Conference Executive Committee Meeting held on March 19, 1954, CAHJP, Claims Conference File no. 16601b.

37. Michael Belzer, "'I Don't Know Whom to Thank': The American Joint Distribution Committee's Secret Aid to Soviet Jewry," *Jewish Social Studies*, 15, no. 2 (2009): 112.

38. Zweig, *German Reparations*, 133 and Letter from Helen Fink to James Rice, JDC Geneva, dated December 1952, JDC Archive, Geneva, Microfilm 025, folders 232 to 244.

39. Discussion of the author with Director of JDC Global Archives on November 16, 2015.

40. *Conference on Jewish Material Claims against Germany – Annual Report 1955* (New York: The Claims Conference, 1956), 15.

41. *Conference on Jewish Material Claims against Germany – Annual Report 1963* (New York: The Organization, 1964), 21.

42. English translation of a letter from Mayer-Lindenburg of the West German Foreign Office to the Claims Conference dated May 8, 1964, [Foreign Office V2 – 84.04/2], JDC Digitized Archives, Item #ID 811922.

43. Claims Conference Board of Directors Meeting held on January 14, 1956, CAHJP, Claims Conference File no. 16604, p. 178–179. On the experiences of Jews of Morocco and Algeria under the Vichy government and Jews of Tunisia under German occupation see Michel Abitbol, *The Jews of North Africa during the Second World War*, trans. Tihanyi Zeitelis (Detroit: Wayne University State Press, 1989).

44. Claims Conference Board of Directors Meeting held on January 14, 1956, CAHJP, Claims Conference File no. 16604, pp. 178–179.

45. Claims Conference Summary of Board of Directors Meeting held on January 25–6, 1958 in Rome, AJCA, CJH, RG 347, Gen. 10, Box 286, Folder 1, p. 23.

46. Claims Conference Board of Directors Meeting held on January 14, 1956, CAHJP, Claims Conference File no. 16603, pp. 150–151.

47. Claims Conference Applications Committee Meeting held on February 3, 1955, CAHJP, Claims Conference File no. 16603, p. 14. Both this allocation and the award to *yeshivot* in the United States discussed above do not appear in the figures of reparation funds spent in different countries in *Twenty Years Later*.

48. See "Saul Kagan, Architect of Holocaust Restitution," *Claims Conference*, n. d., accessed on October 20, 2019, http://www.claimscon.org/about/history/saul-kagan/; "Saul Kagan, Who Won Holocaust Restitution, Is Dead at 91," *New York Times*, November 14, 2013, accessed on October 20, 2019, http://www.nytimes.com/2013/11/15/world/europe/saul-kagan-who-won-holocaust-restitution-is-dead-at-91.html. On the interval in Kagan's service with the Claims Conference see People v. Kagan, 56 N.Y. 2d 193 (N.Y. 1982).

49. Several directors of the Claims Conference, mainly representatives of the organizations of German Jews, had lived under the Third Reich, such as Hendrik George van Dam of the *Zentralrat*, who fled Germany in 1940. Gryn was a survivor of Auschwitz and Mauthausen and Baeck, leader of a member organization, was incarcerated in Theresienstadt.

50. Directors and officers of the Claims Conference who also served in the JRSO included Goldmann, Kagan, Blaustein, Leavitt, Lewin of the *Aguda*, Polier of the American Jewish Congress, Goldstein of the WJC, Janner, and Sir Henry d'Avigdor Goldsmid of the Anglo-Jewish Association. The names of directors of JRSO are listed in the organization's Annual Report for the year of November 1, 1953–November 1, 1954, AJCA, CJH, RG 347, Gen. 10, Box 291, Folder 9.

51. Zweig, "Reparations Made Me," 235.

52. See for example a memorandum sent by Kagan in his capacity of secretary of JRSO to the latter's Board of Directors on January 3, 1957, AJCA, CJH, RG 347, Gen. 10, Box 291, Folder 10.

53. See Report of the Study Committee, September 1958, AJHS, CJH, Conference on Jewish Material Claims Against Germany Collection 1955-1972, Call 1–319, Folder 4, Enclosure 4.

54. *Claims Conference Annual Report 1957* (New York: The Organization, 1958), 35.

55. JDC 1954 Country Directors Conference, JDC Archives, Geneva, File Admin. 30, Film 006, slide 369, p. 158.

56. On life in the *Föhrenwald* camp and the conflicts between the residents and relief organizations see Ronald Webster, "American Relief and Jews in Germany, 1945-1960: Diverging Perspectives," *Leo Baeck Institute Yearbook* 38 (1993): 308.

57. Summary of Proceedings of the Capital Investment Conference held on May 2–3, 1956, Hotel Royal Monceau Paris, American Jewish Historical Society,

Conference on Jewish Material Claims Against Germany Collection 1955–1972, Call 1-319, Folder 2, pp. 4–5.

58. *Claims Conference Annual Report 1960* (New York: The Organization, 1961), 31.

59. Gideon Taylor, Greg Schneider, Saul Kagan z"l and Karen Heilig, "The Claims Conference and the Historic Jewish Efforts for Holocaust-Related Compensation and Restitution," in Carla Ferstman and Mariana Goetz, eds., *Reparations for Victims of Genocide, War Crimes and Crimes against Humanity: Systems in Place and Systems in the Making*, 2nd rev. (Leiden: Nijhoff, 2020), 206.

60. Susan Schrafstetter, "'Gentlemen, the Cheese is All Gone!' British POWS, the 'Great Escape' and the Anglo-German Agreement for Compensation to Victims of Nazism," *Contemporary European History* 17, no. 1 (2008): 37.

61. Jessica Reinisch, "'Auntie UNRRA' at the Crossroads," *Past & Present* 218, suppl. 8 (2013): 89.

Chapter 7

Chief Spokesman for Reparations
A Non-State Actor in the World of International Relations

The Luxembourg Agreement was the first of many rounds of negotiations on reparations for victims of Hitler's war against the Jews. Different groups of survivors excluded from the original settlement sought at least a partial remedy for their losses. Germany repeatedly tried to limit its liability by enacting final legislation and performing last gestures but failed. Growing awareness of the injury to life and property of Holocaust survivors and research that substantiated and quantified the damages provided the grounds for new demands.

After the conclusion of the 1952 round of negotiations with West Germany, the Claims Conference became the principal advocate for Holocaust victims. Direct and open negotiations on reparations between an international nongovernmental organization and governments extended the limits of traditional diplomacy and Jewish internationalism. The term diplomacy is defined as the conduct by government officials of negotiations and other relations between nations.[1] The postwar generation of INGOs performed tasks formerly limited to states. Interactions between the Claims Conference and governments illustrate the workings of a "new public diplomacy," namely the conduct of foreign relations by non-state actors.[2] This chapter examines why the diaspora alliance represented a community seeking reparations and restitution. The diplomatic activities drew on earlier forms of transnational lobbying in the Jewish world but also differed from them in their scope and purpose.

WHY WAS THE CLAIMS CONFERENCE THE CHIEF PROTAGONIST ON COMPENSATION FOR HOLOCAUST VICTIMS?

Victims of Hitler's war against the Jews were citizens or residents of the countries where they lived prior to their deportation, incarceration, or murder. Yet none of these countries submitted claims on behalf of Jewish survivors, past or present citizens, and residents. After the Luxembourg Agreement, Israel ended its involvement in reparations. The Claims Conference filled a void in state-to-state relations. It sought and received reparations for a transnational community, namely Jewish victims of Germany and its allies.

ABSENCE OF A STATE PROTAGONIST FOR HOLOCAUST SURVIVORS

The Luxembourg Agreement set a precedent for the compensation of victims residing outside Germany. In general, individuals in Western Europe who suffered losses or injuries perpetrated by Germany during the Second World War applied to their governments. The governments in turn submitted claims to West Germany for reparations. Between 1958 and 1964, West Germany signed agreements with eleven countries (Norway, France, Greece, Luxembourg, the Netherlands, Belgium, Denmark, the United Kingdom, Italy, Sweden, and Switzerland) for the payment of lump sums to cover damage inflicted on their citizens. Under these agreements (collectively known in German as *Globalabkommen*), West Germany paid a total sum of DM 977 million.[3] The different countries determined criteria and provided medical treatment to their citizens and one-time awards for injuries and losses sustained. These agreements exemplified traditional interstate diplomacy.

The recipient states generally did not grant special compensation to Jewish victims in their legislation. In France, resistance fighters were eligible for the same benefits as veterans of the regular armed forces. Jewish survivors entered a lower category of political victims.[4] The British government prescribed two main criteria for the distribution of the small total sum of one million pounds awarded under the 1964 agreement with West Germany: detention in a concentration camp and acquisition of British citizenship before October 1, 1953. Only 1,015 applicants received payments averaging £985.[5] They included Jews—many from North Africa—and non-Jews, Special Operations Executive agents, and prisoners of war. Tens of thousands of Jewish victims from Austria and Eastern Europe who settled in the United Kingdom and had not been in concentration camps or were naturalized after 1953 (and were not eligible to payments under the BEG) did not receive any compensation.

Countries with large communities of Jewish survivors did not apply for reparations for their citizens. These included the United States and all the countries behind the Iron Curtain. Moreover, the agreements with West European countries recognized only part of the damages incurred and compensated a small minority of the victims. One example of losses not covered is unpaid forced labor. It was not until over fifty years after the end of the war that the German government recognized its liability and set up a foundation to compensate these victims.[6] In the first decades after the Luxembourg Agreement, Holocaust victims who were denied redress for their losses sought a spokesman.

ISRAEL AND HOLOCAUST SURVIVORS

Israel withdrew from its role as reparations advocate after the conclusion of the Luxembourg Agreement. The state came into existence after the Second World War, and Jewish Holocaust survivors were neither citizens nor residents of Palestine at the time of their persecution, except in a very small number of cases. Israeli demands for German compensation were limited to "global recompense for the cost of integration of [destitute Jewish] refugees." Israel made no claims for individual victims either during the negotiations on the Luxembourg Agreement or after its conclusion. Subsequently, it did not apply to other states in the name of survivors for redress of their damages.

The issue of compensation and pensions (*Renten*) was handled by the Office for Handling Personal Claims, a small division in the Ministry of Finance. This office was charged with ensuring the remittance to Israel of compensation and pensions awarded by West Germany to Israeli citizens.[7] The Israeli Foreign Ministry did not have a department that dealt with reparations for Holocaust survivors and did not lobby other perpetrator states for compensation.

The Israeli decision to end its involvement in claims for reparations in the global scene is perhaps surprising in view of the large number of Holocaust survivors who settled there.[8] Furthermore, the economically distressed state benefited from the payment of compensation to its citizens. In the existing literature, scholars do not question why the Claims Conference, instead of Israel, conducted contacts with West Germany and other countries on compensation for individual Jewish victims.

After the Luxembourg Agreement, Israeli politicians and diplomats took it for granted that the state had no role to play in seeking compensation for losses incurred by individuals. Victim associations applied to the Israeli Foreign Ministry for intervention on their behalf but all requests were turned down. Documents from the Ministry reiterated the official line that seeking compensation for victims was in the sole domain of the Claims Conference or other diaspora organizations. For example, in the context of the Austrian refusal to pay compensation to former citizens, the Israeli consul in Vienna stated that "our approach has always been to leave direct contacts to the Jewish organizations."[9] Similarly, the director of the Foreign Minister's office informed the Association of Jews from Austria that the Claims Conference was the most appropriate entity to handle claims for compensation against their former homeland.[10]

Not all officials accepted this non-interventionist approach. In 1958, the Foreign Ministry official Moshe Hess wrote in an internal confidential memo to his superior:

> The official position of the Ministry so far was that the State should not appear as a party to negotiations with the Austrians and the conduct of negotiations should be left to the Jewish organizations. An official statement of the Ministry's spokesman of August 8, 1952 admittedly says that "Israel will not demand reparations from Austria and will demand only restitution of heirless property and individual compensation." Even though this statement would certainly have allowed us to protect the rights of our citizens to compensation, no official step has been taken in this direction so far.
>
> The time has come to act on this matter. Otherwise there is a risk that Israeli citizens born in Austria will charge us of neglect and there is no moral justification for discriminating between Austrian Jews who suffered and were persecuted in the same way as German Jews.[11]

However, no change occurred in the official line and Israel continued to refrain from direct contacts with the governments of Austria or Germany on compensation for individual victims.

Israeli officials gave several reasons for their inaction. One explanation was the transnational nature of the claimants. The Israeli Foreign Ministry informed the Association of Jews from Austria that organizations were more suited to represent victims residing in Israel since they formed part of a larger group.[12] Similarly, in response to a question on the plight of Austrian victims denied compensation, Prime Minister Ben-Gurion said in a *Knesset* debate that the issue applied to all Jews who had lived in Austria before the war and not only Israeli citizens.[13] Another reason put forward at a meeting attended by officials of the Foreign Ministry, Finance Ministry, and representatives of victim associations was that "the signing of the reparations agreement met all claims of Israel against Germany and Austria."[14] In other words, the Luxembourg Agreement addressed outstanding issues between the parties and precluded any further claims. A third explanation was the reticence of legal advisers resulting from a narrow interpretation of international law. These advisers argued, on the basis of the prevailing approach, that only states that had participated in the Second World War were entitled to demand reparations. In an internal memo, the Israeli delegation to Vienna wrote that Israel could not deal directly with Austria since it had not signed a state treaty with the defeated country and therefore had no basis for a compensation claim.[15]

Official explanations do not provide a full picture of the motivations for Israeli resistance to act on behalf of individual victims of National Socialist persecution. The transnational nature of the victims and lack of participation in the war had not prevented the state from demanding and receiving compensation in the framework of the Luxembourg Agreement. In retrospect, it appears that the Israeli decision reflected both the attitude of the ruling Labor Party (*Mapai*) to immigrants and victims of the Holocaust as well as its complex foreign policy vis-à-vis West Germany.

Demands for individual compensation conflicted with the collective ethos that characterized Israeli society in its early years. The Israeli government called for the prioritization of public interests over private rights in light of the pressures facing the fledgling state. These included mass immigration, the need to secure borders, and an economic crisis including food and housing shortages. Prime Minister Ben-Gurion called on members of Israeli society, in particular elites, to bear responsibility for the well-being of other citizens including newly arrived immigrants from Eastern Europe and Muslim-majority countries.[16] In the words of the historian Orit Rozin, after the transition from *Yishuv* to state, the principle of collectivism became "the ethos and logos" of the government.[17] Efforts to obtain compensation for individual victims contradicted this principle. Accordingly, the government framed its demand for compensation for Nazi crimes in terms of strengthening the state that had provided a home for survivors and not as relief for injuries suffered by individuals. Prior to the commencement of negotiations with West Germany, Foreign Minister Sharett stated: "The Israeli government seeks reparations for itself since it views the state of Israel as bearer of the rights of the murdered millions [of Jews] and as entitled and required to avenge their honor since it is the sole sovereign embodiment of the people who were sentenced to extinction."[18]

Benefits to soldiers wounded in action are another example of the prioritization of members of the collective as opposed to victims of the Second World War. In a debate in the *Knesset* on the Disabled Victims of Nazi Persecution Bill, Finance Minister Levi Eshkol announced that the State Attorney had given an opinion concluding that in legal terms, the state was not required to compensate individuals who fought as members of armies or partisans against Germany.[19] Similarly, in response to demands from Jewish soldiers injured in the Second World War to be treated in the same manner as soldiers injured in the Israeli 1948 War, Ben-Gurion said: "I do not accept the claim for them [Second World War veterans] to be covered by the Independence War Disabled Law. Morally, they enter the same category of all disabled people. The state of Israel has no special responsibility toward them."[20]

Knesset members from the Communist and revisionist *Herut* parties submitted motions to compare the rights of combatants in the Second World War to those of the 1948 war. In a session on rehabilitation and payments to veterans of the 1948 War, MK Meir Vilner of the Israeli Communist Party attacked the government policy:

> Who are in fact the injured? They are new immigrants. What is the difference between a person who lost a leg in the war against Nazis in the Soviet army, or the French army, or any other army and those who lost their legs or hands or were injured in any other manner when fighting against the British army? We cannot continue with this situation of abusing anti-Fascist fighters.[21]

The ruling Labor Party rejected the motions on the grounds that veterans of the 1948 War were worthier of compensation than victims of the Third Reich.[22] Another example of this reasoning is the Israeli waiver of its citizens' right to German compensation for disability, which was introduced before the signing of the Luxembourg Agreement. Attempts to place distance between newly arrived survivors and native-born citizens offer an explanation for the lack of government action on behalf of individual victims.

The conflicting interests of the state and its citizens also created a need for a non-state actor. In the period between the reparations agreement and the establishment of diplomatic relations in 1965, Israel pursued a multifaceted policy on Germany. Officially, the state did not have any contact with West Germany, except in connection with the fulfillment of the Luxembourg Agreement. This position was formulated in response to widespread opposition from the Israeli public and media to ties with Germans. In 1953, MK Haim Landau of the *Herut* party described the docking of German ships in Israeli ports as "a disgrace following a disgrace," adding that even before approval of the Luxembourg Agreement by the *Bundestag*, Germany demanded its pound of flesh.[23]

In practice, German and Israeli officials held talks on foreign relations and security matters. In 1952, Adenauer proposed the establishment of diplomatic relations. Israel rejected the offer due to a fear of a public outcry.[24] Three years later, the Czech deal for the sale of Soviet weapons to Egypt prompted a change in Israeli policy.[25] Motivated by the desire to procure weapons from Western powers, Foreign Minister Sharett, with the prime minister's support, applied to West Germany for full diplomatic relations.[26] Both states tentatively examined the possibility of normalizing relations, commencing with the proposal for the establishment of a local liaison office (*Dienststelle*) in Tel Aviv. Cold War politics intervened, and West Germany reneged on its offer. Over the next decade, the Bonn administration's fear that a rapprochement with Israel would result in recognition of

East Germany by Arab states prevented open diplomatic relations between the two states.

During this period, both countries traded in arms. In 1955–1956, West Germany supplied two coastguard boats to Israel, and in 1959, Israel sold 35,000 Uzi submachine guns and 2,515,000 grenades of different types to West Germany.[27] Israeli foreign policy focused on issues directly connected to national security. In the eyes of the country's leaders, negotiations on behalf of citizens for acts committed prior to the establishment of the state took a backseat to obtaining weapons and allies for protection against hostile neighbors. The absence of Israeli diplomacy on behalf of Holocaust victims enabled the Claims Conference to operate in the international arena.

A thawing in the hard line taken by the Israeli government commenced sixty years after the end of the Second World War. The trigger was the plight of elderly impoverished victims, especially immigrants from the former Soviet Union after the fall of the Iron Curtain. These individuals did not receive reparations either from Germany or Israel. In response to public criticism, the *Knesset* adopted the Law on Benefits for Holocaust Survivors in 2007. The act granted financial benefits to citizens who were mainly from Eastern Europe. In January 2008, the government appointed a committee headed by a former Supreme Court judge, Dalia Dorner, to examine state assistance to survivors and the functioning of the Office for Handling Personal Claims.[28] The outcome was the creation of the Authority for Rights of Holocaust Survivors.[29] As the name suggests, the emphasis had moved from the state to individuals. The authority's mandate was to assist the remaining victims in reparations claims, to promote commemoration activities, and initiate welfare projects for survivors. In addition, the *Knesset* enacted an amendment matching the pensions paid by Israel to German pensions. In December 2018, 42,343 Israeli survivors received an average monthly pension of NIS 3,884 (approximately $1,131) pursuant to the Law for Persons Wounded in the War against the Nazis and the Law for Disabled Victims of Nazi Persecution. An additional 19,584 beneficiaries under the 2007 act received an average monthly pension of NIS 3,556 (approximately $1,035).[30] In 2009, following the signing of the non-binding Terezin Declaration calling for the restitution of property seized from Jews during the war, the Israeli Foreign Ministry appointed an official to oversee restitution and compensation for Holocaust victims. Still, to this day, the Claims Conference and not the Jewish state conducts negotiations with Germany on reparations for Holocaust survivors.

GERMANY AND THE CLAIMS CONFERENCE

The status of the Claims Conference as a nongovernmental organization with limited resources made it a more favorable negotiating partner for West

Germany. Clearly, representation of victims by an organization weakened its bargaining power and favored successors of the perpetrator states. This situation enabled countries that had participated in the persecution of Jews to contend that they were conducting negotiations on a voluntary basis and that any agreement they reached did not constitute a precedent for other groups of victims.

Delegating the task of distributing reparations intended for Jewish victims to a nongovernmental organization also promoted German interests. The payment of a lump sum to the Claims Conference fixed the price for the return of West Germany to the family of nations. Another advantage was that the organization, not the state, bore the handling costs involved in processing applications. Moreover, negative publicity following the rejection of claims was directed at the organization, not West Germany.[31] The alternative course of recognizing the eligibility of non-German victims to direct compensation would have greatly increased the state's exposure to claims of survivors persecuted and murdered throughout the territories administered by and in conjunction with Germany during the Second World War. In the aftermath of the Holocaust, it is hard to conceive how the Federal Republic could have drafted legislation for the sole benefit of Jewish victims outside Germany. Assigning to the Claims Conference the allocation of compensation prevented an open-ended undertaking to pay reparations to all Nazi victims.

The Claims Conference was eager and willing to conduct diplomacy with states on behalf of individual victim rights. Officers of the organization had the requisite skills. Goldmann and Robinson had studied law in Germany at the universities of Heidelberg and Jena, respectively. Kagan acquired experience working with German administrators during his service in the United States postwar military government in Berlin. Goldmann and Blaustein were accustomed to dealing with heads of states and governments.

Executives and member organizations of the Claims Conference were experts on the losses and injuries suffered by Jews in the many different countries that came under the control of Nazi Germany. In addition, they collected data on the massive plunder of Jewish property. They received information from organizations that worked closely with or were funded by the Claims Conference, including the JRSO and URO. The qualifications and expertise of Claims Conference leaders and lawyers, together with Goldmann's highly developed personal skills, provided the tools for negotiations on compensation and monitoring the implementation of German legislation on reparations and restitution.

DIPLOMATIC ACTIVITIES OF THE CLAIMS CONFERENCE

The Claims Conference continued to submit demands for survivors. It approached politicians and ministries on indemnification and restitution of property. Furthermore, it oversaw the handling of reparation claims and reported to policy-makers on the hurdles created by recalcitrant German bureaucrats resulting in the rejection of applications for compensation.

The Claims Conference lobbied West Germany for the adoption of the provisions listed in Protocol 1 to the Luxembourg Agreement by federal legislation. These amendments benefited individuals residing outside Germany. Led by lawyer Nehemiah Robinson, representatives of the organization met with German government officials and legislators and negotiated amendments to the state-drafted bill for the Federal Indemnification Law (BEG).[32] Subsequently, West Germany enacted the Federal Restitution Law (*Bundesrückerstattungsgesetz*, known as the "BRüG") in 1957. This legislation was intended to compensate victims including survivors residing outside Germany for household articles, personable valuables, and bank accounts confiscated in Germany and occupied countries.

After the enactment of the Federal Indemnification Law, the Claims Conference set up a legal committee to report on the deficiencies that prevented Jewish victims from obtaining redress for their losses. The committee criticized the short deadlines for filing claims, a low ceiling on total German expenditures, and narrow criteria for indemnification.[33] The organization's lobbying activities, together with those of other groups, led to the adoption of amendments to the BEG in 1956. The revised version included broader definitions of victims entitled to compensation. Deadline requirements for eligibility were extended to everyone who had arrived in West Germany by December 31, 1952 (compared to January 1, 1947, in the original BEG) and to all emigrants who had lived within the 1937 borders of the German Reich. Entitlement to a pension for damage to health began with a twenty-five percent reduction in earnings (compared to thirty percent in the original version), and the upper limits for damages to property and to professional and economic advancement were raised.[34] Another amendment was the extension of the notion of "damage to liberty" to include illegal activity (namely, life in hiding or under a false identity) under inhuman conditions and wearing the Star of David.[35] The organization also negotiated changes to the Federal Restitution Law. The amendments included a waiver of the requirement for proof of shipment to Germany of household furniture seized in Belgium, France, and Holland and the determination of a standard minimum settlement for every room emptied of its contents.[36]

In the next round of negotiations in the years 1964–1965, the Claims Conference demanded compensation for victims who departed Eastern Europe after 1953. They included individuals who left Hungary following the 1956 uprising and had been persecuted as Jews during the Second World War. Negotiators referred to this category of survivors as "late emigrants." In addition, the organization lobbied against the rigid approach adopted by the authorities that processed survivors' claims. One example was the method of proving a causal link between National Socialist persecution and ill health.

The BEG created a legal presumption that ill health suffered by former concentration camp inmates resulted from their incarceration. The authorities refused to apply this presumption to inmates of forced labor camps and ghettos.[37] The German government rejected these demands of the Claims Conference. However, behind-the-scenes contacts between Goldmann and Adenauer resulted in a compromise. A new law adopted in 1965, optimistically entitled the Final Compensation Law (*Bundesentschädigungsschlussgesetz*), provided a hardship fund of DM 1.2 billion for late emigrants who had been persecuted in the war and were in need.[38]

The flight of former victims of the Third Reich from Eastern Europe after 1967 prompted the third round of negotiations between the Claims Conference and West Germany. Israel's victory over its Arab neighbors led to a new wave of official antisemitism in the Soviet bloc. In the wake of the repression in Poland after March 1968, and in Czechoslovakia following the Prague Spring in August 1968, some 20,000 Jews crossed the Iron Curtain. West Germany proposed the release of part of the hardship fund created under the Final Compensation Law to aid resettlement of these refugees. Goldmann insisted on the award of new funds.[39] Eventually, after very protracted negotiations, West Germany adopted a "final indemnification gesture" (*Abschlussgeste der Wiedergutmachung*) in 1979. It allocated an additional sum of DM 440 million for the post-1965 emigrants to be paid over five years. The *Zentralrat* received DM 40 million to assist Jewish communities in Germany and the Claims Conference distributed the balance to post-1965 emigrants, this time according to guidelines prescribed by West Germany.

Another diplomatic task undertaken by the Claims Conference was monitoring the implementation of German legislation. The organization sent representatives to West Germany to review the handling of claims for compensation. In 1957, Robinson and two other lawyers paid a four-week visit to the state of North-Rhine Westphalia to witness the workings of the compensation office.[40] This office handled claims submitted by individuals residing outside Germany. The delegates reported on lengthy proceedings, narrow-minded decisions, and demands for proof that could not be obtained. In a later account of the processing of claims filed by victims of the Third Reich, the German historian Christian Pross described the authorities as a bureaucracy of "hairsplitters" and "quibblers" not subject to direct control by the parliament.[41] Goldmann transmitted the delegation's findings to the West German finance minister and chancellor.[42] The latter promised to intervene and provide funds, if necessary, to expedite the processing of claims.

The Claims Conference conducted negotiations with other states on restitution and compensation. It reached an agreement with the Austrian government in 1956 on the establishment of a $22 million relief fund for needy Austrian Jews living abroad. This fund was created in lieu of legislation on compensation to former citizens and residents. Austria based its refusal to award compensation on its alleged "first-victim" status.[43] The organization also lobbied Greece for use of reparations received from West Germany (under a global agreement) to compensate Jewish survivors. Following this intervention, the Greek government extended eligibility to cover individuals living in Greece at the time of persecution who subsequently migrated to other countries. This amendment benefited Jews who left Greece after the war.[44] Furthermore, the organization made demands to the Greek government for the assignment of Jewish heirless property to the local community. For this purpose, Blaustein conducted discussions with members of the Greek government.[45] In all these cases, representatives of the Claims Conference applied directly to foreign states instead of asking diplomats in their own countries to act on their behalf.

A NEW FORM OF NON-STATE DIPLOMACY

The Claims Conference presents a new model of transnational activism. Traditionally, two forms of cross-border cooperation existed: intergovernmental coalitions and private networks. One or more states created intergovernmental organizations (IGOs) to perform major projects requiring extensive diplomatic interaction between member countries. Examples include the International Monetary Fund, the World Health Organization, and UNRRA. Transnational entities established by individuals to promote an idea or provide information, INGOs, exercised "more of a consultative, knowledge-generating and sharing function."[46] Examples are networks of individuals from different countries who combined forces to promote agendas such as the release of political prisoners (Amnesty International) or environmental protection and diversity (Fauna and Flora International and Greenpeace). These nongovernmental initiatives lobbied for the adoption of a general policy worldwide.

The Claims Conference combined elements of both models. Created by one individual to represent a transnational community, it negotiated with governments, primarily that of West Germany, on an intensive and continuous basis. The object was to alter state behavior. The organization did not promote ideas or generate knowledge. Instead, it directed its efforts to reaching agreements and obtaining amendments to specific and detailed aspects of legislation and policies relating to victims of National Socialism. It also oversaw the implementation of state policies by bureaucrats and reported on their shortcomings. Few other non-domestic private entities conducted similar contacts with foreign states in the 1950s and 1960s. In the context of the Claims Conference, Swiss historian Regula Ludi wrote: "For the first time in modern history, actors representing victims and victimizers, and not states, engaged in direct talks. . . . This novelty eroded clear-cut international law divisions between states and non-state actors."[47]

The blurring of the distinction between states and an INGO occurred due to a lacuna in international law and a vacuum in international relations. Ludi ascribes the innovation to the transnational nature of the victims. Nazi policy targeted the "Jewish race" and treated them as if they were a nation of their own. International law did not recognize this classification and lacked the legal categories to frame the complaints of survivors.[48] This (not unsurmountable) lacuna was compounded by the absence of a state willing to serve as an advocate on behalf of its own former citizens, let alone the entire community of Holocaust victims. Each country had its own priorities and justifications for ignoring the special suffering of present and departed residents. The end result was the same—abandonment of the survivors. The Claims Conference assumed the role ceded by states and promoted the interests of these individuals, first in the West and after the fall of the Iron Curtain, worldwide.

A large part of the success of the Claims Conference is attributable to the special rapport between Goldmann and Adenauer. According to German historian Hockerts, the status of the Claims Conference far exceeded that of a pressure group. This was due to its ability to apply directly to Adenauer (without having to go through lengthy bureaucratic channels).[49] According to Jelinek:

> Adenauer took an immediate liking to Goldmann at their first meeting. Goldmann was known for his charm and brilliance as a negotiator, and understood how to handle his German hosts. For numerous Germans, and perhaps Adenauer himself, Goldmann was a figure representative of that nebulous entity called "world Jewry," that had been frequently feared and over vilified in Germany over many generations. In the framework of this "demonizing" conception of Jewry, Goldmann represented the positive side.[50]

Both men profited from their relationship. Goldmann acquired legitimacy as a spokesman on behalf of victims, inside and outside the Jewish community. Adenauer believed that his friendship with Goldmann would pave the way to acceptance of the successor state by the "international Jewish community." Adenauer's biographer explained:

> Adenauer gained the trust of the international Jewish community—in part for West Germany, but even more so for himself. This trust [of Goldmann] was to be of incalculable value. From now on, in the United States and everywhere

where opinion-formers in the Jewish community gathered together, Goldmann praised Adenauer and defended him against attack.[51]

The relationship between the two leaders contributed to the ability of the Claims Conference to fill an active role in international politics. For instance, following complaints about backlogs in processing claims, Goldmann conducted "a long talk with the Chancellor about some of the *Länder*," and the latter promised to increase the budget for administrative costs from $203 million per annum to $376 million.[52] In conclusion, advocacy by a non-state actor suited the needs of Israel, West Germany, and the Claims Conference.

CHANGES IN JEWISH TRANSNATIONAL ACTIVISM

In the Jewish world, bankers, businessmen, and networks had interceded in the past with leaders on behalf of coreligionists in the Russian, Austro-Hungarian, and Ottoman empires.[53] For instance, in the 1920s, the JDC negotiated with Soviet Russia on large-scale agricultural colonization in Crimea for destitute coreligionists and liaised between "highly ranked Bolsheviks and Herbert Hoover, the secretary of commerce."[54] The Claims Conference did not resemble other advocates on behalf of coreligionists in several aspects. The differences included the object of the intervention, the nature of operations, and activities alongside a sovereign Jewish state.

The focus of Claims Conference diplomacy contrasted with that of earlier and later forms of Jewish activism. Traditionally, individuals and organizations applied to states for the physical protection of coreligionists who were in danger. The arrest of Jews in Damascus by the Ottoman authorities on the charge of ritual murder of an Italian monk in 1840 marked the beginning of modern Jewish transnational activism.[55] The local Jewish community sent a letter to two prominent communal leaders in Constantinople. This letter paved the way for the intercession of Moses Montefiore, the British banker, Adolphe Crémieux, the French-Jewish lawyer and statesman, and members of the Rothschild family.[56] More recently, activists promoted human rights and freedom of movement, such as the Soviet Jewry movement of the 1960s–1980s.[57]

Operations of the Claims Conference (and the successor organizations) concentrated on the material rights of victims of persecution. The generation of organizations set up in the aftermath of the Holocaust negotiated with governments not only for the provision of a better future for victims but also looked backward and claimed monetary redress for past crimes. These activities were unprecedented. The systematic plunder and murder of Jews by a modern, wealthy state offers a possible explanation for this change in the object of transnational activism.

The manner of operations of the Claims Conference also differed from more traditional cross-border activism in the Jewish world. Previously, individuals and organizations lobbied and liaised, frequently behind the scenes on an informal basis. Contrary to the *Alliance* or the JDC, the Claims Conference appealed directly to leaders and governments with demands for compensation. The organization negotiated openly with legislators and administrators on changes to official state policy. This new modus operandi reflected the growing legitimacy of international organizations in global politics as well as the strength of the claims made on behalf of victims of crimes without a parallel.

Another difference between the Claims Conference and previous forms of Jewish transnational activism was the mutual adjustment between diaspora organizations and Israel. In the pre-1948 era, relations between Zionist and non-Zionist activists were characterized by discord and competition. Zionist organizations and leaders concentrated their efforts on rallying support for an internationally recognized sovereign state and viewed resources invested in improving the lives of Jews in the diaspora as a waste.[58] Disputes between organizations committed or opposed to the continued existence of a diaspora undermined attempts to create a broad alliance for the promotion of minority rights after the First World War. Friction between the two camps continued in the first years after the creation of the state of Israel. Even after reaching an understanding with Ben-Gurion, Blaustein continued to criticize Israeli leaders. For instance, he opposed granting the WZO or the Jewish Agency special status either in Israel or in the diaspora.[59]

After the signing of the Luxembourg Agreement, Israel and the Claims Conference developed a working relationship. Israeli officials consulted the Claims Conference regularly on issues relating to compensation and reparations and acted as an intermediary between local associations of victims and officers of the transnational organization. One example is a meeting held by the Central Committee of Jews from Austria in Israel with government officials in 1958 on the Austrian refusal to pay compensation. The meeting ended with a resolution of the Israeli government to inform the Claims Conference of its concern regarding this matter.[60] In the following year, in the context of the delay in obtaining compensation for individual victims from Austria, the Foreign Ministry explained the need to refer the matter to the organization:

> The Foreign Ministry has neither the ability or tools—or authority—in these fields. All aspects of the problem should be discussed in close coordination with the Claims Conference since only with their help will we obtain full representation of the community of claimants not represented by the different associations operating separately in Israel.[61]

Coordination of activities between the Israeli Foreign Ministry and the Claims Conference reflected a shift in Israeli policy toward diaspora organizations. Cooperation between the state and an organization dedicated to the reconstruction and perpetuation of Jewish life outside Israel replaced the former altercations over calls for the ingathering of exiles. There is no explanation for this change, either in official state documents or biographies of the individuals involved. One possible cause was the establishment of two mechanisms by the Luxembourg Agreement for the distribution of reparations. Another factor was the appreciation of both sides of the advantages of diplomacy by a non-state actor.

The separation between funds provided for use inside and outside Israel reduced tensions. Before the Second World War, rivalries frequently arose between Zionists and non-Zionists over the division of communal funds. In the 1920s Zionists criticized the allocation of funds by the JDC to Jewish colonies in Crimea. In their view, money for Palestine was squandered on the Agro-Joint project.[62] The distinction between the reparations for Israel and the diaspora removed a potentially divisive factor. The only exception to the principle of the division of funds was the allocation of funds by the Claims Conference to *Yad Vashem*, a museum located in Israel. Under an agreement made with the *Yad Vashem* Authority in 1954, the organization undertook to contribute up to fifty percent of total expenditures for the construction of a building in Jerusalem and a research and publications center to perpetuate the memory of Holocaust victims.[63] The organization paid over $2 million (equivalent to $17 million today) to *Yad Vashem* out of the reparations between 1954 and 1964.[64]

The passage of time as well as mutual needs also contributed to improved relations between the state and non-Zionist diaspora leaders. By 1953, experience acquired in the first years after the establishment of the state helped allay fears of American communal leaders regarding a potential clash between their duties to the United States and Israel. Moreover, the coordination of actions in the field of compensation for victims served both sides. Negotiations by the Claims Conference benefited Israel and its citizens. According to one estimate, from 1954 to 1959, Israeli citizens received in aggregate, over $250 million in individual compensation following negotiations conducted by the Claims Conference. The state also received much needed foreign currency. In the year 1959 alone, German payments to victims in Israel constituted 17.5 percent of the total foreign currency budget of the state.[65] The government required all citizens to convert German payments into local currency at an unfavorable rate and used the foreign currency for state needs. The decision to assign the conduct of negotiations to an organization enabled Israel to direct its diplomatic efforts to reinforcing the new state. The Claims Conference also gained from the harmonious relationship. Israeli recognition of the organization's status as chief representative of individual victims reinforced its legitimacy and enabled officers to negotiate with heads of state and top-level officials.

CONCLUSION

In the early 1950s, the Claims Conference presented a new model of participation in the world of foreign relations. At the time, the conduct of diplomatic activities by a non-state actor constituted an anomaly. This case illustrates the strengths and weaknesses inherent in this form of diplomacy. A group of individuals joined by past persecution and dispersed across continents benefited from an advocate on their behalf in the international arena.

Diplomatic success depended on a wide range of factors. These included the relative strengths of the negotiating parties, the willingness of perpetrators to recognize wrongs committed by them in the past, and their consent to provide redress for damage caused to former citizens and residents. The main achievements of the Claims Conference in the first decades after the Holocaust resulted from negotiations with politicians and administrators in West Germany. In Austria, a country that outdid Germany in the early persecution of Jews, efforts of the organization led to the creation of a very small fund for needy survivors. The Iron Curtain marked the border of the diplomatic activities of the Claims Conference. Consequently, it did not negotiate with countries in the Soviet bloc, such as East Germany and Poland.

The relative success of the Claims Conference in its dealings with West Germany (and lack of headway with other countries) reflects the importance of personal relations in the world of diplomacy. As stated above in the context of the negotiations on reparations, Goldmann and Adenauer were in close contact and held each other in high esteem. Their close relationship assisted not only in the conclusion of an agreement on reparations but also to narrow gaps in federal legislation and to expedite protracted processing of claims by German authorities. Comparing the organization's achievements in the different countries suggests that personal relations played a larger role in diplomacy than the breadth or strength of the alliance, or the non-state actor.

NOTES

1. See "Diplomacy." *Dictionary.com*, accessed on October 20, 2019, http://www.dictionary.com/browse/diplomacy?s=t.
2. Teresa La Porte, "The Impact of 'Intermestic' Non-State Actors on the Conceptual Framework of Public Diplomacy," *The Hague Journal of Diplomacy* 7 (2012): 443.

3. Schwerin, "German Compensation," 511. According to Hockerts, the total sum was DM 876 million. See Hockerts, "Wiedergutmachung in Deutschland," 192.

4. Ludi, "The Vectors of Postwar Victim Reparations," 445.

5. Susan Schrafstetter, "Gentlemen, the Cheese is All Gone!" 31.

6. On the limited success of victims' claims in the first decades after the war, see Benjamin B. Ferencz, *Less than Slaves: Jewish Forced Labor and the Quest for Compensation* (Cambridge, MA: Harvard University Press, 1979).

7. Katz, *The Forsaken,* 155.

8. According to one estimate, one quarter of the total number of survivors lived in Israel in the first decades after the war. See Shinnar, *Be-Ol Korach U-Regashot,* 75.

9. Internal memorandum from S. Bentsur, Israeli Delegation in Vienna to the Western European Division of the Israeli Foreign Ministry of March 17, 1958, [translation], file on Austria-Personal Compensation, Israel State Archives ("ISA"), HZ- File 3093/17 (hereinafter "File HZ- 3093/17").

10. Letter from M. Gazit of the Israeli Foreign Ministry to the Association of Jews from Austria of September 9, 1959, [translation], ISA, File HZ-3093/17.

11. Confidential memo from Moshe Hess to M. Fischer, deputy director general of the Foreign Ministry of August 28, 1958 [translation], ISA, File HZ-3093/17.

12. See the letter from M. Gazit of the Israeli Foreign Ministry to the Association of Jews from Austria of September 9, 1959, ISA, HZ-File 3093/17.

13. See draft response to the question raised in the *Knesset* (question 892) in ISA, File HZ-3093/17.

14. Summary of a meeting between representatives of the Central Council of Jews from Austria and representatives of the Israeli Finance and Foreign Ministries on Individual Compensation held on September 7, 1958, ISA, File HZ-3093/17.

15. Internal memorandum from S. Bentsur, Israeli Delegation in Vienna to the Western European Division of the Israeli Foreign Ministry of March 17, 1958, [translation], ISA, File HZ-3093/17.

16. Nir Keidar, *Mamlachtiut: HaTefisa HaEzrahit shel David Ben-Gurion (Nationalism: David Ben Gurion's Civil Perception)* (Jerusalem: Ben-Gurion-Institute for Israel Studies and Yad Ben Zvi, 2009), 179.

17. Orit Rozin, *Hovat HaAhava Hakasha: Yahid VeKollektiv BeYisrael Bishnot Hahamishim (The Hard Duty to Love: Individual and Collective in Israel in the 1950s)* (Tel Aviv: Institute for Research of Zionism and Israel, 2008), 11.

18. Session 237 of the First *Knesset* held on March 13, 1951, *Divrei Haknesset,* 8 (January–April 1951): 1320. On the complex relations between veterans and newcomers see *Rozin, Hovat HaAhava HaKasha,* 245.

19. Session 213 of the Third *Knesset* held on December 31, 1956, *Divrei Haknesset,* 21 (October 1956–February 1957): 600.

20. Cited in Hanna Jablonka, "Klitat Nitsolei HaShoah BeMedinat Israel – Heibetim Hadashim," (Absorption of Holocaust Survivors in the State of Israel – New Aspects) *Iyunim Betekumat Israel,* 7 (1997): 293.

21. Session 162 of the Second *Knesset* held on December 30, 1952, *Divrei HaKnesset,* 13, (November 1952–March 1953): 375.

22. See, for instance *Knesset* Session 378 of the Second *Knesset* held on February 22, 1954, *Divrei HaKnesset*,15 (November 1953–April 1954): 953 and *Knesset* Session 396 of the Third *Knesset* held on December 31, 1956, *Divrei HaKnesset*, 21 (October 1956–February 1957): 610.

23. Session 201 of the Second *Knesset* held on March 4, 1953, *Divrei HaKnesset*, 13 (November 1952–March 1953): 863.

24. Asher Ben Natan, "HaDerech LeKinoon Hayahasim: HaHebet HaYisraeli," (The Path to the Establishment of Relations: The Israeli Aspect) in Zimmermann and Heilbronner, *Yahasim "Normaliim": Yahasei Israel-Germania*, 24.

25. Roni Stauber, "Israel's Quest for Diplomatic Relations – The German-Israeli Controversy, " *Tel Aviver Jahrbuch für deutsche Geschichte* 41 (2013): 21.

26. See memo from Israeli Foreign Ministry in Jerusalem (Y. Ilsar) to director of West European Division of May 22, 1956, in Baruch Gilead, ed., *State of Israel, ISA, Documents on the Foreign Policy of Israel, Companion*, vol. 11, *Jan–Oct 1956* (Jerusalem: Government Printer, 2008) (hereinafter *Documents on the Foreign Policy of Israel*), Document 259.

27. Shay Hazkani, "Kalon o Hechreach Bal-Yegune? Iskat Haneshek HaIsraelit-HaGermanit HaRishona" (Disgrace or Unavoidable Necessity? The First Israeli-German Arms Deal). *Zmanim* 102 (2008): 102, 111.

28. *Report of the State Public Inquiry on Aid to Holocaust Survivors* (in Hebrew), *Israel Government website, June 2008,* accessed on October 20, 2019, https://www.gov.il/BlobFolder/generalpage/official_inquiry_committees_holocaust_survivors/he/%D7%95%D7%A2%D7%93%D7%AA%20%D7%94%D7%97%D7%A7%D7%99%D7%A8%D7%94%20%D7%94%D7%9E%D7%9E%D7%9C%D7%9B%D7%AA%D7%99%D7%AA%20%D7%91%D7%A0%D7%95%D7%A9%D7%90%20%D7%94%D7%A1%D7%99%D7%95%D7%A2%20%D7%9C%D7%A0%D7%99%D7%A6%D7%95%D7%9C%D7%99%20%D7%94%D7%A9%D7%95%D7%90%D7%94.pdf.

29. Israeli government decision 4252 dated February 12, 2012.

30. The figures were provided by the Authority for Rights of Holocaust Survivors in response to a request under the Israeli Freedom of Information Law, 1998.

31. An example of this negative publicity is Finkelstein's *The Holocaust Industry*.

32. See chap. 3, p. 69.

33. Claims Conference Executive Committee Meeting, held on October 5, 1954, CAHJP, Claims Conference file 16601b.

34. Pross, *Paying for the Past*, 50.

35. Robinson, *Ten Years of German Indemnification*, 29.

36. *Conference on Jewish Material Claims against Germany – Annual Report 1961* (New York: The Organization, 1962) (hereinafter *the 1961 Annual Report*), 180.

37. Letter from Ernst Katzenstein to Saul Kagan dated May 7, 1963, CZA - NG Archive, Z6\2024.

38. Pross, *Paying for the Past*, 65.

39. Carole Fink, "Negotiations after Negotiations: Nahum Goldmann, West Germany and the Origins of the 1980 Hardship Fund," *Jahrbuch des Simon Dubnow Instituts* 15 (2016): 287–305.

40. Boris Spernol and Matthias Langrock, "Amtliche Wirklichkeit: Die Praxis der Entschädigung aus behördlicher Binnenperspektive," (Bureaucratic Reality: The Practice of Compensation from Official Internal Perspectives) in *Die Praxis der Wiedergutmachung: Geschichte, Erfahrung und Wirkung in Deutschland und Israel*, 600.

41. Pross, *Paying for the Past*, 47. See also a good (but much later) example of the approach of German authorities to Holocaust survivors given by Susan Slymovics who described the 1999 rejection of her mother's application for a German pension on the grounds that when incarcerated in Auschwitz and the concentration camp Markkleeberg, she had not deposited payments in a German pension fund. Susan Slymovics, *How to Accept Reparations* (Philadelphia: University of Pennsylvania Press, 2014), 3–4.

42. Claims Conference Executive Committee Meeting held on May 22, 1958, CAHJP, Claims Conference file 16601b.

43. Israeli Foreign Ministry internal memo in *Documents on the Foreign Policy of Israel*, vol. 13, *1958–1959*, Document 253.

44. *The 1961 Annual Report*, 186.

45. See the discussion of Claims Conference Executive Committee Meeting held on May 22, 1958, CAHJP, Claims Conference file, 16601b.

46. Geoffrey Allen Pigman, "Making Room at the Negotiating Table: The Growth of Diplomacy between Nation-State Governments and Non-State Economic Entities," *Diplomacy and Statecraft* 16 (2005): 388.

47. Ludi, *Reparations for Nazi Victims in Postwar Europe*, 113.

48. Ludi, "The Vectors of Postwar Victim Reparations," 429.

49. Hockerts, "Wiedergutmachung in Deutschland," 181.

50. Jelinek, "Political Acumen," 96.

51. Hans-Peter Schwarz, *Konrad Adenauer: A German Politician and Statesman in a Period of War, Revolution and Reconstruction*, trans. Louise Willmot, vol. 1, *From the German Empire to the Federal Republic, 1876–1952* (Providence and Oxford: Berghahn Books, 1995), 647.

52. Claims Conference Board of Directors Meeting held on January 19–20, 1957, CAHJP, Claims Conference File 16606.

53. On traditional Jewish activism see Dekel-Chen, "Philanthropy, Diplomacy, and Jewish Internationalism," 505–510; Eli Lederhendler, "Shtadlanut and Stewardship: Paternal Diplomacy and Leadership in American Jewry, 1860s to 1920s," *Jewish Culture and History* 19, no. 1 (2018): 97–110.

54. Dekel-Chen, "An Unlikely Triangle," 359.

55. For details of the Damascus Affair and its impact on the development of Jewish transnationalism see Jonathan Frankel, *The Damascus Affair: "Ritual Murder," Politics and the Jews in 1840* (Cambridge: Cambridge University Press, 1997).

56. On the origins of Jewish transnational activism see Abigail Green, "Old Networks, New Connections: The Emergence of the Jewish International," in Abigail Green and Vincent Viaene, eds., *Religious Internationals in the Modern World: Globalization and Faith Communities since 1750* (UK: Palgrave Macmillan, 2012), 53–81.

57. Stuart Altshuler, *From Exodus to Freedom: A History of the Soviet Jewry Movement* (Lanham, MD: Rowman & Littlefield Publishers, 2005), 50.

58. Dekel-Chen, "Philanthropy, Diplomacy, and Jewish Internationalism," 518.

59. Chap. 4, p. 87.

60. Summary of a meeting between Israeli Finance and Foreign Ministries and Central Committee of Jews from Austria in Israel held on September 7, 1958, ISA, File Foreign 3093–17.

61. Letter from the Foreign Ministry to the Office for Personal Compensation from Abroad in the Finance Ministry, dated August 23, 1959, ISA, File HZ-3093/17.

62. Dekel-Chen, *Farming the Red Land*, 73.

63. A draft of the unsigned agreement appears in Claims Conference File no. 16601b.

64. Summary of Annual Budgets of the Claims Conference 1954–1964, CAHJP, Claims Conference File no. 17500.

65. Letter from Association of Recipients of Pensions and Compensation, Tel Aviv District to Levi Eshkol, Minister of Finance dated October 28, 1960, in File on Israel Foreign Representative Offices—Personal Compensation from Abroad, ISA, GL-5990/5.

Conclusion

Millions of women, men, and children were the victims of gross violations of human rights in the twentieth century. One of the earliest state-inflicted atrocities was the Turkish massacre and exile of Armenians from 1915 to 1917. Stalin was a central player in many of the century's violations, including the famine he instigated in Ukraine in the years 1932–1933, incarceration and forced labor in gulags, purges and forcible transfers of entire populations. The century ended with the murder of Muslims and Croatians in the Bosnian wars and the Rwandan slaughter of over half a million Tutsis. The Holocaust overshadowed all other crimes due to the number of victims involved and the planning and execution of mass and industrialized murder by men from one of the richest and most developed countries in the world. Moreover, the breadth of active and passive complicity in the Holocaust distinguished it from earlier and later atrocities.

Only a very small proportion of the century's victims received compensation for their suffering. Recognition by states of wrongdoings against their own citizens or residents of other countries was and still is extremely limited. Victims had to rely on the willingness and capacity of the perpetrator state to provide any sort of justice. Consent to pay reparations was frequently motivated by a state's desire to improve its standing among nations. In other words, reparations for victims were a means to an end, not a recognition of liability for past crimes.

The increasing visibility of gross violations of human rights, together with demands of victims for justice, created new standards of accountability. In 2005, the United Nations General Assembly adopted the Basic Principles and Guidelines on the Right to a Remedy and Reparation for Victims of Gross Violations of International Human Rights Law and Serious Violations of International Humanitarian Law.[1] According to these principles, redressing serious harm suffered by victims is now both a moral and legal imperative for states.² Nevertheless, payment of reparations to individual victims of state-inflicted serious violations of human rights remains the exception, not the rule.

GERMAN REPARATIONS FOR HOLOCAUST SURVIVORS

In the first decades after the Second World War, a small group of Holocaust survivors received reparations from West Germany. Protocol 1 to the Luxembourg Agreement negotiated by the Claims Conference benefited a minority of the victims of National Socialism. The *Bundestag* enacted legislation on reparations and restitution. Jewish beneficiaries mainly originated in Germany or lived in West Germany after 1953. They included Meta Doran. In her testimony, she described how she sued the German government "for some of the reparations that were coming to me ... I was fairly successful. I got some money from the Germans."³ The compensation did not cover the value of her father's confiscated business, jewelry owned by the family, or, more importantly, the loss of her parents and childhood.

The vast majority of Holocaust survivors received nothing for over four decades. East Germany rejected all claims for compensation both at the time of negotiations on the Luxembourg Agreement and subsequently throughout its existence. West Germany did not actively seek a solution for Jewish victims.⁴ The Bonn government made every effort to limit its liability by prescribing narrowly defined categories for eligibility, short deadlines, and onerous burdens of proof. Austria flaunted its false first victim status. As a result, Holocaust survivors from Austria and Eastern Europe did not qualify for compensation.⁵ Nor did Jewish and non-Jewish slave laborers.

The fall of the Iron Curtain in 1989 and German reunification altered the scope of Holocaust victims entitled to reparations. Article II of an agreement between West Germany and East Germany on the implementation of the unification treaty clarified that the federal government would negotiate new funds for victims who had received no compensation or insignificant sums.⁶ The basis was no longer plundered property but instead, bodily damage and suffering . Accordingly, in 1992, Germany established a fund (the Article II Fund), administered by the Claims Conference. The Article II Fund granted a pension to survivors in the West who had been confined in a concentration camp or ghetto during the Holocaust. Eligibility was contingent upon having an income that was less than a given threshold and not receiving compensation under German or Israeli legislation.

Victims of the German program of extermination by labor (*Vernichtung durch Arbeit*) as well as forced laborers were one of the last groups to receive compensation. At the end of the millennium, American lawyers filed class actions in the United States against *Ford Werke* and other German businesses. The lawyers, together with the Claims Conference and Central and East European states, demanded a comprehensive settlement for all forced laborers. The United States government backed up the claims by threatening to impose sanctions and introduce legislation.[7] The outcome was the establishment of a new fund, the Remembrance, Responsibility and Future Foundation (*Stiftung Erinnerung, Verantwortung und Zukunft* known as the "EVZ") in 2000. The object was to make small one-time payments to Jews and non-Jews forced to work without pay and in inhumane conditions by and for the Third Reich.[8] In the case of Jewish former slaves, it was the Claims Conference that determined eligibility and distributed the payments. German chancellor Gerhard Schröder declared that the establishment of this Foundation would close the last chapter of the Nazi past.[9]

Over the years (and contrary to Schröder's declaration), the Claims Conference negotiated changes to the terms of eligibility in order to extend the payment of a pension to remaining impoverished survivors. In April 2020, 38,505 survivors in this category received monthly pensions from funds provided by Germany and administered by the Claims Conference. They included 14,054 recipients residing in Israel, 7,645 residents of France, and 7,604 individuals in the United States. Germany set up a parallel fund (the Central and Eastern European Fund) in 1998 for survivors residing in Eastern Europe. In April 2020, 11,459 Jewish survivors received a pension from this fund, including 4,925 recipients in Hungary and 2,083 in Ukraine. The monthly pension for both categories amounted to €513.[10] In addition, from 2010 onward, the terms of eligibility of the Hardship Fund were extended to provide one-time payments to Jews from North Africa (Tunisia, Morocco, and Algeria) who suffered a restriction of liberty during the Second World War.[11]

Eastern European countries followed the example of the Claims Conference. They demanded compensation for their (non-Jewish) citizens persecuted by Germany during the war. This pressure led to the establishment of five Reconciliatory Funds (*Versöhnungsstiftungen*) that made small "humanitarian payments" to the most severely damaged victims, but excluded forced laborers.

The end of the Cold War and the extension of the scope of German reparations prompted action by other countries that previously refused to pay compensation. In 1995, Japan set up a fund to address its moral responsibility to women from Korea, Singapore, Vietnam, and other countries in Asia, where they were abducted by Japanese occupying forces and held in military sex slave camps during the Second World War (as "comfort women").[12] Three years later, the United States paid compensation to Japanese Americans for their incarceration under the Civil Liberties Act of 1998. Austria belatedly paid small sums to victims as a "voluntary gesture" pursuant to its 2000 Reconciliation Fund Law.[13]

The question of how the reparations impacted the lives of survivors remains open. Literature on the subject is limited, possibly because of the questions of privacy and confidentiality involved. One study of the receipt of reparations is the 2014 book *How to Accept Reparations* by Susan Slymovics. If and when the Claims Conference and the JDC make available to the public files submitted by individuals for allocations, it will be possible to research this issue in depth. Oral testimonies may also illuminate the changes that reparations have made in the lives of survivors. Another direction for future research is the restitution of Jewish property plundered or confiscated by Germany, neutral countries, and the Allies during the Second World War. A decade after the 2009 Terezin Declaration, the US Department of State published the Justice for Uncompensated Survivors Today (JUST) Act Report.[14] This report provides a starting point for further research. It also draws attention to the undertaking included in the Terezin Declaration for the contracting parties to provide access "to the fullest extent possible" to relevant archives.[15] Comparing the treatment (or lack of treatment) by different governments of restitution of confiscated property based on archival material will contribute to a greater understanding of transitional justice.[16]

PROTAGONIST FOR A COMMUNITY

The Claims Conference played a critical role in the campaign for reparations. This non-state actor mediated between victims and former perpetrators, negotiating agreements and financing welfare programs worldwide. Its dealings with states impinged upon the lives of millions of individuals across the globe.

Representation of a transnational community by a non-state actor provided the only means of demanding compensation for Holocaust survivors. International law viewed reparations as "essentially a bilateral matter between the responsible and the injured states."[17] However, Hitler's war against the Jews ignored national borders. Instead, Germany persecuted non-Aryans wherever they were situated and treated them as a separate nation, regardless of their citizenship. Countries where the survivors lived after the war refused to recognize the difference between policies aimed at Jews and non-Jews in territories recently occupied by Germany. No other country volunteered to represent its own present and former citizens who were singled out and persecuted by the Third Reich in their claim for compensation. Israel, a state that did not exist at the time of the atrocities, was struggling to stabilize itself in a hostile region, while facing the challenge of absorbing large numbers of new immigrants. Israeli politicians avoided open, direct contact with Germans for fear of a public outcry. Furthermore, Prime Minister Ben-Gurion and his government viewed reparations in utilitarian terms, as a means of meeting national, not private, ends.

States played an active but unwitting role in the formation of the Claims Conference. Israel's demand for a monopoly of all claims on behalf of Jewish victims of the Third Reich backfired. The German call to negotiate with world Jewry and Israel strengthened the desire of diaspora leaders for separate representation. Chancellor Adenauer's call was motivated by an "exaggerated notion of the power of Jews in the United States."[18] The helplessness of Jews during the twelve-year reign of the Third Reich did not alter this notion. Adenauer believed that connections between Jewish communal leaders and the US State Department would accelerate the restoration of the status of Germany as a world leader. German officials also hoped that the formation of a single entity speaking in the name of the entire collective would expedite a financial reckoning for the past.

The establishment of the Claims Conference attests to the resourcefulness of its founders. Following the failure of Jewish demands in the immediate aftermath of the war, Goldmann and his colleagues, all veterans of communal politics and leaders of organizations, stepped in to fill the void. They set up two committees to negotiate in the name of diaspora organizations and individual victims. The founders' conviction of the justice of their claims and their right to pursue them on the international stage provided the basis for the creation of this self-governing entity.

The Claims Conference focused on one issue, namely redress for Nazi victims. Its negotiators, experts on German law and practices, drafted Protocol 1 to the Luxembourg Agreement. This document laid the foundation for federal compensation of Nazi victims, both Jews and non-Jews. It included provisions that went far beyond those prescribed by the Western Allies during the occupation of Germany.[19] Pursuant to the protocol, West Germany enacted the Federal Indemnification Law (BEG) in 1953 and amended it in 1956 in response to demands made by the Claims Conference. The legislation benefited both members and non-members of the community represented by the Claims Conference. Around one million victims received compensation under the BEG totaling approximately DM 80 billion (approximately $50 billion in nominal terms). Eighty percent of the compensation went to claimants abroad, half of them in Israel.[20] Subsequently, the Claims Conference lobbied for the extension of compensation to other groups of victims not eligible under the BEG.

A NEW MODEL OF AN INTERNATIONAL ORGANIZATION

The Claims Conference was a product of the postwar transnational revolution in world politics. Goldmann used the structure of the institutions created by states and individuals as a model for his new advocacy group. He invited members from a wide range of countries to join the alliance. Americans dominated the Claims Conference, both in executive positions and on the various committees. Moreover, the Claims Conference was incorporated in New York and operated from its offices in Manhattan. These similarities to transnational organizations outside the Jewish world enhanced the legitimacy of the new entity and strengthened the leadership status of its officers. The fact that no other individual or association set up a competing body claiming to speak on behalf of Jewish victims and survivors worldwide until the end of the Cold War is evidence of the success of the structure. Only organizations of Jews in Germany and from Germany, the *Zentralrat* and the Council of Jews from Germany, contested the leadership of the Claims Conference. They were, however, much weaker than the broad alliance and did not have Goldmann's diplomatic skills.

Lobbying states for the payment of reparations to a community was a novelty in international relations. The transnational alliance did not limit its activities to gathering and disseminating information. Instead, it concluded agreements with sovereign states, supervised the implementation of amendments to German federal legislation for the benefit of Jewish victims of National Socialism, and distributed reparation funds. These activities contradict the traditional distinction in international relations between states and organizations. According to this classification, organizations were "mainly influential in pushing an issue onto a political agenda" and unable to affect subsequent decision-making.[21] The case of the Claims Conference shows how an INGO, a private organization, not only put an issue on the agenda but also changed German policy on compensation for non-resident victims. Nevertheless, lack of sovereignty diminished the status of the advocate on behalf of Jewish victims.

The Claims Conference attained its main achievements when a state, Israel or the United States of America, stood by its side. The two protocols signed with West Germany in 1952 were part and parcel of tripartite talks that ended with the execution of the Luxembourg Agreement by the state of Israel. Almost fifty years later, it was America, not the Claims Conference, that exerted pressure on Swiss banks, insurance companies, and German corporations to compensate former victims.

The innovation of diplomacy by a community went hand in hand with second-rate status and weakened bargaining power. West Germany benefited from this weakness. It compensated only a small number of survivors in the years prior to national reunification and for only part of the damage they suffered.[22] Moreover, the categories of damages and sums paid by the perpetrators distorted the horrors of the Holocaust. Compensation for the loss of earnings or potential earnings far exceeded sums paid for incarceration in a concentration camp.[23]

Research on the Claims Conference illustrates the participation of a non-state actor in global politics. Diaspora leaders and associations acted behind the scenes to promote the interests of Jews worldwide, both before and after the establishment of the state of Israel. The case of the Claims Conference extends the range of models that form the basis of international relations theories. The campaign for reparations suggests new possibilities for investigation. Writing individuals and organizations into international relations will enhance our understanding of the exercise of power in transnational settings. In addition, the incorporation of diplomacy on behalf of a community into the field of international affairs will deepen our understanding of both fields.

ISRAEL AND THE CLAIMS CONFERENCE

Israel gained from the activities of the diaspora entity. After the signing of the Luxembourg Agreement, the state and the Claims Conference reached a tacit agreement on a division of labor. The latter remained the sole advocate for victims' rights in the international arena, and Israel referred its citizens and associations of refugees to the organization. The state's *de facto* renouncement of earlier demands to act as sole spokesman for the Jewish people worldwide defused tensions and ended altercations with communal leaders who viewed Judaism in terms of a religious and not ethnic identity. This arrangement improved relations between Israel and American non-Zionist organizations. Assigning the role of victims' advocate to a third party absolved the state of the need to act in this matter. In the 1950s, Israel had limited resources and its foreign officials had little if any diplomatic experience.[24] Moreover, the implicit consent permitted Ben-Gurion and his government to focus their efforts on furthering Israeli security needs and foreign policy. Assuming the responsibility to represent Israeli, as well as other Jewish victims, provided the Claims Conference with a raison d'être for its continued existence and strengthened its legitimacy in global politics.

The earmarking of German reparation funds for use inside and outside Israel removed a source of friction between the state and diaspora organizations. In-fighting had plagued earlier alliances created to dispense money raised from donations. The question of what share of philanthropic funds should be allocated to Jewish settlements in Palestine had been a major source of contention between Zionists and non-Zionists before 1939. German negotiators at Wassenaar created two separate funds: one for Israel pursuant to the Luxembourg Agreement and the other for the diaspora under Protocol 2. In practice, from 1954 to 1964 all reparations in the form of products manufactured in Germany and crude oil were channeled through the Israel

Purchasing Mission. However, the state fulfilled its undertakings and paid in full the share owed to the Claims Conference.[25]

The Claims Conference provides a case study of the conduct of modern Jewish diplomacy. The organization's activities challenge the view that political engagement on behalf of a collective Jewish interest for purposes other than the promotion of the state of Israel ceased to exist in the second half of the twentieth century. One supporter of this view, the historian David Vital, has questioned the relevance of modern Jewish diplomacy since then: "the concept of a collective Jewish national interest is strictly speaking untenable."[26] He based this conclusion on the incompatibility between the interests of the Jewish community in Israel and those elsewhere.[27] Another supporter, Shlomo Avineri, argued that Jewish diplomacy ended with the establishment of Israel. He contended that the existence of traditional politics alongside Israeli statecraft "meant, among other things, the diminution of Jewish sovereignty as epitomized in the state of Israel."[28] Avineri explained the success of the negotiations conducted by Goldmann with West Germany as the product of a moment of transition from pre-state Jewish and Zionist diplomacy to state-driven diplomacy.[29]

The operations of the Claims Conference do not support either contention. Traditional Jewish diplomacy on behalf of victims of National Socialist persecution served both the state and the diaspora. This shared interest relieved the state of the need to seek redress for its citizens and strengthened the organization's authority. The signing of the Luxembourg Agreement, which prevented the bankruptcy of the Israeli economy owed much to Goldmann's ingenuity, charm, and direct access to Adenauer. Moreover, the agreement concluded by the Claims Conference regarding German compensation to individuals and its continued involvement in the implementation of German federal legislation benefited both Israeli citizens and the state. The organization pursued redress for victims not only in the "moment of transition" but also over the course of many decades after the establishment of Israel. In addition to reparations, diaspora Jewish leaders continued to lobby for coreligionists suffering from persecution and discrimination. The Soviet Jewry campaign initiated by individuals and groups in the diaspora in the 1960s offers one example of this form of diplomacy in the international scene.

The number of studies of the transformation of relations between Israel and non-Zionist American leaders and associations is limited. One example of an under-researched topic is the ongoing and complex relationship between the JDC and Israel. The JDC (as well as the AJC) originally rejected the idea of a Jewish homeland. A recent collection of articles on JDC operations during the past century does not contain any discussion of the evolution of its relations with Israel.[30] The organization's digitized archives and Israeli government archives offer new opportunities for research on the interdependence between state and diaspora organizations.

SELF-GOVERNANCE BY AN ELITE

Relations between victims of the Third Reich and the Claims Conference reflected earlier models of self-governance inside and outside the Jewish world. Like the medieval *Landjudenschaften*, a small number of wealthy and influential men set up a self-governing body. They did not seek or receive authorization from the individuals they purported to represent. Furthermore, they distributed funds behind a veil of secrecy. These founders also followed in the footsteps of nineteenth-century community officials who "took for granted their right to govern" and "operated with a heavy hand."[31]

Elite rule in the twentieth century was not limited to the Jewish world and applied to other networks operating across national borders. In the words of the American political scientists Margaret Karns and Karen Mingst: "Often in the case of transnational networks or large international NGOs (INGOs), it is an elite group based in a large Northern city that claims to speak on behalf of poor, disadvantaged people in another part of the world."[32] This form of self-governance continues to characterize large sections of the world of INGOs inside and outside the Jewish world.

A democratic deficit can work in favor of the communities they represent. Transnational organizations, unlike democratic states, do not base their legitimacy on public support and therefore are free to act without regard to the views of the group they claim to represent. The Claims Conference initiated negotiations with Germans less than a decade after the Holocaust. In a later interview, Goldmann boasted that had a Gallup poll been taken on the conduct of direct talks, "the majority of the Jewish people would have been against it, especially the rank-and-file, the masses."[33] Against a backdrop of widespread opposition in Israel to the normalization of relations with West Germany, the Claims Conference led the way to direct talks on reparations. In a decisive debate in the *Knesset*, the support of the diaspora alliance for Israeli demands and its intention to seek compensation for victims provided a rationale and catalyst for the approval of the state's participation in the negotiations.[34] In retrospect, few if any dispute the wisdom of seeking reparations and negotiating compensation with West Germany.

The lack of democracy also contributed to the success of the Claims Conference. Jewish communities and associations from a number of countries and with different ideologies and religious outlooks cooperated on a protracted basis without major dissension or rifts. The alliance exercised far-reaching powers in funding communal activities and welfare. Election of officers by members of the community and disclosure of the organization's inner workings may have endangered the existence of the leadership entity.

The stability of the Claims Conference is striking in view of earlier unsuccessful attempts to create a single, broad coalition to represent Jews worldwide.

Several factors contributed to its longevity. The homogeneity of the alliance's members and executives is one explanation. Middle-aged men directed all constituent organizations. In addition, members were all diaspora-based entities and even associations that supported Zionism were committed to the continuing existence of Jewish communities outside Israel.[35] A majority of the member organizations were created before 1933 and engaged in advocacy, not welfare work. Victim associations, a potential element of discord and opposition, formed a small minority with very limited influence on the alliance. Similarly, women's organizations, another possible opposition group, were and still are totally excluded. The availability of funds from an outside, non-Jewish source reinforced internal cohesion. In the past, members of coalitions had vied with one another on the joint spending of funds raised separately.[36] Payment of reparations by West Germany removed this source of friction and the money was "a wonderful cementing agent."[37] The postwar *Zeitgeist* of cross-border cooperation and spreading American values and modes of operation also contributed to the stability of the alliance. Finally, the management skills of Goldmann and Kagan in handling disputes and adapting to changing circumstances were instrumental to the alliance's smooth running.

The Claims Conference reinforced ties between Jewish communities worldwide. Annual meetings of directors provided a platform for leaders to regularly meet and determine policies. The role of American associations and officers in the Claims Conference attested to the "transatlantic shift" in diaspora politics. Cooperation between communities in the West also benefited Jews behind the Iron Curtain in the form of funding parcels to individuals in Eastern Europe.[38]

The structure of the Claims Conference illustrates the politics of inclusion and exclusion in an entity claiming to represent an entire community. The organization declared that it spoke on behalf of world Jewry. However, it represented and chiefly served its constituent members. The founding organizations did not invite all communities and groups of individuals persecuted as Jews by Germany to participate in the alliance. Consequently, non-affiliated Jews, women and women's organizations played almost no part in the entity purporting to speak in their name. Moreover, the alliance acted as a closed shop and refused to admit new members.[39] The elitist nature of the coalition undermines the claim that it represented a broad community, either of world Jewry or Jewish victims of National Socialism.

Theorists offer different explanations for the authority of institutions created by individuals. The attractiveness of ideas and values promoted by non-governmental organizations is a major source of their influence. In addition, substantive outcomes bolster their legitimacy.[40] Another approach ascribes the power of organizations to two sources: the legitimacy of the rational-legal authority they embody and control over technical expertise and information.[41]

Compensation for the unparalleled damage perpetrated by Germany against Jews was the principal idea advanced by the Claims Conference. Broad support for this cause served as leverage in negotiations with West Germany and resulted in the signing of two protocols. This achievement, together with the ability to overcome internal differences on how to spend the reparations, led to the establishment of a permanent institution. Its authority was invested "rationally" in technical rules and procedures. The organization's lawyers were leading experts on National Socialist persecution directed against Jews throughout the territories controlled by Germany during the twelve-year reign of the Third Reich. Furthermore, Goldmann and Blaustein were well-versed in dealing with heads of states. Their sophistication, together with the knowledge of Robinson and other lawyers involved in German legislation, contributed to the legitimacy of the new organization.

ORGANIZATIONAL CULTURE

Allocations by the Claims Conference in the 1950s and 1960s indicate the problem of distribution of reparations by an organization. West Germany granted the funds as collective compensation for the "relief, rehabilitation and resettlement of Jewish victims of National Socialist persecution." The organization devised a system intended to meet its commitment under Protocol 2 to the Luxembourg Agreement.

Directors and bureaucrats, mostly volunteers without training in welfare work or finance, formulated and applied guidelines. These guidelines created the appearance of a modern organization guided by objective norms. Communal leaders frequently base their legitimacy on the neutral, technical nature of their activities, institutionalized through rules and procedures. They project the image of serving the needs of others without any purpose of their own. The Claims Conference allocation system appeared to be devoid of political considerations. But behind closed doors, senior executives awarded a major share of the funds to the organizations they led. Other recipients were individuals that resembled the directors, former communal leaders, and rabbis. The documents demonstrate that in the period of 1954–1964 victims without connections had little or no chance of receiving grants.

The actual workings of the Claims Conference undermined the concept of depoliticized rules. Officials stressed their professionalism, but lay leaders, not welfare workers, had the final say on allocations. Moreover, the vagueness of allocation rules enabled the organization to disburse funds at its discretion and without the need to ensure compliance with predetermined criteria. The guiding principle that shaped the rules and procedures of the Claims Conference was self-preservation, namely the continued existence of the transnational alliance. Member organizations, not victims, individuals, or associations, determined the use of reparations. The implementation of the organizational rules resulted in the direction of a large share of the funds to member organizations for programs intended to reconstruct communities and promote Jewish culture. In addition, the allocation system set aside considerable funds for the continued existence of the Claims Conference. Max Weber argued that "ideas of culture-values" are the guiding force behind the functional, apparently neutral purposes of bureaucracies.[42] In the case of the Claims Conference, these "culture-values" were the promotion of cooperation between constituent members and self-perpetuation.

Studies of non-profit institutions are frequently funded by the institutions behind them.[43] Analyzing the inner workings of Jewish federations and organizations using theories developed by political scientists or comparisons with non-Jewish counterparts are rare. There is a growing awareness among the Jewish media and the public of the need for greater transparency and accountability for communal leadership entities.[44] The Claims Conference remains an opaque institution. Archival access for independent scholars of the period after 1964 will provide a better understanding of the operations and the manner in which it distributed funds.

THE FUTURE OF THE CLAIMS CONFERENCE

Almost seventy years after the creation of two temporary committees, the Claims Conference continues to demand and distribute reparations. Established for the limited purpose of participating in the 1952 round of negotiations, it completed its mission within one year. Histories of the reparations agency portray its continued existence as predetermined and the only possible outcome of its genesis. This view ignores the desire of member organizations and executives for an eternal life and the measures they took to achieve this goal. Multiple changes in the organization's missions were not the product of a grand plan, but instead were negotiated step by step.

The first transformation of the Claims Conference occurred after the signing of the Luxembourg Agreement and its protocols. German funds and a consensus between founding members on continued cooperation ensured its survival. The temporary negotiating party evolved into a permanent institution. Its object was no longer confined to conducting negotiations but extended to the distribution of German funds.

Payment of the final installment under Protocol 2 in 1964 posed a new challenge to the alliance. Two factors worked against the disbandment of the transnational alliance in 1964: the creation of new tasks requiring ongoing operations and procurement of the means to finance these activities. The hardship fund of DM 1.2 billion set up by West Germany under the Final Compensation Law of 1965 was one justification for the organization's continued existence.[45] The purpose was to compensate late emigrants, former residents of Eastern Europe who had been persecuted in the war and were in need. Again, it was the Claims Conference, not the provider of the money, that determined criteria for allocations and made payments to eligible applicants. Another task was the allocation of funds for cultural programs from the Memorial Foundation for Jewish Culture created by the organization in 1964.[46] The administration of the hardship fund and the Memorial Foundation required a financial source to cover operating costs. The source, the means for self-preservation, was derived from German reparations intended for the benefit of National Socialist victims. The final installment of reparations under Protocol 2, together with the balance in the account of the Claims Conference, totaled between $16–17 million. This sum represented approximately fifteen percent of the total German funds paid during 1954–1964.[47] The reserve of "undistributed funds" now could finance annual board meetings as well as cultural projects.[48]

The fall of the Iron Curtain and the reunification of Germany in 1990 provided new opportunities and a justification for ongoing operations of the Claims Conference. The organization sought and filed claims for property located in East Germany that had been formerly owned by Jews and sold under duress or confiscated after 1933. It also lobbied for compensation for victims who were not eligible under existing laws and rules.

In recent years, the Claims Conference demanded compensation for survivors not covered by existing legislation and agreements. In 2014, in response to lobbying by the organization, Germany established a new fund of $175 million to make one-time payments of €2,500 to child survivors of the Holocaust. According to its latest financial statements, the Claims Conference distributed $14.9 million to child survivors in 2017 and $3.6 million in 2018.[49]

A different challenge to the continued existence of the Claims Conference was the discovery of major fraud involving the diversion of German funds administered by the organization in exchange for kickbacks. The US State Attorney for the Southern District of New York charged thirty-one defendants, including ten former Claims Conference employees, with participation in a scheme to defraud the Claims Conference out of $57.5 million. All the defendants were convicted. In 2013, the court sentenced Semen Domnitser, the highest-ranking insider (director of the Hardship Fund and Article II Fund) to eight years' imprisonment.[50] Considerable negative publicity accompanied the case. One former director accused the organization of mismanagement and nuisance.[51] The Board of Directors appointed an independent ombudsman to investigate the fraud scheme but fired him after the publication of a scathing report. The Claims Conference and its executives did not accept responsibility for the practices that enabled employees to siphon off to accomplices millions of dollars intended for Holocaust survivors.

According to the organization's latest published financial statements, its revenues in 2018 from sold and unsold restituted properties amounted to $36.6 million. It allocated over $42 million to individuals from the Hardship Fund and $405 million to welfare organizations assisting Jewish victims. The organization's net assets without donor restrictions as of December 31, 2018 totaled $425,849,072, with annual administrative costs amounting to $41.6 million.[52] The number of Holocaust survivors declines daily, but the organization created to represent them continues to thrive.

Demographic change have raised questions about the future of the Claims Conference. Since 1952, the declared mission of the organization has been to lobby for and assist Holocaust victims. The performance of this mission depends upon the existence of survivors, the youngest of whom are now over seventy-five years old. Members and executives are (again) faced with two alternatives: termination of operations after distributing remaining funds or the formulation of a new mandate. An interview given by a top-ranking executive in July 2018 indicates that the organization intends to adopt the latter course of action. Greg Schneider, Executive Vice President, acknowledged that there will be a date when no "first generation" survivors remain but added that there will probably always be a role for the Claims Conference. In his words: "We still have so much we need to do for the first generation, we haven't yet broached how best to support their descendants . . . there will probably always be a role for the Claims Conference and other agencies involved in Holocaust education."[53]

Schneider does not spell out the survival strategy envisaged by him, but based on the interview, it appears that the amended goals of the organization are support for descendants of victims (second-generation survivors) and education. In 2017, the organization set up the Ezra Legacy Inc. to promote the provision of relief, support, and assistance for Jewish victims and increase public understanding of the impact of the Holocaust. At this stage, it is unclear whether new resources will be sought or existing funds utilized to accomplish these tasks.

A review of the organization's ground rules in its formative years bridges the gap between self-projected images and public conceptions. In the field of diplomacy, the Claims Conference played a path-breaking role in demanding and receiving reparations for a non-state community and individual victims. In its internal workings, including the selection of members and officers, distribution of funds, and accountability, medieval practices continued to guide the organization in the conduct of its affairs.

Conclusion 175

NOTES

1. "General Assembly 60/147," *United Nations Audiovisual Library of International Law*, 2008, accessed on October 20, 2019, https://legal.un.org/avl/pdf/ha/ga_60-147/ga_60-147_ph_e.pdf.

2. Diana Odier Contreras-Garduno, *Collective Reparations: Tensions and Dilemmas between Collective Reparations with the Individual Right to Receive Reparations* (Cambridge: Intersentia, 2018), 4.

3. Meta Doran, Interview 10878. Tape 3: 12:46–13:30. USC Shoah Foundation Visual History Archive. USC Shoah Foundation. January 13, 1996. Accessed December 30, 2020.

4. Goschler, " German Compensation to Jewish Nazi Victims," 403.

5. The neediest survivors received small handouts from Austria from a fund set up following Claims Conference lobbying. See chap. 7, p. 150.

6. *Vereinbarung zwischen der Bundesrepublik Deutschland und der DDR zur Durchführung und Auslegung des am 31. August 1990 in Berlin unterzeichneten Vertrages zwischen der Bundesrepublik Deutschland und der DDR über die Herstellung der Einheit Deutschland—Einigungsvertrag* (Agreement between the Federal Republic of Germany and the German Democratic Republic on the Implementation and Interpretation of the Treaty signed in Berlin on August 31, 1990, between the Federal Republic of Germany and the German Democratic Republic on the Creation of a Unified Germany—Unification Treaty).

7. Stuart E. Eizenstat, *Imperfect Justice: Looted Assets, Slave Labor and the Unfinished Business of World War II* (New York: Public Affairs, 2003). See also Michael J. Bazyler and Roger P. Alford, *Holocaust Restitution: Perspectives on the Litigation and its Aftermath* (New York: NYU Press, 2006).

8. Anja Hense, "Limitation of Economic Damages as a 'Humanitarian Gesture': The German Foundation 'Remembrance, Responsibility and the Future,'" *Journal of Contemporary History* 46, no. 2 (2011): 407–424.

9. Hense, "Limitation of Economic Damages," 420.

10. All figures in this paragraph were provided to the author by the Claims Conference on April 20, 2020.

11. Taylor, "The Claims Conference and the Historic Jewish Efforts," 205.

12. C. Sarah Soh, "Japan's National/Asian Women's Fund for "Comfort Women," *Pacific Affairs* 76, no. 2 (2003): 209–233. https://www.jstor.org/stable/40024391.

13. See Clemens Jabloner, "The Austrian Historical Commission: Motives, Result and Impact," in Oliver Rathkolb, ed., *Revisiting the National Socialist Legacy: Coming to Terms with Forced Labor, Expropriation, Compensation and Restitution*, (Innsbruck: Studien Verlag, 2002), 51–56; "Reconciliation, Peace and Cooperation," *Fund for Reconciliation, Peace and Cooperation*, n. d., accessed on October 20, 2019, http://www.reconciliationfund.at/db/admin/de/index_main1541.html?cbereich=2&cthema=344&carticle=604&fromlist=1.

14. See "United States Department of State The JUST Act Report," *Office of the Special Envoy for Holocaust Issues Bureau of European and Eurasian Affairs*, 2020,

accessed on April 5, 2020, https://www.state.gov/wp-content/uploads/2020/02/JUST-Act5.pdf.

15. "Terezin Declaration," *EU2009.CZ*, August 16, 2011, accessed on April 5, 2020, http://www.eu2009.cz/en/news-and-documents/news/terezin-declaration-26304/.

16. One example is the Enemy Property Compensation Advisory Panel set up by the British government in 1998. See "Patricia Hewitt Announces Enemy Property Payment Scheme to Close," *Department for Business, Energy & Industrial Strategy*, July 8, 2004, accessed on April 5, 2020, http://www.enemyproperty.bis.gov.uk/inote.html.

17. Shelton, "Righting Wrongs," 839; Contreras-Garduno, *Collective Reparations*, 3; Ludi, "The Vectors of Postwar Victim Reparations," 429.

18. Jeffrey Herf, "Review of *Schuld und Schulden: Die Politik der Wiedergutmachung für NS-Verfolgte seit 1945*," *Journal of Modern History* 79, no. 4 (2007): 948.

19. Hockerts, "Wiedergutmachung in Deutschland," 181.

20. Hockerts, "Wiedergutmachung in Deutschland," 184.

21. Bob Reinalda, "Private in Form, Public in Purpose: NGOs in International Relations Theory," in Bas Arts, Math Noortmann and Bob Reinalda, eds., *Non-State Actors in International Relations* (Hampshire, England: Ashgate Publishing Ltd., 2001), 26. Reinalda states that empirical research rejects the traditional distinction between states and organizations.

22. Other causes of the limited compensation to victims were the priority given by the Bonn administration to rebuilding the German economy and Cold War politics.

23. Goschler, "German Compensation to Jewish Nazi Victims," 393.

24. According to Lewis Brownstein, in its early years the Israeli Foreign Office was staffed by people who lacked "substantial qualifications." See Lewis Brownstein, "Decision Making in Israeli Foreign Policy: An Unplanned Process," *Political Science Quarterly* 92, no. 2 (1977): 269.

25. Funds granted by the Claims Conference for the construction of the *Yad Vashem* museum in Israel were the sole exception to separate use of German reparations by state and organization. See chap. 7, p. 171.

26. David Vital, "Diplomacy in the Jewish Interest," in Ada Rapoport-Albert, and Steven J. Zipperstein, eds., *Jewish History: Essays in Honor of Chimen Abramsky*, eds, (London: P. Halban, 1988), 691.

27. Vital, "Diplomacy in the Jewish Interest," 694.

28. Shlomo Avineri, "Statecraft without a State: A Jewish Contribution to Political History," in Gabriella Gelardini, ed., *Kontexte der Schrift* vol. 1 (Stuttgart: Kohlhammer, 2005), 418.

29. Avineri, "Statecraft without a State," 418.

30. *The JDC at 100*.

31. Hasia Diner, "Jewish Self-Governance, American Style," *American Jewish History* 81, no. 3/4 (1994): 283.

32. Margaret P. Karns and Karen A. Mingst, *International Organizations: The Politics and Processes of Global Governance*, 2nd ed. (Boulder, CO and London, UK: Lynne Rienner Publishers, Inc., 2010), 250–251.

33. Nahum Goldmann in a testimony given to HUJI, on November 14, 1961, 11.

34. The Prime Minister's statement in the *Knesset* on January 7, 1952 concerning reparations. See *Documents Relating to the Agreement,* Document 20, p. 57.

35. One exception was the Jewish Agency, a member organization of the Claims Conference. Originally created to function as a government without a state, the Jewish Agency changed its mission after 1948 to providing a link between Israel and diaspora communities.

36. Marc Lee Raphael, "The Origins of Organized Jewish Philanthropy in the United States 1914–1939," in Moses Rischin, ed., *The Jews of North America* (Detroit: Wayne State University Press, 1987), 217.

37. This phrase was used by an official of the Claims Conference in describing the cooperation between member organizations. See Zweig, *German Reparations,* 191.

38. A full evaluation of the Relief-in-Transit project will have to wait until the parties involved agree to disclose documents on how it worked.

39. Chap. 5, p. 112.

40. Steve Charnovitz, "Nongovernmental Organizations and International Law," *The American Journal of International Law* 100, no. 2 (2006): 348.

41. Barnett and Finnemore, "The Power, Politics and Pathologies of International Organizations," 707.

42. Cited in Robert O. Keohane and Joseph S. Nye, "Transgovernmental Relations and International Organizations," *World Politics* 27, no. 1 (1974): 62.

43. See, for example, Bauer's trilogy on the JDC.

44. The *Forward* newspaper published a comparison of salaries earned by executives in Jewish NPOs in 2017. Unfortunately, the Claims Conference is not included in the review. See Steven Davidson, "How Much Do Top Non-Profit Jewish Leaders Make?" *Forward,* December 11, 2017, accessed on October 20, 2019, https://forward.com/news/388240/how-much-do-top-jewish-non-profit-leaders-make/.

45. See chap. 7, pp. 149–150.

46. Zweig, *German Reparations,* 160.

47. Maurice Boukstein stated that the last installment of the reparations was used for the Memorial Foundation. See his oral testimony given to HUJI on June 28, 1971, 4.

48. The sum and term "undistributed funds" appear in a speech made by Leavitt in a JDC meeting held in Brussels in March 1964. See document headed "CGM-May 27, 1964," in JDC Digitized Archives, Item #ID 811905.

49. See "Conference on Jewish Material Claims Against Germany, Inc. Financial Statements," *Claims Conference,* December 31, 2018 and 2017, accessed on April 5, 2020, n.d.,http://www.claimscon.org/wp-content/uploads/2019/08/Audited-FS-FYE-12-31-18.pdf.

50. Details of the conviction appear at "Former Holocaust Claims Conference Director Sentenced to Eight Years in Prison for $57.3 Million Fraud on Organization That Makes Reparations to Victims of Nazi Persecution," *Federal Bureau of Investigation New York Office,* November 4, 2013, accessed on October 20, 2019, https://archives.fbi.gov/archives/newyork/press-releases/2013/former-holoca

ust-claims-conference-director-sentenced-to-eight-years-in-prison-for-57.3-million-fraud-on-organization-that-makes-reparations-to-victims-of-nazi-persecution; and "Former Holocaust Claims Conference Director and Two Recruiters Convicted in $57.3 Million Fraud on Organization That Makes Reparations to Victims of Nazi Persecution," *Dept. of Justice U.S. Attorney's Office Southern District of New York*, May 8, 2013, accessed on October 20, 2019, https://www.justice.gov/usao-sdny/pr/former-holocaust-claims-conference-director-and-two-recruiters-convicted-573-million.

51. Samuel Norich, "Why I Resigned from Claims Conference Board—And Why You Should Care," *Forward*, July 14, 2013, accessed on October 20, 2019, https://forward.com/opinion/180375/why-i-resigned-from-claims-conference-board-and/; Isi Leibler, "Candidly Speaking: Accountability for Claims Conference," *The Jerusalem Post*, December 2, 2010, accessed on October 20, 2019, https://www.jpost.com/opinion/columnists/candidly-speaking-accountability-for-claims-conference.

52. The financial statements appear on the organization's website. See "Conference on Jewish Material Claims Against Germany, Inc. Financial Statements," *Claims Conference,* December 31, 2018 and 2017, accessed on April 5, 2020, http://www.claimscon.org/wp-content/uploads/2019/08/Audited-FS-FYE-12-31-18.pdf.

53. Greg Schneider in an interview published in the *Association of Jewish Refugees Journal* 18, no. 6 (July 2018): 12–13.

Bibliography

Abitbol, Michel. *The Jews of North Africa during the Second World War.* Translated by Tihanyi Zeitelis. Detroit, MI: Wayne University State Press, 1989.
"About the World Union for Progressive Judaism," *World Union for Progressive Judaism,* n.d., https://wupj.org/about-us/history/.
Adler, H. G. *Der verwaltete Mensch: Studien zur Deportation der Juden aus Deutschland (The Administered Human: Studies on the Deportation of Jews from Germany).* Tübingen, Mohr, 1974.
After Five Years 1948–1953: A Report of the Jewish Restitution Successor Organization on the Restitution of Identifiable Property in the US Zone of Germany. Nuremberg: The Organization, 1953.
"AJC Administrative Committee held on Monday, November 19, 1951," p. 6, *AJC Archives,* http://ajcarchives.org/ajcarchive/DigitalArchive.aspx.
"AJC Administrative Committee held on Wednesday, December 12, 1951," p. 4, *AJC Archives,* http://ajcarchives.org/ajcarchive/DigitalArchive.aspx.
Allwork, Larissa. *Holocaust Remembrance between the National and the Transnational: The Stockholm International Forum and the First Decade of the International Task Force.* London: Bloomsbury Academic, 2015.
Altshuler, Stuart. *From Exodus to Freedom: A History of the Soviet Jewry Movement.* Lanham, MD: Rowman & Littlefield Publishers, 2005.
American Jewish Committee Archives, Center for Jewish History.
American Jewish Joint Distribution Archives.
American Jewish Historical Society Archives, Center for Jewish History, Conference on Jewish Material Claims Against Germany Collection 1955–1972.
"A Portrait of Jewish Americans," *Pew Research Center,* October 1, 2013, https://www.pewforum.org/2013/10/01/jewish-american-beliefs-attitudes-culture-survey/#fn-17239-1.
Arad, Yitzhak. "Plunder of Jewish Property in the Nazi-Occupied Areas of the Soviet Union." *Yad Vashem Studies* 29 (2001): 109–148.

Avineri, Shlomo. "Statecraft without a State: A Jewish Contribution to Political History." In *Kontexte der Schrift*, vol. 1, edited by Gabriella Gelardini, 403–420. Stuttgart: Kohlhammer, 2005.

Bajohr, Franz. "Aryanization and Restitution in Germany." In *Robbery and Restitution: The Conflict over Jewish Property in Europe*, edited by Martin Dean, Constantin Goschler, and Philipp Ther, 33–52. New York: Berghahn Books, 2007.

Balabkins, Nicholas. *West German Reparations to Israel*. New Brunswick, NJ: Rutgers University Press, 1971.

Baranova, Olga. "Early Historiography of the Holocaust: The Example of the Soviet Union." In *Als der Holocaust noch keinen Namen hatte: zur frühen Aufarbeitung des NS-Massenmordes an den Juden (Before the Holocaust Had a Name: On the Early Coming to Terms with NS Mass Murder of Jews)*, edited by Regina Fritz, Éva Kovács, and Béla Rásky, 185–198. Vienna: New Academic Press, 2016.

Barkan, Elazar. *The Guilt of Nations: Restitution and Negotiating Historical Injustices*. New York: Norton, 2000.

Barkan, Elazar, Constantin Goschler, James Waller, eds. *Historical Dialogue and the Prevention of Mass Atrocities*. New York: Routledge, 2020.

Barnett, Michael N., and Martha Finnemore. "The Politics, Power, and Pathologies of International Organizations." *International Organization* 53, no. 4 (1999): 699–732. https://www.jstor.org/stable/2601307.

Barnett, Michael N., and Martha Finnemore. *Rules for the World: International Organizations in Global Politics*. Ithaca and London: Cornell University Press, 2004.

Barnett, Michael N., and Liv Coleman. "Designing Police: Interpol and the Study of Change in International Organizations." *International Studies Quarterly* 49, no. 4 (2005): 593–619. https://www.jstor.org/stable/3693502.

Bartal, Israel. *The Jews of Eastern Europe, 1772–1881*. Translated by Chaya Naor. Philadelphia: University of Pennsylvania Press, 2005.

Barzel, Neima. "Dignity, Hatred and Memory." *Yad Vashem Studies* 24 (1994): 247–280.

Bauer, Yehuda. *American Jewry and the Holocaust: The American Jewish Joint Distribution Committee, 1939–1945*. Detroit: Wayne State University Press, 1981.

———. *Out of the Ashes: The Impact of American Jews on Post-Holocaust European Jewry*. Oxford: Pergamon Press, 1989.

Bazyler, Michael J., and Roger P. Alford. *Holocaust Restitution: Perspectives on the Litigation and its Aftermath*. New York: NYU Press, 2006.

Bazyler, Michael J. *Holocaust, Genocide and the Law: A Quest for Justice in a Post-Holocaust World*. New York, NY: Oxford University Press, 2016.

Belzer, Michael. "'I Don't Know Whom to Thank': The American Joint Distribution Committee's Secret Aid to Soviet Jewry." *Jewish Social Studies* 15, no. 2 (2009): 111–136.

"Benjamin Ferencz: A Former Prosecutor at the Nuremberg War Crimes Trials," *BenFerencz.org*, n. d., https://benferencz.org/biography/.

Ben Natan, Asher. "HaDerech LeKinoon Hayahasim: HaHebet HaYisraeli," (The Path to the Establishment of Relations: The Israeli Aspect). In *Yahasim "Normaliim:"*

Yahasei Israel-Germania. ("Normal" Relations: Israeli-German Relations), edited by Moshe Zimmermann and Oded Heilbronner, 34–31. Jerusalem: Magnes Press, 1993.
Bentwich, Norman. *Siegfried Moses and the United Restitution Organization*. Tel-Aviv: Irgun Olej Merkas Europa, 1962.
———. "Nazi Spoliation and German Restitution: The Work of the United Restitution Office." *Leo Baeck Institute Yearbook* 10 (1965): 204–224.
Berghoff, Harmut, Jürgen Kocka, and Dieter Ziegler, eds. *Business in the Age of Extremes: Essays in Modern German and Austrian Economic History*. Washington, DC: Cambridge University Press, 2013.
Berkovitch, Nitza. "The Emergence and Transformation of the International Women's Movement." In *Constructing World Culture: International Nongovernmental Organizations Since 1875*, edited by John Boli and George M. Thomas, 100–126. Stanford: Stanford University Press, 1999.
Bilsky, Leora. *The Holocaust, Corporations, and the Law: Unfinished Business*. Ann Arbor: University of Michigan Press, 2017.
Bischof, Günter. "Victims? Perpetrators? 'Punching Bags' of European Historical Memory? The Austrians and their World War II Legacies." *German Studies Review* 27, no. 1 (2004): 17–32.
Blaustein, Jacob. *Israel Through American Eyes*. New York: The American Jewish Committee, 1949.
Brautbar, Shirli. *From Fashion to Politics: Hadassah and Jewish American Women in the Post World War II Era*. Boston: Academic Studies Press, 2012.
Brecher, Michael. "Images, Process and Feedback in Foreign Policy: Israel's Decisions on German Reparations." *The American Political Science Review* 67, no. 1 (1973): 73–102.
Breslauer, Walter, and Dr. F. Goldschmidt. *The Work of the Council of Jews from Germany in the Sphere of Indemnification: Report*. London: The Organization, 1966.
Brownstein, Lewis. "Decision Making in Israeli Foreign Policy: An Unplanned Process." *Political Science Quarterly* 92, no. 2 (1977): 259–279.
"Bundesgesetz zur Entschädigung für Opfer der nationalsozialistischen Verfolgung (Bundesentschädigungsgesetz - BEG)," *Bundesministeriums der Justiz und für Verbraucherschutz*, n.d., https://www.gesetze-im-internet.de/beg/BEG.pdf.
Buxbaum, Richard M. "A Legal History of International Reparations." *Berkeley Journal of International Law* 23, no. 2 (2005): 314–346.
Central Zionist Archives – Nahum Goldmann's Offices in New York and Geneva Archives and WJC Archives.
Charnovitz, Steve. "Nongovernmental Organizations and International Law." *The American Journal of International Law* 100, no. 2 (2006): 348–372.
Chouraqui, André. *L'Alliance Israélite Universelle et la Renaissance Juive Contemporaine: Cent Ans d'Histoire (Alliance Israélite Universelle and the Contemporary Jewish Renaissance: A Century of History)*. Paris: Presses Universitaires de France, 1965.
Claims Conference Archives – Central Archives for the History of the Jewish People.

Clavin, Patricia. "Defining Transnationalism." *Contemporary European History* 14, no. 4 (2005): 421–439.

———. "The Role of International Organisations in Europeanization: The Case of the League of Nations and the European Economic Community." In *Europeanization in the Twentieth Century: Historical Approaches*, edited by Martin Conway and Kiran Patel, 110–131. Basingstoke, Hampshire: Palgrave Macmillan, 2010.

———. "International Organizations." In *The Cambridge History of the Second World War*. Vol. II, *Politics and Ideology*, edited by Richard Bosworth and Joseph Maiolo, 39–161. Cambridge: Cambridge University Press, 2015.

Clifford, Rebecca. *Survivors: Children's Lives after the Holocaust*. New Haven, CT: Yale University Press, 2020.

Cohen, Israel. "Jewish Interests in the Peace Treaties." *Jewish Social Studies* 11 (1949): 99–118.

"Conference on Jewish Material Claims Against Germany, Inc. Financial Statements," *Claims Conference*, December 31, 2018 and 2017, n.d., http://www.claimscon.org/wp-content/uploads/2019/08/Audited-FS-FYE-12-31-18.pdf.

Conference on Jewish Material Claims against Germany – Report 1954. New York: The Organization, 1955.

Conference on Jewish Material Claims against Germany – Report 1955. New York: The Organization, 1956.

Conference on Jewish Material Claims against Germany – Report 1956. New York: The Organization, 1957.

Conference on Jewish Material Claims against Germany – Report 1957. New York: The Organization, 1958.

Conference on Jewish Material Claims against Germany – Report 1958. New York: The Organization, 1959.

Conference on Jewish Material Claims against Germany – Report 1959. New York: The Organization, 1960.

Conference on Jewish Material Claims against Germany – Report 1960. New York: The Organization, 1961.

Conference on Jewish Material Claims against Germany – Report 1961. New York: The Organization, 1962.

Conference on Jewish Material Claims against Germany – Report 1962. New York: The Organization, 1963.

Conference on Jewish Material Claims against Germany – Report 1963. New York: The Organization, 1964.

Conference on Jewish Material Claims against Germany – Report 1964. New York: The Organization, 1965.

Conradi Gerstbauer, Loramy. "The Whole Story of NGO Mandate Change: The Peacebuilding Work of World Vision, Catholic Relief Services and Mennonite Central Committee." *Nonprofit & Voluntary Sector Quarterly* 39 (2010): 844–865.

Coontz, Stephanie. *The Way We Never Were: American Families and the Nostalgia Gap*. New York: Basic Books, 1993.

"Corporation and Business Entity Database." *NYS Division of Corporations, State Records and UCC*, n.d., https://www.dos.ny.gov/corps/bus_entity_search.html.

Crawford, James. *Brownlie's Principles of Public International Law*, 8th ed. Oxford: Oxford University Press, 2012.

Davidson, Steven. "How Much Do Top Non-Profit Jewish Leaders Make?" *Forward*, December 11, 2017, https://forward.com/news/388240/how-much-do-top-jewish-non-profit-leaders-make/.

De Waal, Edmund. *The Hare with Amber Eyes: A Family's Century of Art and Loss*. New York: Farrar, Straus and Giroux, 2010.

Dean, Martin, Constantin Goschler, and Philipp Ther, ed. *Robbery and Restitution: The Conflict over Jewish Property in Europe*. New York: Berghahn Books, 2007.

Dekel, Ephraim. *B'riha: Flight to the Homeland*. Translated by Dina Ettinger. New York: Herzl Press, 1972.

Dekel-Chen, Jonathan. "An Unlikely Triangle: Philanthropists, Commissars and American Statesmanship Meet in Soviet Crimea, 1922–37." *Diplomatic History* 27, no. 3 (2003): 353–376.

———. *Farming the Red Land: Jewish Agricultural Colonization and Local Soviet Power, 1924–1941*. New Haven and London: Yale University Press, 2005.

———. "One Big Agrarianizing Family." *Jewish History*, 21 (2007): 263–278.

———. "Philanthropy, Diplomacy and Jewish Internationalism." In *Cambridge History of Judaism*. Vol. 8, edited by Mitchell Hart and Tony Michels, 505–528. Cambridge: Cambridge University Press, 2017.

DellaPergola, Sergio. "Reflections on the Multinational Geography of Jews After World War II." In *Postwar Jewish Displacement and Rebirth, 1945–1967*, edited by Françoise S. Ouzan and Manfred Gerstenfeld, 11–33. Leiden, Boston: Brill, 2014.

Dembowski, Peter F. *Christians in the Warsaw Ghetto: An Epitaph for the Unremembered*. Notre Dame, IN: University of Notre Dame Press, 2005.

Diner, Hasia. "Jewish Self-Governance, American Style." *American Jewish History* 81, no. 3/4 (1994): 277–296.

Dinnerstein, Leonard. *America and the Survivors of the Holocaust*. New York: Columbia University Press, 1982.

Documents Relating to the Agreement between the Government of Israel and the Government of the Federal Republic of Germany. Jerusalem: Ministry of Foreign Affairs, 1953.

Draft of an Indemnification Law for Germany Submitted by the Council for the Protection of the Rights and Interests of Jews from Germany. London: n. p. 1947.

Dreifuss, Havi. "The Leadership of the Jewish Combat Organization during the Warsaw Ghetto: A Reassessment." *Holocaust and Genocide Studies* 31, no. 1 (2017): 24–48.

Drori, Gili S., John W. Meyer, and Hokyu Hwang, eds. *Globalization and Organization: World Society and Organizational Change*. Oxford: Oxford University Press, 2006.

Eizenstat, Stuart E. *Imperfect Justice: Looted Assets, Slave Labor and the Unfinished Business of World War II*. New York: Public Affairs, 2003.

Feinstein, Margarete Myers. *Holocaust Survivors in Postwar Germany, 1945–1957*. Cambridge and New York: Cambridge University Press, 2010.

Feldman, Lily Gardner. *The Special Relationship between West Germany and Israel*. Boston: George Allen & Unwin, 1984.

Ferencz, Benjamin B. *Less than Slaves: Jewish Forced Labor and the Quest for Compensation*. Cambridge, MA: Harvard University Press, 1979.

Ferstman, Carla, and Mariana Goetz, eds. *Reparations for Victims of Genocide, War Crimes and Crimes Against Humanity: Systems in Place and Systems in the Making*. Leiden and Boston: Nijhoff, 2020.

Fink, Carole. *Defending the Rights of Others: The Great Powers, the Jews, and International Minority Protection, 1878–1938*. Cambridge: Cambridge University Press, 2004.

———. "Negotiations after Negotiations: Nahum Goldmann, West Germany and the Origins of the 1980 Hardship Fund." *Jahrbuch des Simon Dubnow Instituts* 15 (2016): 287–305.

Finkelstein, Norman. *The Holocaust Industry: Reflections on the Exploitation of Jewish Suffering*. London: Verso, 2000.

Fischer, Wolfgang Georg. *Wohnungen (Apartments)*. Munich: C. Hanser, 1969.

Five Years Later: Activities of the Conference of Jewish Material Claims Against Germany, 1954–1958. New York: The Claims Conference, 1959.

"Former Holocaust Claims Conference Director and Two Recruiters Convicted in $57.3 Million Fraud on Organization That Makes Reparations to Victims of Nazi Persecution," *Dept. of Justice U.S. Attorney's Office Southern District of New York*, May 8, 2013, https://www.justice.gov/usao-sdny/pr/former-holocaust-claims-conference-director-and-two-recruiters-convicted-573-million.

"Former Holocaust Claims Conference Director Sentenced to Eight Years in Prison for $57.3 Million Fraud on Organization That Makes Reparations to Victims of Nazi Persecution," *Federal Bureau of Investigation New York Office*, November 4, 2013, https://archives.fbi.gov/archives/newyork/press-releases/2013/former-holocaust-claims-conference-director-sentenced-to-eight-years-in-prison-for-57.3-million-fraud-on-organization-that-makes-reparations-to-victims-of-nazi-persecution.

Fraenkel, Josef. "Noah Barou: The Man from Poltava." In *Essays in Jewish Sociology, Labour and Co-operation in Memory of Dr. Noah Barou 1889–1955*, edited by Henrik F. Infield, 3–8. London and New York: Thomas Yoseloff, 1962.

Frankel, Jonathan. *The Damascus Affair: "Ritual Murder," Politics, and the Jews in 1840*. Cambridge: Cambridge University Press, 1997.

———. "The Jewish Socialists and the American Jewish Congress Movement." *YIVO Annual of Jewish Social Science* 16 (1976): 288–302.

Franklin, William M., and E. R. Perkins. *Foreign Relations of the United States: Diplomatic Papers, 1943, General*, vol. 1. Washington, DC: US Government Printing Office, 1963.

Frei, Norbert, José Brunner, and Constantin Goschler, eds. *Die Praxis der Wiedergutmachung: Geschichte, Erfahrung und Wirkung in Deutschland und Israel (Compensation Practice: History, Experience, and Outcome)*. Göttingen: Wallstein Verlag, 2009.

Friedan, Betty. *The Feminine Mystique*. New York: W.W. Norton & Co., 1963.

Friedlander, Saul. *Nazi Germany and the Jews, 1933–1945*. New York: Harper, 2009.
Frohn, Axel., ed. *Holocaust and Shilumim: The Policy of Wiedergutmachung in the Early 1950s*. Washington, DC: German Historical Institute, 1991.
Frojimovics, Kinga. "Different Interpretations of Reconstruction: The AJDC and the WJC in Hungary after the Holocaust." In *The Jews are Coming Back: The Return of the Jews to their Countries of Origin after WWII*, edited by David Bankier, 286–292. Jerusalem: Yad Vashem, 2005.
Gallas, Elisabeth, Anna Holzer-Kawalko, Caroline Jessen, and Yfaat Weiss, eds. *Contested Heritage: Jewish Cultural Property after 1945*. Göttingen, Germany: Vandenhoeck & Ruprecht, 2020.
Ganin, Zvi. *An Uneasy Relationship: American Jewish Leadership and Israel, 1948–1957*. New York: Syracuse University Press, 2005.
Geller, Jay Howard. *Jews in Post-Holocaust Germany, 1945–1953*. Cambridge: Cambridge University Press, 2005.
"General Assembly 60/147," *United Nations Audiovisual Library of International Law*, 2008, https://legal.un.org/avl/pdf/ha/ga_60-147/ga_60-147_ph_e.pdf.
Gillessen, Günther. *Konrad Adenauer and Israel, The Konrad Adenauer Memorial Lecture 1986*. Oxford: St. Anthony's College, 1986.
Gmür, Priska. "'It Is Not up to Us Women to Solve Great Problems': The Duty of the Zionist Woman in the Context of the First Ten Zionist Congresses." In *The First Zionist Congress in 1897: Causes, Significance, Topicality*, edited by Heiko Haumann, Wayne van Dalsum, and Vivian Kramer, 292–296. Basel: Karger, 1997.
Goldmann, Nahum. "A Noble Son of Jewry." In *Essays in Jewish Sociology, Labour and Co-Operation in Memory of Dr. Noah Barou 1889–1955*, edited by Henrik F. Infield, 9–13. London and New York: Thomas Yoseloff, 1962.
———. *The Autobiography of Nahum Goldmann: Sixty Years of Jewish Life*. New York: Holt, Rinehart and Winston, 1969.
———. *The Autobiography of Nahum Goldmann: The Story of a Lifelong Battle by World Jewry's Ambassador at Large*. Translated by Helen Sabba. London: Weidenfeld and Nicolson, 1970.
———. *Community of Fate: Jews in the Modern World, Essays, Speeches, and Articles*. Jerusalem: Israel Universities Press, 1977.
Goossen, Ben. "The Real History of the Mennonites and the Holocaust," *Tablet Magazine*, tabletmag.com, November 17, 2020, https://www.tabletmag.com/sections/history/articles/heinrich-hamm-mennonite-holocaust.
Goschler, Constantin. *Schuld und Schulden: Die Politik der Wiedergutmachung für NS-Verfolgte seit 1945* (*Guilt and Debt: The Politics of Reparation for Victims of National Socialism since 1945*). Göttingen: Wallstein, 2005.
———. "German Compensation to Jewish Nazi Victims." In *Lessons and Legacies: New Currents in Holocaust Research*, vol. VI, edited by Jeffry M. Diefendorf, 373–412. Evanston, IL: Northwestern University Press, 2004.
"Grants Process," *Claims Conference*, n. d., http://www.claimscon.org/for-agencies/applications/process/.
Gray, Julia. "Life, Death or Zombie? The Vitality of International Organizations." *International Studies Quarterly* 62 (2018): 1–13.

Green, Abigail. "Old Networks, New Connections: The Emergence of the Jewish International." In *Religious Internationals in the Modern World: Globalization and Faith Communities since 1750*, edited by Abigail Green and Vincent Viaene, 53–81. UK: Palgrave Macmillan, 2012.

Grubel, Herbert G., ed. *World Monetary Reform: Plans and Issues*. Stanford: Stanford University Press, 1963.

Haron, Miriam. "Britain and Israel, 1948–1950." *Modern Judaism* 3, no. 2 (1983): 217–223.

Hawkins, Darren, David Lake, Daniel Nielson, and Michael Tiernet, eds. *Delegation and Agency in International Organization*. New York: Cambridge, 2006.

Hazkani, Shay. "Kalon o Hechreach Bal-Yegune? Iskat Haneshek Haisraelit-Hagermanit Harishona." (Disgrace or Unavoidable Necessity? The First Israeli-German Arms Deal) *Zmanim* 102 (2008): 102–111.

Hebrew University of Jerusalem – Oral History Division.

Heilig, Karen. "From the Luxembourg Agreement to Today Representing a People." *Berkeley Journal of International Law*, 20, no. 1 (2002): 176–196.

Heller, Henry. *The Cold War and the New Imperialism: A Global History, 1945–2005*. New York: Monthly Review Press, 2006.

Henry, Marilyn. *Confronting the Perpetrators: A History of the Claims Conference*. London: Vallentine Mitchell, 2007.

Hense, Anja. "Limitation of Economic Damages as a 'Humanitarian Gesture': The German Foundation 'Remembrance, Responsibility and the Future.'" *Journal of Contemporary History* 46, no. 2 (2011): 407–424.

Herf, Jeffrey. "Review of *Schuld und Schulden: Die Politik der Wiedergutmachung für NS-Verfolgte seit 1945*, by Constantin Goschler." *Journal of Modern History* 79, no. 4 (2007): 947–948.

Hilberg, Raul. *The Destruction of the European Jews*. New York and London: Holmes & Meier, 1985.

Hockerts, Hans Günter. "Anwälte der Verfolgten, Die URO" (Representatives of the Victims: The URO). In *Wiedergutmachung in der Bundesrepublik Deutschland (Reparations in the Federal Republic of Germany)*, edited by Ludolf Herbst and Constantin Goschler, 249–271. Munich: R. Oldenbourg, 1989.

———. "Wiedergutmachung in Deutschland: Eine historische Bilanz 1945–2000" ("Reparations in Germany: A Historical Balance 1945–2000"). *Vierteljahrshefte für Zeitgeschichte* 49, no. 2 (2001): 167–214.

Hofmannsthal, Emilio von. *Draft of a Restoration Law for Axis and Axis Occupied Countries*. Translated by Ferdinand W. Coudert. Baltimore, MD: University of Maryland, 1944.

Holub, Robert C. "Germans as Victims in 1995." *Colloquia Germanica* 48, no. 1/2 (2015): 23–33. https://www.jstor.org/stable/44478221.

Hopkinson, Chris. *Terezín Declaration—Ten Years Later: 7th International Conference: The Documentation, Identification and Restitution of the Cultural Assets of WWII Victims: Proceedings of an International Academic Conference Held in Prague on 18–19 June, 2019*. Prague: Documentation Centre for Property Transfers of Cultural Assets of WWII Victims, 2019.

Howard-Hassmann, Rhoda E. "Getting to Reparations: Japanese Americans and African Americans." *Social Forces* 83, no. 2 (2004): 823–840.
"Inter-Allied Declaration Against Acts of Dispossession Committed in Territories Under Enemy Occupation or Control." *U.S. Department of State Office of the Historian*, n. d., https://history.state.gov/historicaldocuments/frus1943v01/d456.
Israel State Archives – Files of the Israeli Ministry of Foreign Affairs.
Jabloner, Clemens. "The Austrian Historical Commission: Motives, Result and Impact." In *Revisiting the National Socialist Legacy: Coming to Terms with Forced Labor, Expropriation, Compensation, and Restitution*, edited by Oliver Rathkolb, 51–56. Innsbruck: Studien Verlag, 2002.
Jablonka, Hanna. "Klitat Nitsolei HaShoah BeMedinat Israel – Heibetim Hadashim" ("Absorption of Holocaust Survivors in the State of Israel – New Aspects"). *Iyunim Betekumat Israel* 7 (1997): 285–299.
Jelinek, Yeshayahu A. "Leo Baeck, Nahum Goldmann and the Money from Germany (A Document)." *Studies in Contemporary Jewry* 5 (1989): 236–241.
———. "Political Acumen, Altruism, Foreign Pressure or Moral Debt – Konrad Adenauer and the 'Shilumim.'" *Tel Aviver Jahrbuch für deutsche Geschichte* 19 (1990): 77–102.
———. "Implementing the Luxembourg Agreement: The Purchasing Mission and the Israeli Economy." *Journal of Israeli History* 18 (1997): 191–209.
"Jewish Population in Germany Greatly Reduced Since 1950," *Jewish Telegraphic Agency*, May 16, 1952, https://www.jta.org/1952/05/16/archive/jewish-population-in-germany-greatly-reduced-since-1950.
Judt, Tony. *Postwar: A History of Europe since 1945*. New York: Penguin Books, 2005.
Junz, Helen B. "Report on the Pre-War Wealth Position of the Jewish Population in Nazi-Occupied Countries, Germany and Austria." Appendix S to *Report on Dormant Accounts of Victims of Nazi Persecution in Swiss Banks*. Berne: Staempfli, 1999.
Kapralik, C. I. *Reclaiming the Nazi Loot: The History of the Work of the Jewish Trust Corporation for Germany*. London: The Sidney Press Ltd., 1962.
Karns, Margaret P. and Karen A. Mingst. *International Organizations: The Politics and Processes of Global Governance*. 2nd ed. Boulder, CO and London, UK: Lynne Rienner Publishers, Inc., 2010.
Katz, Yossi. *Al Heshbon Hakorbanot: Iyunim Hadashim Besugiyot Heskem Hashilumim, Hapitsuim Haishiim Vehashavat Rechush Hakorbanot BeIsrael (The Forsaken: Israel, the Reparations Agreement, and the Question of Compensation and Restitution for Nazi Survivors)*. Tel Aviv: Ministry of Defense Press, 2009.
Kauffman, Christopher J. "Politics, Programs and Protests: Catholic Relief Services in Vietnam, 1954–1975." *Catholic Historical Review* 91, no. 2 (2005): 223–250.
Kaufman, Menahem. *An Ambiguous Relationship: Non-Zionists and Zionists in America, 1939–1948*. Jerusalem: Magnes Press, 1991.
Keidar, Nir. *Mamlachtiut: Hatefisa Haezrahit shel David Ben-Gurion (Nationalism. David Ben Gurion's Civil Perception)*. Jerusalem: Ben-Gurion-Institute for Israel Studies and Yad Ben Zvi, 2009.

Keohane, Robert O., and Joseph S. Nye. "Transgovernmental Relations and International Organizations." *World Politics* 27, no. 1 (1974): 39–62.

Kittel, Manfred. *Die Legende von der „Zweiten Schuld": Vergangenheitsbewältigung in der Ära Adenauer* (*The Legend of the "Second Guilt": Dealing with the Past in the Adenauer Era*). Berlin: Ullstein, 1993.

Köhler, Ingo. "Business as Usual? Aryanization in Practice, 1933–1938." In *Business in the Age of Extremes: Essays in Modern German and Austrian Economic History*, edited by Harmut Berghoff, Jürgen Kocka, and Dieter Ziegler, 172–188. Washington, DC: Cambridge University Press, 2013.

Kohut, Rebekah. "Jewish Women's Organizations in the United States." *The American Jewish Year Book*. September 12, 1931–September 31, 1932/5692.

Kolinsky, Eva. *After the Holocaust: Jewish Survivors after 1945*. London: Pimlico, 2004.

Klüger, Ruth. *Still Alive: A Holocaust Girlhood Remembered*. New York: Feminist Press, 2012.

Knight, Robert. "National Construction Work and Hierarchies of Empathy in Postwar Austria." *Journal of Contemporary History* 49, no. 3 (2014): 491–513.

Kracauer, Isidor. "Rabbi Joselmann de Rosheim." *Revue des Études Juives* 16 (1888).

Krajewski, André. *Die Geschichte der jüdischen Warenhäuser in Deutschland* (*The History of Jewish Department Stores in Germany*), Self-published, 2011, https://andre-krajewski.de/content/pdf/warenhaus.pdf.

Kubowitzki, Aryeh Leon. *Unity in Dispersion: A History of the World Jewish Congress*. New York: World Jewish Congress, 1948.

Kurz, Nathan. "In the Shadow of Versailles: Jewish Minority Rights at the 1946 Paris Peace Conference." *Simon Dubnow Institute Yearbook* (2017): 187–209.

Lang, Berel. *Post-Holocaust: Interpretation, Misinterpretation and the Claims of History*. Bloomington: Indiana University Press, 2005.

Lange, Carolin Dorothée. "After they Left: Looted Jewish Apartments and the Private Perception of the Holocaust." *Holocaust and Genocide Studies* 34, no. 3 (2020): 431–449.

La Porte, Teresa. "The Impact of 'Intermestic' Non-State Actors on the Conceptual Framework of Public Diplomacy." *The Hague Journal of Diplomacy* 7 (2012): 441–458.

Larres, Klaus, and Ann Lane, eds. *The Cold War: The Essential Readings*. Oxford. UK: Blackwell Publishers, 2001.

Laskier, Michael M. "Aspects of the Activities of the Alliance Israélite Universelle in the Jewish Communities of the Middle East and North Africa: 1860–1918." *Modern Judaism* 3, no. 2 (1983): 147–171.

Lavsky, Hagit. *New Beginnings: Holocaust Survivors in Bergen-Belsen and the British Zone in Germany, 1945–1950*. Detroit: Wayne State University Press, 2002.

Lederhendler, Eli. *Jewish Responses to Modernity: New Voices in America and Eastern Europe*. New York and London: NYU Press, 1994.

———. "Shtadlanut and Stewardship: Paternal Diplomacy and Leadership in American Jewry, 1860s to 1920s." *Jewish Culture and History* 19, no. 1 (2018): 97–110.
Leff, Lisa Moses. *Sacred Bonds of Solidarity: The Rise of Jewish Internationalism in Nineteenth-Century France*. Stanford: Stanford University Press, 2006.
Lehrman, Hal. "The New Germany and the Remaining Jews," *Commentary*, December 1953, https://www.commentarymagazine.com/articles/the-new-germany-and-her-remaining-jewsa-reporters-notebook/.
Leibler, Isi. "Candidly Speaking: Accountability for Claims Conference," *The Jerusalem Post*, December 2, 2010, https://www.jpost.com/opinion/columnists/candidly-speaking-accountability-for-claims-conference.
Lieberman, Charles S. "Diaspora Influence on Israel: The Ben-Gurion-Blaustein "Exchange" and its Aftermath." *Jewish Social Studies* 36, no. 3/4 (1974): 271–280.
Ludi, Regula. *Reparations for Nazi Victims in Postwar Europe*. Cambridge: Cambridge University Press, 2012.
———. "The Vectors of Postwar Victim Reparations: Relief, Redress and Memory Politics." *Journal of Contemporary History* 41, no. 3 (2006): 421–450.
Marrus, Michael R. *Some Measure of Justice: The Holocaust Era Restitution Campaigns of the 1990s*. Madison, Wisconsin: University of Wisconsin Press, 2009.
Marx, Hugo. *The Case of the German Jews vs. Germany: A Legal Basis for the Claims of the German Jews Against Germany*. New York: Egmont Press, 1944.
May, Larry. *After the War: A Philosophical Perspective*. Cambridge: Cambridge University Press, 2012.
McCune, Mary. "Formulating the 'Women's Interpretation of Zionism': Hadassah Recruitment of Non-Zionist American Women, 1914–1930." In *American Jewish Women and the Zionist Enterprise*, edited by Shulamit Reinharz and Mark A. Raider, 89–111. Waltham, Mass: Brandeis University Press, 2005.
———. *The Whole Wide World without Limits: International Relief, Gender Politics and American Jewish Women, 1893–1930*. Detroit: Wayne State University Press, 2005.
McFadden, Margaret. *Golden Cables of Sympathy: The Transatlantic Sources of Nineteenth-Century Feminism*. Lexington, KY: University Press of Kentucky, 1999.
Melville, Rose. "Nonprofit Umbrella Organisations in a Contracting Regime: A Comparative Review of Australian, British and American Literature and Experiences." *International Journal of Not-for-Profit Law* 1, no. 4 (1999).
"Member Organizations," *Conference of Presidents of Major American Jewish Organizations*, n. d., https://www.conferenceofpresidents.org/about/members.
Meng, Michael L. "After the Holocaust: The History of Jewish Life in West Germany." *Contemporary European History* 14, no. 3 (2005): 403–413.
Meyer, John W., and Brian Rowan. "Institutional Organizations: Formal Structures as Myth and Ceremony." *American Journal of Sociology* 83, no. 2 (1977): 340–363.
Meyer, Michael A., ed. *German-Jewish History in Modern Times*. Volume I, *Tradition and Enlightenment 1600–1780*. New York: Columbia University Press, 1996.

Meyerowitz, Joanne. *Not June Cleaver: Women and Gender in Postwar America, 1945–1961*. Philadelphia: Temple University Press, 1994.

Michalczyk, John., ed. *Nazi Law: From Nuremberg to Nuremberg*. London: Bloomsbury Academic, 2018.

Miller, Israel. "The Conference on Jewish Material Claims against Germany." *Cardozo Law Review* 20 (1998): 579–582.

"Minutes of Government Meeting 5/312, Section 7, Israel Enlists Jewish Organizations," *Sharett.org.il*, n.d., http://www.sharett.org.il/cgi-webaxy/sal/sal.pl?lang=he&ID=880900_sharett_new&act=show&dbid=bookfiles&dataid=2212.

"Mischlinge," *Holocaust Education & Archive Research Team*, n. d., http://www.holocaustresearchproject.org/holoprelude/mischlinge.html.

Moeller, Robert G. "The Politics of the Past in the 1950s: Rhetorics of Victimization in East and West Germany." In *Germans as Victims: Remembering the Past in Contemporary Germany*, edited by Bill Niven, 26–42. New York: Palgrave Macmillan, 2006.

Moisel, Claudia, and Tobias Winstel, eds. *Grenzen der Wiedergutmachung: Die Entschädigung für NS-Verfolgte in West- und Osteuropa 1945–2000 (Limits of Reparations: Compensation for Victims of National Socialism in Western and Eastern Europe 1945–2000)*. Göttingen: Wallstein Verlag, 2006.

Moravcsik, Andrew. "Theory and Method in the Study of International Negotiation: A Rejoinder to Oran Young." *International Organization* 53, no. 4 (1999): 811–814. https://doi.org/10.1162/002081899551084.

Moses, Siegfried. *Jewish Post-War Claims*. Tel Aviv: Irgun Olej Merkaz Europa, 1944.

———. "Salman Schocken: His Economic and Zionist Activities." *Leo Baeck Institute Yearbook* 5 (1960): 73–104.

Murray, "Alice Yang. Review of *"Military Necessity," World War II Internment, and Japanese American History, American History"* 25, no. 2 (1997): 319–325. https://www.jstor.org/stable/30030791?seq=1.

Nadell, Pamela. "Rereading Charles S. Liebman: Questions from the Perspective of Women's History." *American Jewish History* 80, no. 4 (1991): 502–516.

Nasaw, David. *The Last Million: Europe's Displaced Persons from World War to Cold War*. New York: Penguin Press, 2020.

Neiberg, Michael. *Potsdam: The End of World War II and the Remaking of Europe*. New York: Basic Books, 2015.

Nelson, Deborah L. "Introduction." *Women's Studies Quarterly*, 33, no. 3/4 (2005): 10–23.

"No Compensation for Lebensborn Children Abducted by SS," *Deutsche Welle*, July 6, 2018, https://www.dw.com/en/no-compensation-for-lebensborn-children-abducted-by-nazi-ss/a-44556995.

Norich, Samuel. "Why I Resigned from Claims Conference Board — And Why You Should Care," *Forward*, July 14, 2013, https://forward.com/opinion/180375/why-i-resigned-from-claims-conference-board-and/.

Odier Contreras-Garduno, Diana. *Collective Reparations: Tensions and Dilemmas between Collective Reparations with the Individual Right to Receive Reparations*. Cambridge: Intersentia, 2018.

Ohanyan, Anna. "Policy Wars for Peace: Network Model of NGO Behavior." *International Studies Review* 11, no. 3 (2009): 475–501.

"Patricia Hewitt Announces Enemy Property Payment Scheme to Close." *Department for Business, Energy & Industrial Strategy*, July 8, 2004, http://www.enemyproperty.bis.gov.uk/inote.html.

Pendas, Devin O. *Democracy, Nazi Trials, and Transitional Justice in Germany, 1945–1950*. New York: Cambridge University Press, 2020.

Pigman, Geoffrey Allen. "Making Room at the Negotiating Table: The Growth of Diplomacy between Nation-State Governments and Non-State Economic Entities." *Diplomacy and Statecraft* 16 (2005): 385–401.

Pinkus, Benjamin. *The Soviet Government and the Jews, 1948-1967: A Documented Study*. Cambridge: Cambridge University Press, 1984.

Pinson, Koppel S. "Jewish Life in Liberated Germany – A Study of Jewish DPs." *Jewish Social Studies* 9 (1947): 101–126.

Pohl, Dieter. "The Robbery of Jewish Property in Eastern Europe under German Occupation, 1939–1942." In *Robbery and Restitution: The Conflict over Jewish Property in Europe*, edited by Martin Dean, Constantin Goschler, and Philipp Ther, 68–80. New York: Berghahn Books, 2007.

Pross, Christian. *Paying for the Past: The Struggle over Reparations for Surviving Victims of the Nazi Terror*. Translated by Belinda Cooper. Baltimore and London: John Hopkins University Press, 1998.

Protocole du Premier Congrès Juif Mondial: Genève, 8–15 Août 1936 (Minutes of First World Jewish Congress: Geneva, August 8–15. 1936). Geneva: WJC, 1936.

Proudfoot, Malcolm J. *European Refugees: 1939–1952: A Study in Forced Population Movement*. London: Faber and Faber, 1957.

Raider, Mark A., ed. *Nahum Goldmann: Statesman without a State*. Albany: SUNY Press, 2009.

Raphael, Marc Lee. "The Origins of Organized Jewish Philanthropy in the United States, 1914-1939." In *The Jews of North America*, edited by Moses Rischin, 213–223. Detroit: Wayne State University Press, 1987.

Rauschenberger, Katharina. "The Restitution of Jewish Cultural Objects and the Activities of Jewish Cultural Reconstruction, Inc." *Leo Baeck Institute Year Book* 53 (2008): 191–211. https://doi.org/10.1093/leobaeck/53.1.191.

"Reconciliation, Peace and Cooperation," *Fund for Reconciliation, Peace and Cooperation*, n. d., http://www.reconciliationfund.at/db/admin/de/index_main1541.html?cbereich=2&cthema=344&carticle=604&fromlist=1.

Redlich, Shimon. "The Jewish Antifascist Committee in the Soviet Union." *Jewish Social Studies* 31, no. 1 (1969): 25–39.

Reinalda, Bob. "Private in Form, Public in Purpose: NGOs in International Relations Theory." In *Non-State Actors in International Relations*, edited by Bas Arts, Math Noortmann, and Bob Reinalda, 11–28. Hampshire, England: Ashgate Publishing Ltd., 2001.

———. *Routledge History of International Organizations: From 1815 to the Present Day*. London, New York: Routledge, 2009.

Reinharz, Jehuda, and Evyatar Friesel. "Nahum Goldmann, Jewish and Zionist Statesman – An Overview." In *Nahum Goldmann: Statesman without a State*, edited by Mark A. Raider, 3–49. Albany: SUNY Press, 2009.

Reinisch, Jessica. "'Auntie UNRRA' at the Crossroads." *Past & Present* 218, suppl. 8 (2013): 70–97.

Report of the State Public Inquiry on Aid to Holocaust Survivors (in Hebrew), Israel Government website, June 2008, https://www.gov.il/BlobFolder/generalpage/official_inquiry_committees_holocaust_survivors/he/%D7%95%D7%A2%D7%93%D7%AA%20%D7%94%D7%97%D7%A7%D7%99%D7%A8%D7%94%20%D7%94%D7%9E%D7%9E%D7%9C%D7%9B%D7%AA%D7%99%D7%AA%20%D7%91%D7%A0%D7%95%D7%A9%D7%90%20%D7%94%D7%A1%D7%99%D7%95%D7%A2%20%D7%9C%D7%A0%D7%99%D7%A6%D7%95%D7%9C%D7%99%20%D7%94%D7%A9%D7%95%D7%90%D7%94.pdf.

Report on Conference of Jewish Educational Reconstruction. Paris: n. p., 1946.

Riegner, Gerhart. *Never Despair: Sixty Years in the Service of the Cause of Human Rights.* Chicago: Ivan R. Dee, 2006.

Robinson, Nehemiah. *Indemnification and Reparations: Jewish Aspects.* New York: Institute of Jewish affairs of AJC and WJC, 1944.

———. *Ten Years of German Indemnification.* New York: Claims Conference, 1964.

Ro'i, Yaacov. "The Reconstruction of Jewish Communities in the USSR, 1944–1947." In *The Jews are Coming Back: The Return of the Jews to their Countries of Origin after WWII*, edited by David Bankier, 186–206. Jerusalem: Yad Vashem, 2005.

Rosand, Eric. "Confronting the Nazi Past at the End of the 20th Century: The Austrian Model." *Berkeley Journal of International Law* 20, no. 1 (2002): 202–211.

Rosenthal, Jemima, ed. *Foreign Policy Documents of the State of Israel.* Jerusalem: Government Printer, 1991.

Rozin, Orit. *Hovat Haahava Hakasha: Yahid Vekollektiv Beyisrael Bishnot Hahamishim (The Hard Duty to Love: Individual and Collective in Israel in the 1950s).* Tel Aviv: Institute for Research of Zionism and Israel, 2008.

Rubinstein, Alvin Z. *The Soviets in International Organizations: Changing Policy Toward Developing Countries, 1953–1963.* Princeton, NJ: Princeton University Press, 1964.

Sagi, Nana. *German Reparations: A History of the Negotiations.* Translated by Dafna Alon. Jerusalem: Magnes Press, 1980.

Sands, Philippe. *East West Street: On the Origins of Genocide and Crimes Against Humanity.* London: Weidenfeld & Nicolson, 2016.

"Saul Kagan, Architect of Holocaust Restitution," *Claims Conference*, n. d., http://www.claimscon.org/about/history/saul-kagan/.

"Saul Kagan, Who Won Holocaust Restitution, Is Dead at 91," *New York Times*, November 14, 2013, http://www.nytimes.com/2013/11/15/world/europe/saul-kagan-who-won-holocaust-restitution-is-dead-at-91.html.

Saunders-Hastings, Emma. "Plutocratic Philanthropy." *The Journal of Politics* 80, no. 1 (2018): 149–161. https://doi.org/10.1177%2F002083451806800201.

Schrafstetter, Susan. "'Gentlemen, the Cheese is All Gone!' British POWS, the 'Great Escape' and the Anglo-German Agreement for Compensation to Victims of Nazism." *Contemporary European History* 17, no. 1 (2008): 23–43.

Schwarz, Géraldine. *Those Who Forget: One Family's Story – A Memoir, A History, A Warning*. Translated by Laura Marris. London: Pushkin Press, 2020.

Schwarz, Hans-Peter. *Konrad Adenauer: A German Politician and Statesman in a Period of War, Revolution and Reconstruction*. Vol. 1, *From the German Empire to the Federal Republic, 1876–1952*. Translated by Louise Willmot. Providence and Oxford: Berghahn Books, 1995.

Schwerin, Kurt. "German Compensation for Victims of Nazi Persecution." *Northwestern University Law Review* 67, no. 4 (1972): 479–527.

Segev, Tom. *The Seventh Million: The Israelis and the Holocaust*. Translated by Haim Watzman. New York: Hill and Wang, 1993.

Segev, Zohar. *The World Jewish Congress During the Holocaust: Between Activism and Restraint*. Berlin and Boston: De Gruyter Oldenbourg, 2014.

Shain, Yossi and Aharon Barth. "Diasporas and International Relations Theory." *International Organization* 57, no. 3 (2003): 449–479.

Shelton, Dinah. "Righting Wrongs: Reparations in the Articles on State Responsibility." *The American Journal of International Law* 96, no. 4 (2002): 833–856.

Shephard, Ben. *The Long Road Home: The Aftermath of the Second World War*. London: Vintage Books, 2011.

Shiff, Ofer, Adi Sherzer, Talia Gorodess. "The Ben-Gurion-Blaustein Exchange: Ben-Gurion's Perspective Between an Ideological Capitulation and a Strategic Alliance." *Israel Studies* 25, no. 3 (2020): 15–32.

Shinnar, Felix. *Be-Ol Korach U-regashot, Bishelichut Hamedina, Yahasei Israel-Germanyah, 1951–1966*. (*The Burden of Necessity and Feelings, On Behalf of the State: Israel-German Relations, 1951–1966*). Jerusalem: Schocken, 1967.

Shirer, William. *Berlin Diary: The Journal of a Foreign Correspondent, 1934-1941*. New York: Alfred A. Knopf, 1941.

Slymovics, Susan. *How to Accept Reparations*. Philadelphia: University of Pennsylvania Press, 2014.

Smith, Brian H. *More than Altruism: The Politics of Private Foreign Aid*. Princeton NJ: Princeton University Press, 2014.

Soh, C. Sarah. "Japan's National/Asian Women's Fund for 'Comfort Women.'" *Pacific Affairs* 76, no. 2 (2003): 209–233. https://www.jstor.org/stable/40024391.

Sommer Schneider, Anna. "Behind the Iron Curtain: The Communist Government in Poland and its Attitude towards the Joint's Activities, 1944–1989." In *The JDC at 100: A Century of Humanitarianism*, edited by Avinoam Patt, Atina Grossmann, Linda G. Levi, and Maud S. Mandel, 316–360. Detroit: Wayne State University Press, 2019.

"Speech by Menahem Begin in the *Knesset* on January 7, 1952," *Knesset.gov.il*, n.d., http://main.knesset.gov.il/About/Occasion/Pages/BeginSpeech4.aspx.

Spernol, Boris, and Matthias Langrock. "Amtliche Wirklichkeit: Die Praxis der Entschädigung aus behördlicher Binnenperspektive" (Bureaucratic Reality: The Practice of Compensation from Official Internal Perspectives). In *Die Praxis der Wiedergutmachung: Geschichte, Erfahrung und Wirkung in Deutschland und Israel,* edited by state Norbert Frei, José Brunner, and Constantin Goschler, 600–634. Göttingen: Wallstein Verlag, 2009.

Stauber, Roni. "Israel's Quest for Diplomatic Relations – The German-Israeli Controversy." *Tel Aviver Jahrbuch für deutsche Geschichte* 41 (2013): 215–228.

Steinweis, Alan E., and Robert D. Rachlin, eds. *Ideology, Opportunism, and the Perversion of Justice.* New York and Oxford: Berghahn, 2013.

Stiebel, Joan. "The Central British Fund for World Jewish Relief: Transactions & Miscellanies." *Jewish Historical Society of England* 27 (1978): 51–60.

Strum, Harvey. "Henry Stimson's Opposition to American Jews and Zionism." *Patterns of Prejudice* 18, no. 4 (1984): 17–24.

Szajkowski, Zosa. "'Reconstruction' vs. 'Palliative Relief' in American Jewish Overseas Work (1919–1939)." *Jewish Social Studies* 32, no. 1 (1970): 14–42.

Takei, Ayaka. "The 'Gemeinde Problem': The JRSO and the Postwar Jewish Communities in Germany, 1947–54." *Holocaust and Genocide Studies* 16, no. 2 (2002): 266–288.

Taylor, Gideon, Greg Schneider, Saul Kagan, and Karen Heilig. "The Claims Conference and the Historic Jewish Efforts for Holocaust-Related Compensation and Restitution." In *Reparations for Victims of Genocide, War Crimes and Crimes against Humanity: Systems in Place and Systems in the* Making, edited by Carla Ferstman and Mariana Goetz, 2nd rev. version, 203–214. Leiden and Boston: Nijhoff, 2020.

Teitelbaum, Raul. *Hapitaron Habiologi: Shaaruriat Hapitsuim Haishiim Lenitsolei Hashoah* (*The Biological Solution: The Scandal of Individual Compensation for Holocaust Survivors*). Israel: Hakibbutz Hameuchad, 2008.

"Terezin Declaration," *EU2009.CZ*, August 16, 2011, http://www.eu2009.cz/en/news-and-documents/news/terezin-declaration-26304/.

Timm, Angelika. *Jewish Claims against East Germany: Moral Obligations and Pragmatic Policy.* Budapest: Central European University Press, 1997.

Troen, Ilan. *Jewish Centers and Peripheries: Europe between America and Israel Fifty Years after World War II.* New Brunswick, NJ: Transaction, 1998.

Tsur, Yaron. "Reshito shel Ha-irgun Ha-kehilati Be'Casablanca" (The Beginning of the Communal Organization in Casablanca). In *Kehal Yisra'el: Ha-shilton Ha-'atsmi Ha-Yehudi Le-dorotav,* edited by Israel Bartal, vol. 3, 165–189. Jerusalem: Merkaz Zalman Shazar, 2001.

———. *Kehilah Keru'ah: Yehude Maroko veha-le'umiyut, 1943–1954* (*A Torn Community: Moroccan Jews and Nationalism, 1943–1954*). Tel Aviv: Am Oved, 2001.

Twenty Years Later: Activities of the Conference of Jewish Material Claims against Germany, 1952–1972. New York: The Claims Conference, 1973.

"United States Department of State The JUST Act Report," *Office of the Special Envoy for Holocaust Issues Bureau of European and Eurasian Affairs,* 2020, https://www.state.gov/wp-content/uploads/2020/02/JUST-Act5.pdf.

USC Shoah Foundation Visual History Archive.

Van der Steen, Eric. "Culture Clash: The Costs and Benefits of Homogeneity." *Management Science* 56, no. 10 (2010): 1718–1738.

Vital, David. "Diplomacy in the Jewish Interest." In *Jewish History: Essays in Honor of Chimen Abramsky*, edited by Ada Rappoport-Albert and Steven Zipperstein, 683–695. London: P. Halban, 1988.

———. *A People Apart – A Political History of the Jews in Europe, 1789–1939*. Oxford: Oxford University Press, 1999.

Vogel, Rolf., ed. *The German Path to Israel: A Documentation*. London: Oswald Wolff, 1969.

Waite, Robert G. "Returning Jewish Cultural Property: The Handling of Books Looted by the Nazis in the American Zone of Occupation, 1945 to 1952." *Libraries & Culture* 37, no.3 (2002): 213–228.

Webster, Ronald. "American Relief and Jews in Germany, 1945–1960: Diverging Perspectives." *Leo Baeck Institute Yearbook* 38 (1993): 293–321.

Weil, Bruno. "Review." *The American Journal of International Law* 39 (1945): 362–364.

———. "Review." *The American Journal of International Law* 40 (1946): 221–227.

Weiner, Amir. *Making Sense of War: The Second World War and the Fate of the Bolshevik Revolution*. Princeton, NJ: Princeton University Press, 2001.

Weinryb, Bernard D. "East European Immigration to the United States." *The Jewish Quarterly Review* 45, no. 4 (1955): 497–528.

———. *The Jews of Poland: A Social and Economic History of the Jewish Community in Poland from 1100 to 1800*. Philadelphia: Jewish Publication Society, 1973.

Weitz, Yechiam. "Haderech LeWassenaar: Keitsad Ushra Hahachlata al Masa uMatan Yashir ben Yisrael leGermania" (The Way to Wassenaar: How the Decision on Negotiations between Israel and Germany was Approved). *Yad Vashem* 28 (2000): 247–275.

Werker, Eric and Faisal Z. Ahmed. "What do Nongovernmental Organizations Do?" *The Journal of Economic Perspectives* 22, no. 2 (2008): 73–92.

Wieters, Heike. "Reinventing the Firm: From Post-War Relief to International Humanitarian Agency." *European Review of History* 23, no. 1–2 (2016): 116–135. https://doi.org/10.1080/13507486.2015.1117424.

Wyman, Mark. *Displaced Persons: Europe's Displaced Persons, 1945–1951*. Philadelphia: Balch Institute Press, 1989.

Young, Dennis R. "Organizational Identity and the Structure of Nonprofit Umbrella Associations." *Nonprofit Management and Leadership* 11, no. 3 (2001): 289–304.

Young, Oran R. *Governance in World Affairs*. Ithaca and London: Cornell University Press, 1999.

Zahra, Tara. *The Lost Children: Reconstructing Europe's Families after World War II*. Cambridge, MA: Harvard University Press, 2011.

Zentralrat der Juden in Deutschland-Geschichte, n.d., https://www.zentralratder juden.de/der-zentralrat/geschichte/.

Zimmermann, Moshe and Oded Heilbronner, eds. *Yahasim 'Normaliim:' Yahasei Israel-Germania*" (*"Normal" Relations: Israeli-German Relations*). Jerusalem: Magnes Press, 1993.

Zweig, Ronald W. *German Reparations and the Jewish World, A History of the Claims Conference*, 2nd ed. London: Portland, 2001.

———. "Review of *Confronting the Perpetrators: A History of the Claims Conference*, by Marilyn Henry." *American Jewish History* 94 (2008): 344–346.

———. "'Reparations Made Me,' Nahum Goldmann, German Reparations and the Jewish World." In *Nahum Goldmann: Statesman without a State*, edited by Mark A. Raider, 233–253. Albany: SUNY Press, 2009.

Index

Please note that page numbers in bold direct the reader to photographs, diagrams or other images, and that acronyms and abbreviations are used wherever possible for the sake of brevity.

Abs, Hermann, 67
Acheson, Dean, 46, 135
Adenauer, Konrad, 48–53, 99, 146, 165; friendship with Goldmann, 57, 66–68, 150–53, 156, 168
Adler-Rudel, Shalom, 20
Algeria, 137, 163
Allies. *See* Second World War
American, Sadie, 109
antisemitism, 8, 24, 57, 94, 107, 150
anti-slavery conference (1840), 25
Arendt, Hannah, 29
Argentina, 35, 100–101, 104
Armenian massacre, 161
Australia, 100, 104, 109, 127
Austria, 27, 44; annexation of (*Anschluss*), 70; reparations, refusal to pay, 47, 143–45, 150–51, 154, 162–64; survivors originating from, 67, 70, 84, 112, 142, 156; Vienna, 4–5, 143
Austro-Hungarian Empire, 26, 153

Baeck, Leo, 84
Baron, Salo, 29, 32, 94
Barou, Noah, 44, 49, 85, 91–93

Beckelman, Moses, 87, 121, 125
Begin, Menahem, 51
Belgium, 11, 142, 149
Ben-Gurion, David, 20, 55, 144–45, 154, 164–65, 167; speeches of, 10, 46–47, 55, 86–87
Bentwich, Norman, 30, 71
Bernstein, Bernard, 111
Blankenhorn, Herbert, 49, 84
Blaustein, Jacob, 46–47, 74, 113, 132; allocation of reparations, 86–88, 91–94, 126, 131; attitude to Israel, 46–47, 54, 154; background of, 103, 132, 148; diplomatic skill of, 148, 151, 171
Böhm, Franz, 66–67, 106
Bosnia, 161
Boukstein, Maurice, 132
Brill, Hermann, 48
Brunschvig, Jules, 124
Bulgaria, 22

Callman, Rudolph, 93, 132
Canada, 23, 27, 35, 91, 100–101, 104, 129; refugees to, 128–30

197

Churchill, Winston, 22
Claims Conference (Conference on Jewish Material Claims against Germany): accountability, lack of, 123–24, 171–72; allocation of reparations, **128** (for all Jews (*Judentum*), 125; for "Christian Jews," 107; for cultural and education activities, 89, 93–94, 122, 126, 131–33, 172–74; for displacement, 83, 133; for German Jews, 35–36, 83–84, 148–49; for individuals, 35, 68–72, 81, 85–87, 93, 120–22, 125–26, 133–35, 143–45, 148–49, 155–56, 165, 171; for organizations, 35, 72, 85–87, 125–26; for rabbis and communal leaders, 92–94, 171; for reconstruction, 86–89, 133; for relief, rehabilitation, and resettlement, 83, 123, 171; for slave labor, 7; for stolen property. *See* reparations, for stolen property; for survivors in United Kingdom, 127–30; for survivors in United States, 91, 129, 131; Board of Directors, 120–22, 125, 173–74; establishment of, 6–9, 31, 41–59 (founding meeting (Waldorf-Astoria Hotel, New York, 1951), 53–59, 65, 100–102); expertise, 12, 119–35, 171; Ezra Legacy Inc., 174; inclusion and exclusion, 12, 99–114, 133, 141; legal status of, 41; lobbying by, 13, 149–51, 166, 173–74; Luxembourg Agreement. *See* Luxembourg Agreement; membership, 10, 26, 73, 99–106, **105**, 110, 113, 120–31, 148, 171; Memorial Foundation for Jewish Culture, 173; mismanagement of, 173–74; objectivity, lack of, 119–21, 124–31, 134; organizational logic, 119–35; permanence of, 12, 65–76, 171–74; scholarly neglect of, 7–10, 143; as spokesman for all Jews (*Judentum*), 7–8, 12, 41–46, 49–50, 59, 65–68, 101, 106, 120, 141, 165–67, 170; transparency, 123–24, 172

Cohen, Israel, 23

Cold War, 47, 51, 70, 104, 146; end of, 76, 163, 166; Iron Curtain, 33, 44, 89–90, 107, 130, 142, 150, 156, 170 (fall of, 147, 152, 162, 173); Soviet Union. *See* Soviet Union

Comité des Délégations auprès de la Conférence de la Paix, 27

Communism, 48, 100; collectivization, 90–91; Israeli Communist Party, 146; Soviet. *See* Soviet Union

Conference on German External Debts (London), 67

Crémieux, Adolphe, 153

Czechoslovakia, 27, 113, 150

Denmark, 142
de Waal, Edmund, 4
diplomacy, 19–21, 165; new forms of, 13, 123, 141, 148–53, 156, 166–68. *See also* Claims Conference
displaced persons. *See* Holocaust, survivors, stateless
Domnitser, Semen, 173
Doran, Meta, 1, 162
Dorner, Dalia, 147
Dzialowski, Dina, 11

Easterman, Alex, 56
East Germany (German Democratic Republic, GDR), 47, 147, 156; refusal to pay reparations, 47, 67
Eban, Abba, 54
Eden, Anthony, 24
Egypt, 146
Ehrenburg, Ilya, 107–8
Emerson, Sir Herbert, 20
Eshkol, Levi, 145

Fagin, Helen, 5
famine, 65, 161
Ferencz, Benjamin, 30, 34, 45, 57, 66–67
Finland, 22

First World War: aftermath of, 88, 154 (Minorities Treaties, 27, 120; Versailles, Treaty of, 24, 43, 67); veterans of, 71
Fischer, Wolfgang Georg, 4
France, 23, 31, 34, 47, 104, 142, 149, 163; Jews, treatment of, 71–72; Normandy, 34; resistance fighters, 142

Gaster, Theodor H., 29, 32
Germany, 27, 31, 104; Baden-Württemberg, 5; Berlin, 20, 30, 148; *Bundestag*, 51, 70, 146, 162; Cologne, 71; Dresden, 11; East. *See* East Germany; *Ford Werke*, 163; Frankfurt, 28; German language, 66, 69–70, 93; Gold Discount Bank (Dego), 3; Hamburg, 1; Heidelburg, 28, 148; Holocaust. *See* Holocaust; Jena, 148; Jews, treatment of (concentration camps. *See* Holocaust, concentration and labor camps; confiscation of property (*Arisierung*), 1–6, 20, 47, 84, 148–49, 153, 162, 173. *See also* reparations, for stolen property; restitution of stolen property; Decree on the Registration of Jewish property, 4; deportation, 4–5, 112; expiation levy, 3–4; genocide. *See* Holocaust; Nuremberg Race Laws, 4, 29, 104–6; Reich Flight Tax, 3–4; "wild" Aryanization, 4); Ministry of Foreign Affairs, 44, 49, 84, 130; Munich, 45; Nazi regime (Third Reich), 1, 23, 28 (concentration camps. *See* Holocaust; forced sterilization, 71; homosexuals, persecution of, 71; *Lebensborn*, 71; SS officers, 4, 71); occupied, 35–36, 43–44, 47–48, 67–69, 112. *See also* East Germany; West Germany; reparations laws and agreements. reunification of, 7, 48, 75, 162, 173; Weimar Republic, 67; West. *See* West Germany

globalization, 76
Goebbels, Joseph, 4
Goldmann, Nahum, 10, **28**, 53, 66–68, **69**, 91–94, **102**; Adenauer, friendship with, 57, 66–68, 150–53, 156, 168; childhood and education, 28; coalitions, creation of, 100–103; Claims Conference, establishment of, 6–9, 29, 43–46, 54–58, 65, 83; Claims Conference, selection of members, 99–103. *See also* Claims Conference, membership; as dealmaker, 2, 66–68; diplomatic skill of, 103, 120, 148, 152, 166, 170–71; Luxembourg Agreement, role in, 49, 72–74; organizational skill of, 100–103, 113, 120–21, 128–31; and reparations allocations policy, 82–86, 92–94, 123–24
Goldstein, Israel, 74, 111–12, 132
Goodman, Harry, 123
Goodman, Romana, 109
Gottheil, Emma, 109
Gottlieb, Isak, 5
Great Britain. *See* UK
Greece, 27, 142, 151
Grossman, Vasily, 107–8
Grotius, Hugo, 19, 67
Grünstein, Sarah, 5
Gryn, Hugo, 132
Guriel, Boris, 52
Gutmann, Baron, 4

Hallstein, Walter, 125
Halprin, Rose Luria, 109–10
Hamm, Heinrich, 5
Haskalah, 88
Held, Adolph, 111–12
Herzl, Theodore, 26
Hess, Moshe, 144
Himmler, Heinrich, 5
Holland (the Netherlands), 47, 142; Jews, treatment of, 71–72, 149; Wassenaar, 45, 66–67, 82, 167
Holocaust, 21–24, 31, 65, 161; concentration and labor camps, 2,

5, 71, 132, 142, 149–50, 162, 166 (Auschwitz, 1, 11, 22; Bergen-Belsen, 1, 44; forced labour (*Vernichtung durch Arbeit*), 44, 71, 142, 161–63; gas chambers, 1, 30; Sachsenhausen, 134; Salzwedel, 1; Theresienstadt, 84); ghettoization, 1, 11, 70, 132, 150, 162; nonrecognition of, 47; survivors, 2, 5–7, 11–12, 31, 35–36, 41, 44, 52, 123, 143–47; aged, 31, 147; *Föhrenwald*, 133; "late emigrants," 149–50, 173; mentally disabled, 31, 45, 70, 133, 145; physically disabled, 31, 45, 70, 75, 133, 145, 149–50, 162; stateless, 21, 24, 31, 44–45, 65, 70, 94; underrepresentation of, 104, 110, 170
Hoover, Herbert, 153
Hungarian Empire. *See* Austro-Hungarian Empire
Hungary, 22, 88, 149, 163

intergovernmental organizations (IGOs), 120; International Monetary Fund, 151; League of Nations. *See* League of Nations; North Atlantic Treaty Organization (NATO), 32; UNRRA. *See* UN, UNRRA; World Health Organization, 151
international law, 19, 23, 41–43, 152, 164
international non-governmental organizations (INGOs) and non-governmental organizations (NGOs), 33–34, 94, 120, 123, 141, 148, 151–52, 166, 169; CARE (Cooperative for American Remittances to Europe), 74–75; Caritas, 81; Claims Conference. *See* Claims Conference; CRS (Catholic Relief Services), 32; ICRC (International Committee of the Red Cross), 25, 129; JDC. *See* JDC; Jewish. *See* Jewish organizations; LWR (Lutheran World Relief), 32, 75–76; Socialist First International,

25; Young Men's Christian Association, 25
Israel, 30, 33–35, 66–69; Authority for Rights of Holocaust Survivors, 147; *Beth Hatefusoth*, 93; Claims Conference, relations with, 89, 154–56, 165–67; establishment of, 41–43, 154, 164, 167–68; foreign policy, 146–47; *Herut* party, 51, 146; Holocaust survivors, 54, 67, 133, 143–46, 163–64; Israeli Communist Party, 146; Israel Purchasing Mission, 167–68; Jerusalem, 86, **102** (Bezalel School of Art, 30); Jewish leadership, relations with, 46–47, 53–56, 86–87, 154–56, 167–69; *Knesset*, 51, 55–58, 70, 144–47, 169; *Mapai* party, 145; *Mapam* party, 52; Ministry of Foreign Affairs, 11, 52–53, 58, 144, 147, 154–55; Office for Handling Personal Claims, 143, 147; reparations laws and agreements. *See* reparations, laws and agreements (Israeli); as spokesman for all Jews (*Judentum*), 2, 41–54, 87, 143; Tel Aviv, 146; West Germany, relations with, 2, 7, 45, **56**, 146, 164
Italy, 22, 27, 44, 133, 142

Janner, Barnett, 84–85, 92–93, 130–32
Japan, 163
JDC (Joint Distribution Committee), 30–35, 45, 52, 55–58, 66, 81–85, 100, 108, 121–33, 153–55, 163, 168; Agro-Joint, 88–90, 155; conference of country directors (1954), 126; creation, 26; Relief-in-Transit program, 129–30; reparations, role in, 88–94, 124–28
Jewish Agency for Palestine/Israel, 26–32, 35, 44–45, 50–58, 91, 100, 103–4, 132, 154
Jewish diaspora, 11, 26–28; *Encyclopedia Judaica*, 93; Hebrew language, 93; Israel, relations with, 2, 10, 46–47; leadership. *See* Jewish

leadership; Jewish organizations; postwar, 7, 101; religious and national/ethnic identity, tension between, 46–47, 167
Jewish leadership, 9, 12, 19–21, 29, 41, 46, 99, 155, 165–67; American, 2, 26, 83–84, 101, 166; medieval, 103, 174; non-Zionist, 46, 103, 155, 167–68; postwar organizing and impact on Jewish organizations, 32–35; Zionist, 27–28, 31, 86–87, 109, 154–55, 167, 170. *See also* Jewish organizations
Jewish organizations, 11, 22–24, **26**–29, 32–33, 41–54, 58, 84, 165–68; *Aguda* (*Agudas* Israel World Organization), 53, 85, 92–93, 99, 103–4, 109, 122–23; AJC (American Jewish Committee), 46, 49, 54, 57, 86–87, 94, 100, 103–4, 126, 132, 168; *Alliance* (*Alliance Israélite Universelle*), 25–27, 33, 92, 103, 108–9, 124, 154; American Council for Judaism, 46; American Jewish Congress, 27, 85, 122, 132; American Jewish Relief Committee, 26; American Zionist Council, 103; Anglo-Jewish Association, 104; Association of Jews from Austria, 144; Berlin Jewish Community Department of Productive Welfare, 20; B'nai B'rith, 111, 122, 131; Board of Deputies of British Jews, 23, 84, 109, 129, 132; British Relief Committee of Jews from Czechoslovakia, 112; Canadian Jewish Congress, 104; CBF (Central British Fund for German Jews, later World Jewish Relief), 20, 30, 35, 52, 100, 112; Central Committee for the Relief of Jews, 26; Central Committee of Jews from Austria, 154; Claims Conference. *See* Claims Conference; COJO (Conference of Jewish Organizations), 101; Conference of Presidents of Major American Jewish Organizations (1955), 101–3; Council for Jews from Germany (Council for the Protection of the Rights and Interests of Jews from Germany), 21–23, 30, 35, 84, 92–93, 104, 129, 132, 166; Council of Australian Jewry, 111; Federation of Women Zionists, 109; *Fonds Social Juif Unifié*, 134; International Council of Jewish Women, 109; JCR (Jewish Cultural Reconstruction, Inc.), 29–33; JDC. *See* JDC; Jewish Agency for Palestine/Israel. *See* Jewish Agency for Palestine/Israel; Jewish Antifascist Committee (Soviet Union), 107; JLC (Jewish Labor Committee), 103, 111; JRSO. *See* JRSO; Hadassah, Women's Zionist Organization of America, 109–10; Labor Zionist Alliance, 132; NCJW (National Council of Jewish Women), 109; South African Jewish Board of Deputies, 122; Synagogue Council of America, 112; UJA (United Jewish Appeal), 89; URO. *See* URO; WIZO (Women's International Zionist Organization), 109; WJC. *See* WJC; WUPJ (World Union of Progressive Judaism), 99–100, 113; WZO (World Zionist Organization), 10, 26, 86–87, 101, 154; *Zentralrat*. *See Zentralrat*; ZOA (Zionist Organization of America), 109
Jewish refugees. *See* Holocaust, survivors, stateless
Jewish Restitution Successor Organization (JRSO), 45, 52, 57, 66, 91, 132, 148; establishment, 30–31; allocations by, 31–32, 35–36; postwar organizing, impact of, 32–35
Jordan, Charles, 121
Josel of Rosheim, 103
Josephthal, Giora, 66, **69**

Kagan, Saul, 68, 83–84, 87, 91–92, 99, 126–27; background of, 34, 132, 148; diplomatic skill of, 170
Kindertransport, 112
Klatzkin, Jacob, 93
Klüger, Ruth, 5
Korea, 51, 75, 163
Küster, Otto, 66–67

Landau, MK Haim, 146
Landauer, Georg, 35
Latvia, 5
Lauterpacht, Hersch, 23
League of Nations, 27–29; Inter-Governmental Committee for Refugees, 20; structure of, 120, 165–66
Leavitt, Moses, 85, 89–93, **90**, 99, 106–7, 122–24; background of, 132; diplomatic skill of, 66, 82
Lewin, Isaac, 2, 85, 92–93, 130
Lithuania, 28, 34
Luxembourg, 142
Luxembourg Agreement, 13, 41, **42**, 65–76, 84, 141–45, 155, 166; payments to the Claims Conference, 72–73, 119–21, 133, 171–73; Protocol 1, 68–72, 149, 162, 165; Protocol 2, 81–86, 94, 107, 129–32, 167; signing of, 6–7, 65, **69**, 146, 154, 167–68, 172

Marx, Hugo, 44
McCloy, John J., 67
Mennonites, 5
Methodists, 25
Mexico, 32
Michael, Jerome, 33
Mischlinge, 106
Moldova, 33
Montefiore, Moses, 153
Morocco, 108, 130, 163
Moses, Siegfried, 20, 23, 44

National Socialists. *See* Germany, Nazi regime

non-governmental organizations (NGOs). *See* INGOs and NGOs
non-state actors, 6, 9, 10, 13, 24, 81, 141, 146, 151–53, 155–56, 164, 167, 174
Norway, 142

organizational theory, 65, 74–75, 82, 119–21, 170–72
Ottoman Empire, 25–26, 153

Palestine, 23, 27–30, 50, 143, 155, 167; British Mandate, 22–26, 50; *Etzel*, 24; refugees to, 31–32, 45, 109; *Yishuv*, 20, 145
Pappenheim, Bertha (Anna O), 109
Perlzweig, Maurice, 111
Peru, 35
philanthropy and philanthropic practices, 33, 46, 81, 88, 94, 112, 167
Poland, 27, 156; invasion of, 5; Katowice, 53; Lodz, 1, 5; Polish Jews, 5, 32, 150; Radomski, 5; Warsaw, 106
Polier, Shad, 85, 122–24, 127, 132
Portugal, 127
Presbyterians, 25

Quakers, 25

reparations: Claims Conference. *See* Claims Conference; guilt, feelings of, 2; Hardship Fund, 150, 163, 173–74; in international law, 19, 67; Japanese American rights to, 72, 125; Justice for Uncompensated Survivors Today Act Report (JUST, USA), 164; pensions (*Renten*), 147–49, 162–63; resistance fighters, right to, 142); for stolen property, 2–3, 19, 33–36, 43–44, 72, 84 (heirless property, 29–31, 50, 56, 67, 107, 132, 144, 151; refusal to acknowledge, 21, 24; restitution of. *See* restitution of stolen property); Terezin Declaration, 147, 164; laws and agreements (German/

West-German) Anglo-German Agreement for Compensation to Victims of Nazism, 135; Article II Fund, 162, 173; Federal Law on Compensation of Victims of Nation Socialist Persecution (*Bundesentschädigungsgesetz*, BEG), 69–71, 75, 125, 142, 149, 162, 165; Federal Restitution Law (*Bundesrückerstattungsgesetz*, BRüG), 149; Final Compensation Law (*Bundesentschädigungss-chlussgesetz*), 150, 173; "final indemnification gesture" (*Abschlussgeste der Wiedergutmachung*), 150; *Globalabkommen* (West German reparation treaties with states), 142; Reconciliation Fund Law (*Versöhnungsstiftungen*), 163–64; Remembrance, Responsibility and Future Foundation (*Stiftung Erinnerung, Verantwortung und Zukunft*, EVZ), 163; laws and agreements (Israeli), Law for Disabled Victims of Nazi Persecution, 147; Law for Persons Wounded in the War against the Nazis, 147; Law on Benefits for Holocaust Survivors, 147

restitution of stolen property, 19–23, 30, 34–35, 67, 112, 164, 174; Washington Conference on Principles of Nazi-Confiscated Art (1998), 9

Robinson, Jacob, 23

Robinson, Nehemiah, 6, 20, 23, 44, 66; background of, 148–50; diplomatic skill of, 171

Roman Catholics, 106

Romania, 22, 25–27, 33, 57

Roma people, persecution of, 48

Roosevelt, Franklin Delano, 22

Rosenwald, Julius, 46, 91

Rosenwald, Lessing J., 46

Rothschild, Alphonse, 4

Russia, 25–27; Soviet. *See* Soviet Union

Rwanda, 161

Schiff, Otto, 112

Schneider, Greg, 174

Schocken, Simon and Salman, 3–4

Schröder, Gerhard, 163

Schwartz, Joseph, 45

Second World War: aftermath of, 19, 22, 29, 129, 135, 165; Council of Foreign Ministers of the Allied Powers, 22–23; Moscow Declaration on Austria, 47; Nuremberg war trials, 34; Paris Peace Conference (1946), 19, 22–24, 27–29; Potsdam conference (1945), 22; Yalta conference (1945), 22; Inter-Allied Declaration against Acts of Dispossession Committed in Territories Under Enemy Occupation or Control (1943), 21; outbreak of, 20, 31; prisoners of war, 44, 134, 142; veterans of, 142, 145–46

Sieff, Rebecca, 109

Shapiro, Judah, 126, 132

Sharett, Moshe, 53–55, 66, **69**, 145–46

Shinnar, Felix, 53, 58, 66–68

Shirer, William, 4

Shuster, Zachariah, 126

Sinti people, persecution of, 48

Solomon, Hannah, 109

South Africa, 23, 35, 100, 104, 109

Soviet Union (USSR), 19, 24, 32, 90, 153; Black Book of Soviet Jewry, 107; Cold War. *See* Cold War; collectivization, 90–91; Crimea, 153–55; international organizations, 32–33; Jewish organizations, 33, 107; nonrecognition of the Holocaust, 47; Soviet bloc. *See* Cold War, Iron Curtain; Soviet/Russian Jewry, 29, 33, 52, 88–91, 107–8, 129, 147, 150, 168. *See also* Russia

Spain, 127, 131

Stalin, Joseph, 22–24, 52, 90, 107, 161

Stimson, Henry, 24
Strauss, Isak, 5
successor organizations, 30–35, 83, 85, 128, 153; allocations principles, 35–36, 45, 57; *Branche Française de la Jewish Trust Corporation*, 30; Jewish Trust Corporation, 30–31, 35, 52, 112; JRSO. *See* JRSO
Sweden, 127, 142
Switzerland, 47, 83, 127, 142
Szold, Henrietta, 109

Terezin Declaration. *See* reparations, Terezin Declaration
Third Reich. *See* Germany, Nazi regime
Truman, Harry S., 22, 52
Tunisia, 163

Ukraine, 27, 33, 161–63
UN (United Nations), 20, 32–34, 54; General Assembly, 161; membership, 52; UNESCO (United Nations Educational, Scientific, and Cultural Organization), 32; UNICEF (United Nations Children's Emergency Fund), 32; UNRRA (United Nations Relief and Rehabilitation Administration), 32, 44–45, 74, 81, 89, 135
Unitarians, 25
United Kingdom, 19, 23, 34, 67, 100, 104, 129, 142; Foreign Office, 134; internment of enemy aliens, 72; London, 30, 45, 67. *See also* Palestine, British Mandate
United States (US), 19–23, 27, 29, 30, 52, 91, 100, 129; Civil Liberties Act (1988), 72, 125, 163; Columbia University, 29, 32; Harvard Law School, 34; Japanese Americans, treatment of, 72, 163; JUST. *See* reparations, JUST; Library of Congress, 29–32; New Jersey, 131; New York, 30, 133, 166; Office of Military Government, 29, 34–35; postwar organizing, 32–35; State Department, 9, 22, 35, 68, 76, 101, 164–65; US Army, 34, 74, 132
URO (United Restitution Organization), 30–31, 34, 45, 52, 71, 148
USSR. *See* Soviet Union

van Dam, Hendrik G., 35, 84
Versailles. *See* First World War, aftermath of
Vietnam, 163
Vilner, MK Meir, 146
von Hofmannsthal, Emilio, 21

Waldorf-Astoria Hotel. *See* Claims Conference, establishment of, founding meeting
Weber, Max, 172
Weiner, Eva, 11
Weiss, Horst, 11
Weizmann, Chaim, 24, 46, 50
Weizmann, Vera, 109
West Germany (Federal Republic of Germany, DDR), 2, 156; establishment of, 48; Foreign Office, 125; Israel, relations with, 2, 7, 45, 146, 164; *Länder*, 36, 57, 69, 152; reparations laws and agreements. *See* reparations, laws and agreements (German/West German); Union of Persecutees of the Nazi Regime, 48
Wiedergutmachung, 48
Wise, Rabbi Stephen, 28, 104–5
women: "comfort women," 163; exclusion from anti-slavery movement, 25; exclusion from Claims Conference, 104, 108–11, 133, 169–70; feminism, 110; suffrage, 25; women's organizations, 109–10, 170; World Conference of Jewish Women, Vienna (1923), 109
World Jewish Congress (WJC), 66–67, 74, 83, 85, 92, 93, 101–6, 110–11,

120, 122; calls for reparations, 43–44; Claims Conference, not WJC as spokesman on reparations, 56–57; conference, Atlantic City (1944), 43; creation, 28–29
World Zionist Congress, Jerusalem (1951), 86

Yad Vashem, 155
yeshivot, 89, 122, 128, 133
Yugoslavia, 27

Zentralrat der Juden in Deutschland (Zentralrat), 35–36, 84, 100, 104, 112, 150, 166

About the Author

Rachel Blumenthal is a lawyer and a historian. She is a fellow at the Avraham Harman Research Institute of Contemporary Jewry at the Hebrew University of Jerusalem.

www.ingramcontent.com/pod-product-compliance
Lightning Source LLC
Chambersburg PA
CBHW020118010526
44115CB00008B/883